INTERNATIONAL CLASSIFICATION FOR INDUSTRIAL DESIGNS

国际外观设计分类表

（第13版）中英文对照版

(LOCARNO CLASSIFICATION)
THIRTEENTH EDITION

世界知识产权组织　编
国家知识产权局专利局　译

知识产权出版社
全国百佳图书出版单位
—北京—

图书在版编目（CIP）数据

国际外观设计分类表：第 13 版：汉、英/世界知识产权组织编；国家知识产权局专利局译. —北京：知识产权出版社，2021.1

ISBN 978-7-5130-7317-2

Ⅰ. ①国… Ⅱ. ①世…②国… Ⅲ. ①造型设计—专利分类法—世界—汉、英 Ⅳ. ①G255.53

中国版本图书馆 CIP 数据核字（2020）第 228602 号

内容摘要

本分类表为第 13 版《国际外观设计分类表》（《洛迦诺分类表》）的中英文对照版。在世界知识产权组织公布的《国际外观设计分类表（第 13 版）》官方版本的基础上，我国将分类表的历次修订内容的整理成果编撰在本次出版的分类表中，以方便读者对分类表的理解和使用。

第 13 版《国际外观设计分类表》（《洛迦诺分类表》）于 2020 年 6 月以两种正式文本（英文和法文）公布，于 2021 年 1 月 1 日正式实施，同时废止前一版本。

责任编辑：王玉茂　王瑞璞	责任校对：潘凤越
封面设计：博华创意·张　冀	责任印制：刘译文
执行编辑：武　伟	

国际外观设计分类表（第 13 版）中英文对照版

世界知识产权组织　编

国家知识产权局专利局　译

出版发行：知识产权出版社有限责任公司	网　　址：http://www.ipph.cn
社　　址：北京市海淀区气象路 50 号院	邮　　编：100081
责编电话：010-82000860 转 8116	责编邮箱：wangruipu@cnipr.com
发行电话：010-82000860 转 8101/8102	发行传真：010-82000893/82005070/82000270
印　　刷：天津嘉恒印务有限公司	经　　销：各大网上书店、新华书店及相关专业书店
开　　本：889mm×1194mm　1/16	印　　张：17.5
版　　次：2021 年 1 月第 1 版	印　　次：2021 年 1 月第 1 次印刷
字　　数：490 千字	定　　价：88.00 元

ISBN 978-7-5130-7317-2

出版权专有　侵权必究

如有印装质量问题，本社负责调换。

总目录

PREFACE	(1)
序　言	(3)
LOCARNO AGREEMENT	(5)
建立工业品外观设计国际分类洛迦诺协定	(14)
GUIDANCE FOR THE USER	(20)
使用指南	(22)
RECOMMENDATIONS CONCERNING THE APPLICATION OF THE LOCARNO CLASSIFICATION	(24)
关于使用洛迦诺分类表的标注说明	(25)
LOCARNO CLASSIFICATION（13th EDITION）	
洛迦诺分类表（第13版）	(27)
LIST OF CLASSES	(29)
大类表	(30)
LIST OF CLASSES AND SUBCLASSES,WITH EXPLANATORY NOTES	
大类和小类表（含注释）	
GENERAL REMARKS	(31)
概　述	(32)
LIST OF CLASSES AND SUBCLASSES, WITH EXPLANATORY NOTES	(33)
大类和小类表（含注释）	(52)
LIST OF GOODS IN CLASS ORDER	
按类别顺序排列产品项列表	(67)

* * *

编译说明	(270)
第11版《国际外观设计分类表》已删除产品项列表	(271)
第12版《国际外观设计分类表》已删除产品项列表	(272)
第13版《国际外观设计分类表》已删除产品项列表	(275)
后　记	(276)

PREFACE[1]

A diplomatic conference, to which all the countries that were members of the Paris Convention for the Protection of Industrial Property were invited and which was held in Locarno (Switzerland), adopted, on October 8, 1968, the Locarno Agreement Establishing an International Classification for Industrial Designs (Locarno Classification).

The Locarno Classification comprises:

(i) a list of classes and subclasses;

(ii) an alphabetical list of goods which constitute industrial designs, with an indication of the classes and subclasses into which they fall;

(iii) explanatory notes.

The original list of classes and subclasses was attached to the Locarno Agreement when it was adopted.

The Locarno Agreement set up a Committee of Experts, in which each contracting country is represented. The Agreement empowered the Committee to make "amendments" or "additions" to the original list of classes and subclasses, to establish the alphabetical list and the explanatory notes (which were not established in the diplomatic conference), and to amend and supplement each and any of the three parts (list of classes and subclasses, alphabetical list of goods, explanatory notes) of the Locarno Classification.

Use of the Locarno Classification

The Locarno Classification is "solely of an administrative character" and does not bind the contracting countries "as regards the nature and scope of the protection afforded to the design in those countries" (Locarno Agreement, Article 2 (1)).

The Locarno Agreement requires the industrial property office of each contracting country to "include in the official documents for the deposit or registration of designs, and, if they are officially published, in the publications in question, the numbers of the classes and subclasses of international classification into which the goods incorporating the designs belong" (Article 2 (3)). Recommendations of the Committee of Experts deal with the manner in which the classes and subclasses should be indicated in the said documents and publications.

On July, 2020, the following 58 countries were party to the Locarno Agreement: Albania, Argentina, Armenia, Austria, Azerbaijan, Belarus, Belgium, Bosnia and Herzegovina, Bulgaria, China, Croatia, Cuba, Czech Republic, Democratic People's Republic of Korea, Denmark, Estonia, Finland, France, Germany, Greece, Guinea, Hungary, Iceland, India, Iran (Islamic Republic of), Ireland, Italy, Japan, Kazakhstan, Kyrgyzstan, Latvia, Malawi, Mexico, Mongolia, Montenegro, Netherlands, North Macedonia, Norway, Poland, Republic of Korea, Republic of Moldova, Romania, Russian Federation, Serbia, Singapore, Slovakia, Slovenia, Spain, Sweden, Switzerland, Tajikistan, Trinidad and Tobago, Turkey, Turkmenistan, Ukraine, United Kingdom, Uruguay, Uzbekistan.

---

1 http://www.wipo.int/classifications/locarno/en/preface.html, https://www.wipo.int/treaties/en/showResults.jsp?lang=en&treaty_id=14.

PREFACE

Besides the competent offices of the contracting countries, the African Intellectual Property Organization (OAPI), the African Regional Intellectual Property Organization (ARIPO), the Benelux Office for Intellectual Property (BOIP), the European Union Intellectual Property Office (EUIPO) and the International Bureau of WIPO also use the Locarno Classification in their registers and in the publications they issue.

Revisions and editions of the Locarno Classification

The Locarno Classification has been revised several times by the Committee of Experts. The current edition incorporates all the revisions made in previous editions and replaces them. It contains classes and subclasses, with explanatory notes, as the case may be. The alphabetical list of goods, which contains more than 5,000 entries in English, is presented in alphabetical order irrespective of the class to which each good belongs, as well as in the order of classes and subclasses, alphabetically under each subclass.

The authentic versions of the Locarno Classification, in English and French, are published online by the International Bureau of WIPO.

The thirteenth edition was published in June 2020 and entered into force on January 1, 2021. It replaces the previous editions.

* * *

Geneva, July 2020

序　言[1]

1968年10月8日，《保护工业产权巴黎公约》全体成员国在瑞士洛迦诺召开外交会议，缔结了《建立工业品外观设计国际分类洛迦诺协定》（下文分别称为《洛迦诺协定》和《洛迦诺分类表》）。

《洛迦诺分类表》包括以下内容：

（Ⅰ）大类和小类表；

（Ⅱ）依字母编序的外观设计产品项列表，并标示出其所属大类和小类；

（Ⅲ）注释。

《洛迦诺协定》缔结时附有初版大类和小类表。

《洛迦诺协定》成立了由各缔约国代表组成的专家委员会。该专家委员会由《洛迦诺协定》授权负责初版大类和小类表的修订或增补工作，并制定未在外交会议上确定的依字母编序的产品项列表和注释，同时负责修正和补充（增加）《洛迦诺分类表》的大类和小类目录、依字母编序的产品项列表、注释三部分内容。

《洛迦诺分类表》的使用

《洛迦诺分类表》"纯粹属管理性质"，不约束各缔约国"给予外观设计的保护性质和保护范围"（《洛迦诺协定》第2（1）条）。

《洛迦诺协定》要求各缔约国的工业产权局"在外观设计保存或注册的官方文件上以及在正式公布这些文件时在有关刊物上标明使用该外观设计的产品所属洛迦诺分类表的大类和小类号"（《洛迦诺协定》第2（3）条）。专家委员会议案中制定了使用于上述文件和出版物中的大类和小类的标示方法。

至2020年7月，以下58个国家加入了《洛迦诺协定》：阿尔巴尼亚、阿根廷、亚美尼亚、奥地利、阿塞拜疆、白俄罗斯、比利时、波斯尼亚和黑塞哥维那、保加利亚、中国、克罗地亚、古巴、捷克、朝鲜、丹麦、爱沙尼亚、芬兰、法国、德国、希腊、几内亚、匈牙利、冰岛、印度、伊朗、爱尔兰、意大利、日本、哈萨克斯坦、吉尔吉斯斯坦、拉脱维亚、马拉维、墨西哥、蒙古、黑山、荷兰、北马其顿、挪威、波兰、韩国、摩尔多瓦、罗马尼亚、俄罗斯、塞尔维亚、新加坡、斯洛伐克、斯洛文尼亚、西班牙、瑞典、瑞士、塔吉克斯坦、特立尼达和多巴哥、土耳其、土库曼斯坦、乌克兰、英国、乌拉圭、乌兹别克斯坦。

除了上述缔约国的主管局，非洲知识产权组织（OAPI）、非洲地区工业产权组织（ARIPO）、比荷卢知识产权局（BOIP）、欧盟知识产权局（EUIPO）和世界知识产权组织（WIPO）国际局也在注册簿和发行的出版物中使用《洛迦诺分类表》。

《洛迦诺分类表》的修订及版本[2]

专家委员会已多次修订《洛迦诺分类表》，当前版本分类表体现了对上一版本的所有修订内容，并进行了替换。本版分类表包括大类和小类，并视情况附有注释。依字母编序的产品项列表包含超过5000

---

[1] 自第11版《洛迦诺分类表》起，世界知识产权组织仅采用网页形式公布，序言的相关内容来源于http://www.wipo.int/classifications/locarno/en/preface.html 和 https://www.wipo.int/treaties/en/ShowResults.jsp?lang=en&treaty_id=14。

[2] 第13版《洛迦诺分类表》包括32个大类和237个小类。

个英文条目，依字母编序进行排列而不考虑产品所属的类别顺序，在按大类和小类顺序排列的产品项列表中，每一个小类下产品项按字母编序排列。

世界知识产权组织（WIPO）国际局以英文和法文两种语言在网站上发布《洛迦诺分类表》的正式版本。

第13版《洛迦诺分类表》于2020年6月公布，于2021年1月1日正式实施，同时废止前一版本。

日内瓦，2020年7月

LOCARNO AGREEMENT

Establishing an International Classification
for Industrial Designs

*Signed at Locarno on October 8, 1968
as amended on September 28, 1979*

Article 1

Establishment of a Special Union; Adoption of an International Classification

(1) The countries to which this Agreement applies constitute a Special Union.

(2) They adopt a single classification for industrial designs (hereinafter designated as "the international classification").

(3) The international classification shall comprise:

(i) a list of classes and subclasses;

(ii) an alphabetical list of goods in which industrial designs are incorporated, with an indication of the classes and subclasses into which they fall;

(iii) explanatory notes.

(4) The list of classes and subclasses is the list annexed to the present Agreement, subject to such amendments and additions as the Committee of Experts set up under Article 3 (hereinafter designated as "the Committee of Experts") may make to it.

(5) The alphabetical list of goods and the explanatory notes shall be adopted by the Committee of Experts in accordance with the procedure laid down in Article 3.

(6) The international classification may be amended or supplemented by the Committee of Experts, in accordance with the procedure laid down in Article 3.

(7) (a) The international classification shall be established in the English and French languages.

(b) Official texts of the international classification, in such other languages as the Assembly referred to in Article 5 may designate, shall be established, after consultation with the interested Governments, by the International Bureau of Intellectual Property (hereinafter designated as "the International Bureau") referred to in the Convention Establishing the World Intellectual Property Organization (hereinafter designated as "the Organization").

Article 2

Use and Legal Scope of the International Classification

(1) Subject to the requirements prescribed by this Agreement, the international classification shall be solely of an administrative character. Nevertheless, each country may attribute to it the legal scope which it considers appropriate. In particular, the international classification shall not bind the countries of the Special Union as regards the nature and scope of the protection afforded to the design in those countries.

(2) Each country of the Special Union reserves the right to use the international classification as a principal or as a subsidiary system.

(3) The Offices of the countries of the Special Union shall include in the official documents for the deposit or registration of designs, and, if they are officially published, in the publications in question, the numbers of the classes and subclasses of the international classification into which the goods incorporating the designs belong.

(4) In selecting terms for inclusion in the alphabetical list of goods, the Committee of Experts shall exercise reasonable care to avoid using terms in which exclusive rights may exist. The inclusion of any word in the alphabetical index, however, is not an expression of opinion of the Committee of Experts on whether or not it is subject to exclusive rights.

Article 3

Committee of Experts

(1) A Committee of Experts shall be entrusted with the tasks referred to in Article 1 (4), 1 (5) and 1 (6). Each country of the Special Union shall be represented on the Committee of Experts, which shall be organized according to rules of procedure adopted by a simple majority of the countries represented.

(2) The Committee of Experts shall adopt the alphabetical list and explanatory notes by a simple majority of the votes of the countries of the Special Union.

(3) Proposals for amendments or additions to the international classification may be made by the Office of any country of the Special Union or by the International Bureau. Any proposal emanating from an Office shall be communicated by that Office to the International Bureau. Proposals from Offices and from the International Bureau shall be transmitted by the latter to the members of the Committee of Experts not later than two months before the session of the Committee at which the said proposals are to be considered.

(4) The decisions of the Committee of Experts concerning the adoption of amendments and additions to be made in the international classification shall be by a simple majority of the countries of the Special Union. Nevertheless, if such decisions entail the setting up of a new class or any transfer of goods from one class to another, unanimity shall be required.

(5) Each expert shall have the right to vote by mail.

(6) If a country does not appoint a representative for a given session of the Committee of Experts, or if the expert appointed has not expressed his vote during the session or within a period to be prescribed by the rules of procedure of the Committee of Experts, the country concerned shall be considered to have accepted the decision of the Committee.

Article 4

Notification and Publication of the Classification and of Amendments and Additions Thereto

(1) The alphabetical list of goods and the explanatory notes adopted by the Committee of Experts, as well as any amendment or addition to the international classification decided by the Committee, shall be communicated to the Offices of the countries of the Special Union by the International Bureau. The decisions of the Committee of Experts shall enter into force as soon as the communication is received. Nevertheless, if such decisions entail the setting up of a new class or any transfer of goods from one class to another, they shall enter into force within a period of six months from the date of the said communication.

(2) The International Bureau, as depositary of the international classification, shall incorporate therein the amendments and additions which have entered into force. Announcements of the amendments and additions shall be published in the periodicals to be designated by the Assembly.

Article 5

Assembly of the Special Union

(1) (a) The Special Union shall have an Assembly consisting of the countries of the Special Union.
(b) The Government of each country of the Special Union shall be represented by one delegate, who may be assisted by alternate delegates, advisors, and experts.
(c) The expenses of each delegation shall be borne by the Government which has appointed it.
(2) (a) Subject to the provisions of Article 3, the Assembly shall:
(i) deal with all matters concerning the maintenance and development of the Special Union and the implementation of this Agreement;
(ii) give directions to the International Bureau concerning the preparation for conferences of revision;
(iii) review and approve the reports and activities of the Director General of the Organization (hereinafter designated as "the Director General") concerning the Special Union, and give him all necessary instructions concerning matters within the competence of the Special Union;
(iv) determine the program and adopt the biennial budget of the Special Union, and approve its final accounts;
(v) adopt the financial regulations of the Special Union;

(vi) decide on the establishment of official texts of the international classification in languages other than English and French;

(vii) establish, in addition to the Committee of Experts set up under Article 3, such other committees of experts and working groups as it deems appropriate to achieve the objectives of the Special Union;

(viii) determine which countries not members of the Special Union and which intergovernmental and international non-governmental organizations shall be admitted to its meetings as observers;

(ix) adopt amendments to Articles 5 to 8;

(x) take any other appropriate action designed to further the objectives of the Special Union;

(xi) perform such other functions as are appropriate under this Agreement.

(b) With respect to matters which are of interest also to other Unions administered by the Organization, the Assembly shall make its decisions after having heard the advice of the Coordination Committee of the Organization.

(3) (a) Each country member of the Assembly shall have one vote.

(b) One-half of the countries members of the Assembly shall constitute a quorum.

(c) Notwithstanding the provisions of subparagraph (b), if, in any session, the number of countries represented is less than one-half but equal to or more than one-third of the countries members of the Assembly, the Assembly may make decisions but, with the exception of decisions concerning its own procedure, all such decisions shall take effect only if the conditions set forth hereinafter are fulfilled. The International Bureau shall communicate the said decisions to the countries members of the Assembly which were not represented and shall invite them to express in writing their vote or abstention within a period of three months from the date of the communication. If, at the expiration of this period, the number of countries having thus expressed their vote or abstention attains the number of countries which was lacking for attaining the quorum in the session itself, such decisions shall take effect provided that at the same time the required majority still obtains.

(d) Subject to the provisions of Article 8(2), the decisions of the Assembly shall require two-thirds of the votes cast.

(e) Abstentions shall not be considered as votes.

(f) A delegate may represent, and vote in the name of, one country only.

(4) (a) The Assembly shall meet once in every second calendar year in ordinary session upon convocation by the Director General and, in the absence of exceptional circumstances, during the same period and at the same place as the General Assembly of the Organization.

(b) The Assembly shall meet in extraordinary session upon convocation by the Director General, at the request of one-fourth of the countries members of the Assembly.

(c) The agenda of each session shall be prepared by the Director General.

(5) The Assembly shall adopt its own rules of procedure.

Article 6

International Bureau

(1) (a) Administrative tasks concerning the Special Union shall be performed by the International Bureau.

(b) In particular, the International Bureau shall prepare the meetings and provide the secretariat of the Assembly, the Committee of Experts, and such other committees of experts and working groups as may have been established by the Assembly or the Committee of Experts.

(c) The Director General shall be the chief executive of the Special Union and shall represent the Special Union.

(2) The Director General and any staff member designated by him shall participate, without the right to vote, in all meetings of the Assembly, the Committee of Experts, and such other committees of experts or working groups as may have been established by the Assembly or the Committee of Experts. The Director General, or a staff member designated by him, shall be ex officio secretary of those bodies.

(3) (a) The International Bureau shall, in accordance with the directions of the Assembly, make the preparations for the conferences of revision of the provisions of the Agreement other than Articles 5 to 8.

(b) The International Bureau may consult with intergovernmental and international non-governmental organizations concerning preparations for conferences of revision.

(c) The Director General and persons designated by him shall take part, without the right to vote, in the discussions at those conferences.

(4) The International Bureau shall carry out any other tasks assigned to it.

Article 7

Finances

(1) (a) The Special Union shall have a budget.

(b) The budget of the Special Union shall include the income and expenses proper to the Special Union, its contribution to the budget of expenses common to the Unions, and, where applicable, the sum made available to the budget of the Conference of the Organization.

(c) Expenses not attributable exclusively to the Special Union but also to one or more other Unions administered by the Organization shall be considered as expenses common to the Unions. The share of the Special Union in such common expenses shall be in proportion to the interest the Special Union has in them.

(2) The budget of the Special Union shall be established with due regard to the requirements of coordination with the budgets of the other Unions administered by the Organization.

(3) The budget of the Special Union shall be financed from the following sources:

(i) contributions of the countries of the Special Union;

(ii) fees and charges due for services rendered by the International Bureau in relation to the Special Union;

(iii) sale of, or royalties on, the publications of the International Bureau concerning the Special Union;

(iv) gifts, bequests, and subventions;

(v) rents, interests, and other miscellaneous income.

(4) (a) For the purpose of establishing its contribution referred to in paragraph (3) (i), each country of the Special Union shall belong to the same class as it belongs to in the Paris Union for the Protection of Industrial Property, and shall pay its annual contributions on the basis of the same number of units as is fixed for that class in that Union.

(b) The annual contribution of each country of the Special Union shall be an amount in the same proportion to the total sum to be contributed to the budget of the Special Union by all countries as the number of its units is to the total of the units of all contributing countries.

(c) Contributions shall become due on the first of January of each year.

(d) A country which is in arrears in the payment of its contributions may not exercise its right to vote in any organ of the Special Union if the amount of its arrears equals or exceeds the amount of the contributions due from it for the preceding two full years. However, any organ of the Special Union may allow such a country to continue to exercise its right to vote in that organ if, and as long as, it is satisfied that the delay in payment is due to exceptional and unavoidable circumstances.

(e) If the budget is not adopted before the beginning of a new financial period, it shall be at the same level as the budget of the previous year, as provided in the financial regulations.

(5) The amount of the fees and charges due for services rendered by the International Bureau in relation to the Special Union shall be established, and shall be reported to the Assembly, by the Director General.

(6) (a) The Special Union shall have a working capital fund which shall be constituted by a single payment made by each country of the Special Union. If the fund becomes insufficient, the Assembly shall decide to increase it.

(b) The amount of the initial payment of each country to the said fund or of its participation in the increase thereof shall be a proportion of the contribution of that country for the year in which the fund is established or the decision to increase it is made.

(c) The proportion and the terms of payment shall be fixed by the Assembly on the proposal of the Director General and after it has heard the advice of the Coordination Committee of the Organization.

(7) (a) In the headquarters agreement concluded with the country on the territory of which the Organization has its headquarters, it shall be provided that, whenever the working capital fund is insufficient, such country shall grant advances. The amount of those advances and the conditions on which they are granted shall be the subject of separate agreements, in each case, between such country and the Organization.

(b) The country referred to in subparagraph (a) and the Organization shall each have the right to denounce the obligation to grant advances, by written notification. Denunciation shall take effect three years after the end of the year in which it has been notified.

(8) The auditing of the accounts shall be effected by one or more of the countries of the Special Union or by external auditors, as provided in the financial regulations. They shall be designated, with their agreement, by the Assembly.

Article 8

Amendment of Articles 5 to 8

(1) Proposals for the amendment of Articles 5, 6, 7, and the present Article, may be initiated by any country of the Special Union or by the Director General. Such proposals shall be communicated by the Director General to the countries of the Special Union at least six months in advance of their consideration by the Assembly.

(2) Amendments to the Articles referred to in paragraph (1) shall be adopted by the Assembly. Adoption shall require three-fourths of the votes cast, provided that any amendment to Article 5, and to the present paragraph, shall require four-fifths of the votes cast.

(3) Any amendment to the Articles referred to in paragraph (1) shall enter into force one month after written notifications of acceptance, effected in accordance with their respective constitutional processes, have been received by the Director General from three-fourths of the countries members of the Special Union at the time the amendment was adopted. Any amendment to the said Articles thus accepted shall bind all the countries which are members of the Special Union at the time the amendment enters into force, or which become members thereof at a subsequent date, provided that any amendment increasing the financial obligations of countries of the Special Union shall bind only those countries which have notified their acceptance of such amendment.

Article 9

Ratification and Accession; Entry Into Force

(1) Any country party to the Paris Convention for the Protection of Industrial Property which has signed this Agreement may ratify it, and, if it has not signed it, may accede to it.

(2) Instruments of ratification and accession shall be deposited with the Director General.

(3) (a) With respect to the first five countries which have deposited their instruments of ratification or accession, this Agreement shall enter into force three months after the deposit of the fifth such instrument.

(b) With respect to any other country, this Agreement shall enter into force three months after the date on which its ratification or accession has been notified by the Director General, unless a subsequent date has been indicated in the instrument of ratification or accession. In the latter case, this Agreement shall enter into force with respect to that country on the date thus indicated.

(4) Ratification or accession shall automatically entail acceptance of all the clauses and admission to all the advantages of this Agreement.

Article 10

Force and Duration of the Agreement

This Agreement shall have the same force and duration as the Paris Convention for the Protection of Industrial Property.

Article 11

Revision of Articles 1 to 4 and 9 to 15

(1) Articles 1 to 4 and 9 to 15 of this Agreement may be submitted to revision with a view to the introduction of desired improvements.

(2) Every revision shall be considered at a conference which shall be held among the delegates of the countries of the Special Union.

Article 12

Denunciation

(1) Any country may denounce this Agreement by notification addressed to the Director General. Such denunciation shall affect only the country making it, the Agreement remaining in full force and effect as regards the other countries of the Special Union.

(2) Denunciation shall take effect one year after the day on which the Director General has received the notification.

(3) The right of denunciation provided by this Article shall not be exercised by any country before the expiration of five years from the date upon which it becomes a member of the Special Union.

Article 13

Territories

The provisions of Article 24 of the Paris Convention for the Protection of Industrial Property shall apply to this Agreement.

Article 14

Signature, Languages, Notifications

(1) (a) This Agreement shall be signed in a single copy in the English and French languages, both texts being equally authentic, and shall be deposited with the Government of Switzerland.

(b) This Agreement shall remain open for signature at Berne until June 30, 1969.

(2) Official texts shall be established by the Director General, after consultation with the interested Governments, in such other languages as the Assembly may designate.

(3) The Director General shall transmit two copies, certified by the Government of Switzerland, of the signed text of this Agreement to the Governments of the countries that have signed it and, on request, to the Government of any other country.

(4) The Director General shall register this Agreement with the Secretariat of the United Nations.

(5) The Director General shall notify the Governments of all countries of the Special Union of the date of entry into force of the Agreement, signatures, deposits of instruments of ratification or accession, acceptances of amendments to this Agreement and the dates on which such amendments enter into force, and notifications of denunciation.

Article 15

Transitional Provision

Until the first Director General assumes office, references in this Agreement to the International Bureau of the Organization or to the Director General shall be deemed to be references to the United International Bureaux for the Protection of Intellectual Property (BIRPI) or its Director, respectively.

建立工业品外观设计国际分类洛迦诺协定

(1968年10月8日签订，1979年9月28日修订)

第一条 建立专门联盟；采用国际分类

（1）适应本协定的国家组成专门联盟。

（2）上述国家采用统一的外观设计分类（以下简称"国际分类法"）。

（3）国际分类法应包括：

（i）大类和小类表；

（ii）结合外观设计的按字母顺序排列的产品项列表，包括这些产品分成大类和小类的分类标记；

（iii）用法说明。

（4）大类和小类表作为本协定的附件，根据第三条规定所设立的专家委员会（以下简称"专家委员会"）可以对其作出修正和补充。

（5）按字母顺序排列的产品项列表和用法说明应由专家委员会依照第三条规定的程序通过。

（6）专家委员会可以依照第三条规定的程序对国际分类法进行修正和补充。

（7）（a）国际分类法应用英语和法语制定。

（b）第五条所述大会可以指定的其他语言的国际分类法正式文本，应由建立世界知识产权组织（以下简称"本组织"）公约所述知识产权国际局（以下简称"国际局"）与有关国家政府协商后制定。

第二条 国际分类法的使用和法定范围

（1）除本协定另有规定的要求应适用该规定的要求外，国际分类法纯属管理性质。然而，每个国家可以将其认为适当的法定范围归属于国际分类法。特别是本专门联盟各国对本国给予外观设计的保护性质和范围应不受国际分类法的约束。

（2）本专门联盟的每一国家保留将国际分类法作为主要的分类系统或者作为辅助的分类系统使用的权利。

（3）本专门联盟国家的主管局应在外观设计保存或注册的官方文件上以及在正式公布这些文件时在有关刊物上标明使用外观设计的产品所属国际分类法的大类和小类号。

（4）在选择按字母顺序排列的产品项列表中的用语时，专家委员会应相当谨慎，避免使用含有专有权的用语。但是按字母顺序排列的索引中所列的任何用语并不表示专家委员会对该用语是否属于专有权的意见。

第三条 专家委员会

（1）专家委员会应承担第一条第（4）款、第（5）款和第（6）款所述的任务。本专门联盟的每一国家，在专家委员会都应有代表，该委员会应按照出席国家的简单多数所通过的议事规则进行组织。

（2）专家委员会应依本专门联盟国家的简单多数票通过按字母顺序排列的产品项列表和用法说明。

（3）国际分类法的修正和补充的建议可由本专门联盟的任何国家主管局或由国际局提出。由主管局提出的任何建议应由该局通知国际局。由主管局以及由国际局提出的建议应由国际局在不迟于审议该建议的专家委员会会议开会前2个月送交专家委员会的每一成员国。

（4）专家委员会关于国际分类法的修正和补充的决议应由本专门联盟国家的简单多数通过。然而，如果决议涉及建立新的大类或将一些产品由一大类转移至另一大类时，需要全体一致同意。

（5）每位专家应有通过邮寄投票的权利。

（6）如果一个国家未指派代表参加专家委员会的一届会议，或指派的专家在会议期间或在专家委员会议事规则所规定的期间未表示投票，该有关国家应认为已接受专家委员会的决议。

第四条 国际分类法及其修正和补充的通知和出版

（1）专家委员会所通过的按字母顺序排列的产品项列表和用法说明，以及该委员会所决定的国际分类法的修正或补充应由国际局通知本专门联盟各国主管局。通知一经收到，专家委员会的决议就应开始生效。然而，如果决议涉及建立新的大类，或将一些产品从一个大类转移至另一大类时，该决议应自发出上述通知之日起6个月内开始生效。

（2）国际局作为国际分类法的保存机构，应将已开始生效的修正和补充编入国际分类法中。修正和补充的宣告应在大会指定的期刊上公布。

第五条 本专门联盟大会

（1）（a）本专门联盟应设立大会，由本专门联盟各国组成。

（b）本专门联盟每一国家的政府应有1名代表，可辅以若干名副代表、顾问和专家。

（c）每一代表团的费用应由委派代表团的政府负担。

（2）（a）除第三条另有规定外，大会应当：

（i）处理有关维持和发展本专门联盟以及执行本协定的一切事项；

（ii）就有关修订会议的筹备事项对国际局给予指示；

（iii）审查和批准本组织总干事（以下简称"总干事"）关于本专门联盟的报告和活动，并就本专门联盟职权范围内的事项对总干事给予一切必要的指示；

（iv）决定本专门联盟的计划和通过2年预算，并批准决算；

（v）通过本专门联盟的财务规则；

（vi）决定英语和法语以外语言的国际分类法正式文本的制定；

（vii）除按第三条所设立的专家委员会以外，建立为实现本专门联盟目标而认为适当的其他专家委员会和工作组；

（viii）决定接受哪些非本专门联盟成员的国家以及哪些政府间组织和非政府间国际组织为观察员；

（ix）通过第五条至第八条的修正案；

（x）采取旨在促进实现本专门联盟的目标的任何其他适当的行动；

（xi）履行按照本协定是适当的其他职责。

（b）关于与本组织管理的其他联盟共同有关的事项，大会应在听取本组织协调委员会的意见后作出决议。

（3）（a）大会的每一成员国应有一票表决权。

（b）大会成员国的半数构成开会的法定人数。

（c）尽管有（b）项的规定，如任何一次会议出席的国家不足大会成员国的半数，但达到三分之一或三分之一以上时，大会可以作出决议，但是，除有关大会本身议事程序的决议外，所有其他决议只有符合下述条件才能生效。国际局应将上述决议通知未出席的大会成员国，请其在通知之日起 3 个月的期限内，以书面表示是否赞成或弃权。如该期限届满时，这些表示是否赞成或弃权的国家数目达到会议本身开会法定人数所缺少的国家数目，只要同时也取得规定的多数票，这些决议即应生效。

（d）除第八条第（2）款另有规定外，大会的决议需有所投票数的三分之二。

（e）弃权不应认为是投票。

（f）一名代表仅可以一国名义代表一个国家投票。

（4）（a）大会应每 2 年由总干事召开一次通常会议，如无特殊情况，应与本组织的大会在同一期间和同一地点召开。

（b）大会的临时会议应由总干事根据大会四分之一成员国的请求召开。

（c）每届会议的议程应由总干事准备。

（5）大会应通过自己的议事规程。

第六条 国际局

（1）（a）有关本专门联盟的行政工作应由国际局执行。

（b）国际局特别应负责筹备各种会议，并为大会、专家委员会以及由大会或专家委员会所设立的其他专家委员会和工作组设置秘书处。

（c）总干事是本专门联盟的最高行政官员，并代表本专门联盟。

（2）总干事及其指定的职员均应参加大会、专家委员会以及由大会或专家委员会所设立的其他专家委员会或工作组的所有会议，但无表决权。总干事或其指定的职员应是这些机构的当然秘书。

（3）（a）国际局应依照大会的指示，为修订本协定除第五条至第八条以外各规定的会议进行筹备工作。

（b）国际局可以就修订会议的筹备工作与政府间组织及非政府间国际组织进行磋商。

（c）总干事及其指定的人员应参加修订会议的讨论，但无表决权。

（4）国际局应执行指定的其他工作。

第七条 财 务

（1）（a）本专门联盟应有预算。

（b）本专门联盟的预算应包括本专门联盟的专有的收入和支出。对各联盟共同支出预算的摊款，以及在需要时包括向本组织成员国会议预算提供的款项数。

（c）对于不是专属于本专门联盟的支出，而是与本组织管理下的一个或一个以上的其他联盟有关的支出，应视为各联盟的共同支出。本专门联盟在该项共同支出中的摊款，应与本专门联盟在其中所享有的利益成比例。

（2）制订本专门联盟的预算，应适当考虑到本组织管理的其他联盟预算相协调的需要。

（3）本专门联盟预算的财政来源如下：

（i）本专门联盟国家的会费；

（ii）国际局提供的与本专门联盟有关的服务应收的各种费用；

（iii）国际局有关本专门联盟出版物的售款或版税；

（iv）赠款、遗赠和补助金；

（v）租金、利息以及其他杂项收入。

（4）（a）为了确定第（3）款（i）项所指的会费数额，本专门联盟每一国家应与其在保护工业产权巴黎联盟属于同一等级，并应以该联盟对该等级所确定的单位数字为基础缴纳其年度会费。

（b）本专门联盟每一国家年度会费的数额在所有国家向本专门联盟预算缴纳的会费总额中所占的比例，应与该国的单位数额在所有缴纳会费国家的单位总数中所占的比例相同。

（c）会费应在每年的1月1日缴纳。

（d）一个国家欠缴的会费数额等于或超过其前两个整年的会费数额的，不得在本专门联盟的任何机构内行使表决权。但是，如果本专门联盟的任何机构证实延迟缴费是由于特殊的和不可避免的情况，则在这期间内，可以允许该国在该机构内继续行使其表决权。

（e）如果预算在新财政年度开始以前尚未通过，预算应与上一年度预算的水平相同。

（5）国际局提供的与本专门联盟有关的服务应收的各种费用数额，应由总干事确定并报告大会。

（6）（a）本专门联盟应设工作基金，由本专门联盟的每一国家一次缴纳组成，如果基金不足，大会就决定予以增加。

（b）每一国家对上述基金初次缴纳的数额或在基金增加时缴纳的数额，应与建立基金或决定增加基金的当年该国缴纳的会费成比例。

（c）缴款的比例和条件，应由大会根据总干事的建议，并听取本组织协调委员会的意见后确定。

（7）（a）在本组织与本组织总部所在地国家签订的总部协定中应规定：工作基金不足时，该国应予贷款。该项贷款的数额和条件，每一次应由本组织与该国签订单独的协定。

（b）上列（a）项所指的国家与本组织都各自有权以书面通知废除贷款的义务。废除应在发出通知当年年底起 3 年后生效。

（8）账目的审核工作应按财务规则的规定，由本专门联盟一个或一个以上国家或外界的审计师进行。审计师应由大会在征得其同意后指定。

第八条 第五条至第八条的修正

（1）本专门联盟任何国家或总干事均可对第五条、第六条、第七条和本条提出修正案。修正案至少应在提交大会审议前 6 个月，由总干事通知本专门联盟各国。

（2）对第（1）款所指各条的修正案，应由大会通过。通过需有投票数的四分之三。但对第五条和本款的任何修正案，需有所投票数的五分之四。

（3）对第（1）款所指各条的任何修正案，应在总干事收到修正案通过时的本专门联盟四分之三国家按其各自宪法程序表示接受修正案的书面通知日起 1 个月后生效。对上述各条的任何修正案经依上述规定接受后，对修正案生效时本专门联盟的成员国或在此后日期成为成员国的所有国家都有约束力，但增加本专门联盟国家财政义务的修正案，只对已经通知接受该修正案的国家有约束力。

第九条 批准和加入；生效

（1）《保护工业产权巴黎公约》的任何缔约国家已在本协定签字的都可批准本协定，未在本协定签字的，可以加入本协定。

（2）批准书和加入书均应递交总干事保存。

（3）（a）对于最先递交其批准书或加入书的 5 个国家，本协定应在递交第 5 份批准书或加入书的 3 个月后开始生效。

（b）对于任何其他国家，本协定应自总干事就其批准书或加入书发出通知之日起 3 个月后生效，除非批准书或加入书已经指定以后的日期。在后一种情况下，本协定应在指定的日期对该国生效。

（4）批准或加入本协定，应自动接受本协定的全部条款，并享有本协定的一切利益。

第十条 本协定的效力和有效期

本协定的效力和有效期应与《保护工业产权巴黎公约》的效力和有效期相同。

第十一条 第一条至第四条和第九条至第十五条的修订

（1）对第一条至第四条和第九条至第十五条都可提出修订，以便采用适当的改进。

（2）每项修订应在本专门联盟国家的代表会议上予以审议。

第十二条　退　出

（1）任何国家均可通知总干事退出本协定。退出仅对发出此通知的国家生效，对于本专门联盟的其他国家，本协定仍保持其全部效力。

（2）退出应自总干事收到通知之日起 1 年后生效。

（3）任何国家在成为本专门联盟成员国之日起 5 年届满以前，不得行使本条规定的退出的权利。

第十三条　领　地

《保护工业产权巴黎公约》第二十四条的规定适用于本协定。

第十四条　签字、语言、通知

（1）（a）本协定应在一份用英语和法语写成的文本上签字，两种文本均为同等的正本，并应由瑞士政府保存。

（b）本协定于 1969 年 6 月 30 日以前在伯尔尼开放签字。

（2）总干事在与有关政府协商后，应制定大会指定的其他语言的正式文本。

（3）总干事应将经瑞士政府证明的本协定签字文本两份送给各签字国政府，并根据请求送交任何其他国家政府。

（4）总干事应将本协定向联合国秘书处登记。

（5）总干事应将本协定的生效日期、签字、批准书或加入书的交存、本协定修正案的接受、该修正案的生效日期以及退出的通知等，通知本专门联盟所有国家政府。

第十五条　过渡条款

在第一任总干事就职前，本协定所指本组织的国际局或总干事应认为分别指保护知识产权联合国际局（BIRPI）或其总干事。

GUIDANCE FOR THE USER[1]

Version 2.1.25

The Locarno Classification consists of a list of classes and subclasses with, as the case may be, explanatory notes, and a list of goods with an indication of the class and subclass in which each good is classified (see Article 1 (3) of the *Locarno Agreement*).

Class and Subclass Headings

The Class Headings indicate in a general manner the fields to which the goods in principle belong.

The Subclass Headings give further specification as to the type of goods included in each class.

Explanatory Notes and General Remarks

For ascertaining the correct classification of a good, the Explanatory Notes relating to the various classes and subclasses, as well as the List of Goods should be consulted.

The Explanatory Notes can refer to a class or a subclass. The notes of a class apply to all subclasses within that class.

If a good cannot be classified with the aid of the List of Classes and Subclasses, the Explanatory Notes and the List of Goods, the General Remarks set forth the criteria that should be applied.

List of Goods

The List of Goods is presented in class and subclass order in the "Classes" tab and in alphabetical order in the "Alphabetical" tab. Each indication of good has a six-digit identification number (ID No.). Different indications of the same good (synonyms or indications with variant spellings) share the same ID No. The ID No. enables the user to find the equivalent good in the lists of goods of other language versions of the Classification.

(i) List of Goods in class order ("Classes" tab)

The list is presented in two columns; the first column shows the ID No. for each good and the second column shows the indication of the good. When an indication has synonyms and/or spelling variants, the second column contains the master indication on the first line, and the synonyms and/or spelling variants on the following lines, e.g.:

Class 03-01

ID No.   Indication (EN)

100325	**Vanity** cases
	Toilet cases

The alphabetical order within the subclass is determined by a keyword marked in bold in the master indication, in the example above "**Vanity**".

In the bilingual version (English/French), the list is presented in three columns, the third column containing the French version of the English indication appearing in the second column, e.g.:

---

[1] This guidance is about using the Locarno Classification. Information about using LOCPUB can be obtained by clicking on "Help" in the left upper corner of the screen.

Class 03-01

ID No.	Indication (EN)	Indication (FR)
100325	**Vanity** cases	**Vanity-cases**
	Toilet cases	**Nécessaires** de toilette [contenants]

(ii) List of Goods in alphabetical order ("Alphabetical" tab)

The list is presented in three columns, under each letter of the alphabet; the first column shows the class and subclass to which each good belongs, the second column shows the indication of the good, and the third column shows the ID No. for each good. The alphabetical order is determined by keywords marked in bold in each indication, whether master, synonym or spelling variant, e.g.:

Letter C

Cl.-Subcl.	Indication	ID No.
03-01	**Vanity** cases	100325
03-01	**Toilet** cases	100325

Letter T

Cl.-Subcl.	Indication	ID No.
03-01	**Toilet** cases	100325

Letter V

Cl.-Subcl.	Indication	ID No.
03-01	**Vanity** cases	100325

In the bilingual version (English/French), the list is presented in four columns, the fourth column containing the master indication in French of the English indication (s) appearing in the second column, e.g.:

Letter C

Cl.-Subcl.	Indication (EN)	ID No.	Indication (FR)
03-01	**Vanity** cases	100325	**Vanity-cases**
03-01	**Toilet** cases	100325	**Vanity-cases**

Letter T

Cl.-Subcl.	Indication (EN)	ID No.	Indication (FR)
03-01	**Toilet** cases	100325	**Vanity-cases**

Letter V

Cl.-Subcl.	Indication (EN)	ID No.	Indication (FR)
03-01	**Vanity** cases	100325	**Vanity-cases**

<u>Square brackets</u>

In the List of Goods, an expression between square brackets is in most cases intended to define more precisely the text preceding the brackets, since the said text is ambiguous or too vague for classification purposes.

* * *

使用指南[1]

第 2.1.25 版

《洛迦诺分类表》包括视情况而含有注释的大类和小类表，以及标示出所属大类和小类的产品项列表（参见《洛迦诺协定》第 1（3）条）。

大类和小类标题

大类标题规定该类产品的所属领域。

小类标题对每个大类中的产品类型作进一步阐述。

注释和概述

为确定产品的正确类别，应当查看与各个大类和小类相关的注释以及产品项列表。

大类或者小类均可包含注释。大类的注释适用于该大类中的所有小类。

如果依据大类和小类表、注释以及产品项列表仍然无法对产品进行分类，应当适用概述中阐明的标准。

产品项列表

产品项列表在"类别"标签中以大类和小类顺序进行排列，而在"字母"标签中以字母顺序排列。每个产品名称有一个六位的编码（ID No.）。相同产品的不同名称（同义词或具有变体拼写的名称）使用相同的编码。编码有助于使用者在其他语言版本分类表的产品项列表中找到相对应的产品。

（1）以类别排序排列的产品项列表（"类别"标签）

列表分为两栏，第一栏是每种产品的编码，第二栏是该产品的名称。 当一个名称具有同义词和/或拼写变体时，第二栏的第一行是主名称，下面是同义词和/或拼写变体，例如：

Class 03-01

ID No.	Indication（EN）
100325	**Vanity** cases
	Toilet cases

小类中的字母顺序根据主名称中粗体标示的关键词进行排序，比如上例中的 Vanity。

在双语版本（英文/法文）中，列表分为三栏，第三栏为第二栏英文名称的法文版，例如：

Class 03-01

ID No.	Indication（EN）	Indication（FR）
100325	**Vanity** cases	**Vanity**-cases
	Toilet cases	**Nécessaires** de toilette [contenants]

（2）按字母表顺序排列的产品项列表（"字母"标签）

在字母表的每个字母下，列表分为三栏：第一栏标示产品所属的大类和小类，第二栏是产品的名称，第三栏是该产品的编码。不论是主名称、同义词还是拼写变体，其字母排序都是以每种名称中粗体标示的关键词来进行的，例如：

---

[1] 该使用指南涉及《洛迦诺分类表》的使用，文中的有关 LOCPUB 的使用信息，可点击网页中的"帮助"标签。

Letter C

Cl.-Subcl.	Indication	ID No.
03-01	Vanity **cases**	100325
03-01	Toilet **cases**	100325

Letter T

Cl.-Subcl.	Indication	ID No.
03-01	**Toilet** cases	100325

Letter V

Cl.-Subcl.	Indication	ID No.
03-01	**Vanity** cases	100325

在双语版本（英文/法文）中，列表分为四栏，第四栏为第二栏英文名称的法文主名称，例如：

Letter C

Cl.-Subcl.	Indication（EN）	ID No.	Indication（FR）
03-01	Vanity **cases**	100325	**Vanity-cases**
03-01	Toilet **cases**	100325	**Vanity-cases**

Letter T

Cl.-Subcl.	Indication（EN）	ID No.	Indication（FR）
03-01	**Toilet** cases	100325	**Vanity-cases**

Letter V

Cl.-Subcl.	Indication（EN）	ID No.	Indication（FR）
03-01	**Vanity** cases	100325	**Vanity-cases**

方括号

在产品项列表中，由于方括号前用于分类的文字存在歧义或不明确，方括号内的短语通常用来更精确地解释方括号前的文字内容。

* * *

RECOMMENDATIONS CONCERNING THE APPLICATION OF THE LOCARNO CLASSIFICATION

The Committee of Experts set up under Article 3 of the Locarno Agreement recommended, at its sessions in September 1971 and March 1993, to the member countries of the Locarno Union that they apply, in their official documents and publications relating to registrations and renewals of industrial designs, the International Classification for Industrial Designs in the following manner:

(a) the class number should be indicated in Arabic figures; the subclass number should also be indicated in Arabic figures and it must always contain two digits; for the subclasses, therefore, the numbers 1 to 9 should be preceded by a 0; the class number should be separated from the subclass number by a dash (for example, Subclass 4 of Class 1 should be indicated as "1-04");

(b) the class and subclass numbers should be preceded by the indication "Cl." (for example, Cl. 1-04);

(c) if the numbers of several classes or subclasses must be indicated for one and the same deposit or registration, the classes should be separated by semicolons and subclasses by commas (for example, Cl. 8-05, 08; 11-01);

(d) the numbers of the classes and subclasses should be preceded by the abbreviation "LOC" and the edition according to which the industrial designs have been classified should be indicated by an Arabic figure in round brackets (for example, LOC (11) Cl. 8-05).

关于使用洛迦诺分类表的标注说明

依照《洛迦诺协定》第三条设立的专家委员会在其 1971 年 9 月和 1993 年 3 月召开的会议上建议，洛迦诺联盟成员国在外观设计注册及续期的官方文件和出版物中用如下方法标示国际外观设计分类号：

（a）大类号用阿拉伯数字表示，小类号也用阿拉伯数字表示并且应当包含两位数字，对于小类号，数字 1 到 9 之前应当加 0；大类号与小类号之间用破折号连接（例如：1 大类的 4 小类用"01-04"表示）；[1]

（b）大类和小类的分类号前应加标示"Cl."（例如：Cl.01-04）；

（c）若同一外观设计有多个分类号，应该用分号分隔其大类，用逗号分隔其小类（例如：Cl.08-05，08；11-01）；

（d）大类和小类的分类号前应加缩写词"LOC"和置于圆括号内以阿拉伯数字表示的外观设计分类表的版本号（例如：LOC（11）Cl.08-05）。

---

[1] 国际上通常也将大类号用两位数字表示，在数字 1 到 9 之前加 0。我国遵照此惯例执行。

LOCARNO CLASSIFICATION
(13th EDITION)

洛迦诺分类表
(第13版)

LIST OF CLASSES

Class 1	Foodstuffs
Class 2	Articles of clothing and haberdashery
Class 3	Travel goods, cases, parasols and personal belongings, not elsewhere specified
Class 4	Brushware
Class 5	Textile piece goods, artificial and natural sheet material
Class 6	Furnishing
Class 7	Household goods, not elsewhere specified
Class 8	Tools and hardware
Class 9	Packaging and containers for the transport or handling of goods
Class 10	Clocks and watches and other measuring instruments, checking and signalling instruments
Class 11	Articles of adornment
Class 12	Means of transport or hoisting
Class 13	Equipment for production, distribution or transformation of electricity
Class 14	Recording, telecommunication or data processing equipment
Class 15	Machines, not elsewhere specified
Class 16	Photographic, cinematographic and optical apparatus
Class 17	Musical instruments
Class 18	Printing and office machinery
Class 19	Stationery and office equipment, artists' and teaching materials
Class 20	Sales and advertising equipment, signs
Class 21	Games, toys, tents and sports goods
Class 22	Arms, pyrotechnic articles, articles for hunting, fishing and pest killing
Class 23	Fluid distribution equipment, sanitary, heating, ventilation and air-conditioning equipment, solid fuel
Class 24	Medical and laboratory equipment
Class 25	Building units and construction elements
Class 26	Lighting apparatus
Class 27	Tobacco and smokers' supplies
Class 28	Pharmaceutical and cosmetic products, toilet articles and apparatus
Class 29	Devices and equipment against fire hazards, for accident prevention and for rescue
Class 30	Articles for the care and handling of animals
Class 31	Machines and appliances for preparing food or drink, not elsewhere specified
Class 32	Graphic symbols and logos, surface patterns, ornamentation

大 类 表

01 类　　食品

02 类　　服装、服饰用品和缝纫用品

03 类　　其他类未列入的旅行用品、箱包、阳伞和个人用品

04 类　　刷子

05 类　　纺织品，人造或天然材料片材

06 类　　家具和家居用品

07 类　　其他类未列入的家用物品

08 类　　工具和五金器具

09 类　　用于商品运输或装卸的包装和容器

10 类　　钟、表及其他测量仪器，检测仪器，信号仪器

11 类　　装饰品

12 类　　运输或提升工具

13 类　　发电、配电或变电设备

14 类　　记录、电信或数据处理设备

15 类　　其他类未列入的机械

16 类　　照相设备、电影摄影设备和光学设备

17 类　　乐器

18 类　　印刷和办公机械

19 类　　文具、办公用品、美术用品和教学用品

20 类　　销售设备、广告设备和标志物

21 类　　游戏器具、玩具、帐篷和体育用品

22 类　　武器，烟火用品，用于狩猎、捕鱼及捕杀有害动物的用具

23 类　　流体分配设备、卫生设备、加热设备、通风和空气调节设备、固体燃料

24 类　　医疗设备和实验室设备

25 类　　建筑构件和施工元件

26 类　　照明设备

27 类　　烟草和吸烟用具

28 类　　药品，化妆品，梳妆用品和设备

29 类　　防火灾、防事故、救援用的装置及设备

30 类　　动物照管与驯养用品

31 类　　其他类未列入的食品或饮料制备机械和设备

32 类　　图形符号、标识、表面图案、纹饰

LIST OF CLASSES AND SUBCLASSES, WITH EXPLANATORY NOTES

GENERAL REMARKS

(a) The titles of the classes and subclasses provide a general indication as to the area to which the goods belong. Some goods may be covered by more than one such title, however. It is therefore advisable to consult the Alphabetical List to make sure of the classification of various goods.

(b) Explanatory notes relating to a class are not repeated in the subclasses which they concern. It is therefore advisable to consult them when studying the notes appearing in the subclasses themselves.

(c) In principle, goods are classified first according to their purpose and subsidiarily, if this is possible, according to the object that they represent. This latter classification is optional.

(d) Where there is no special classification provided for goods intended to form part of another product, those goods are placed in the same class and subclass as the product of which they are intended to form part, if they cannot normally be used for another purpose.

(e) Goods, which are multipurpose composite objects are, with the exception of multipurpose composite pieces of furniture, placed in all the classes and subclasses that correspond to each of the intended purposes.

大类和小类表（含注释）

概　述

（a）大类和小类的标题概括规定了该类产品所属的领域。对于可能被多个标题所涵盖的产品，可以参考按字母顺序排列的产品项列表确定产品的分类。

（b）大类的注释不在涉及的小类中重复，因此研究小类时应参考大类的注释。

（c）原则上，首先，根据产品的用途进行分类，其次，在可能的情况下也可以根据其所代表的对象进行分类。后者是可选的。

（d）对于可以作为其他产品部件的产品，若无专属类别，而通常也不被用于其他用途，则分入其构成产品所属的类别中。

（e）对于多用途的复合产品（多用途复合家具除外），应分在与每种用途相应的类别中。

LIST OF CLASSES AND SUBCLASSES, WITH EXPLANATORY NOTES

CLASS 1

Foodstuffs

Notes: (a) Including foodstuffs for human beings, foodstuffs for animals and dietetic foods.
(b) Not including packaging (Cl. 09).

01-01	BAKERS' PRODUCTS, BISCUITS, PASTRY, PASTA AND OTHER CEREAL PRODUCTS, CHOCOLATES, CONFECTIONERY, ICES	(69)
01-02	FRUIT, VEGETABLES AND PRODUCTS MADE FROM FRUITS AND VEGETABLES	(70)
01-03	CHEESES, BUTTER AND BUTTER SUBSTITUTES, OTHER DAIRY PRODUCE	(70)
01-04	BUTCHERS' MEAT (INCLUDING PORK PRODUCTS), FISH	(71)
01-05	TOFU AND TOFU PRODUCTS	(71)
01-06	ANIMAL FOODSTUFFS	(71)
01-99	MISCELLANEOUS	(71)

CLASS 2

Articles of clothing and haberdashery

Note: Not including articles of clothing for dolls (Cl. 21-01), special equipment for protection against fire hazards, for accident prevention and for rescue (Cl. 29), and animal clothing (Cl. 30-01).

02-01　UNDERGARMENTS, LINGERIE, CORSETS, BRASSIÈRES, NIGHTWEAR　(72)
　　　Notes: (a) Including orthopedic corsets and body linen.
　　　　　　(b) Not including household linen (Cl. 06-13).
02-02　GARMENTS　(73)
　　　Notes: (a) Including all sorts of garments, and furs, bathing costumes, sports clothing and orthopedic garments, subject to the exceptions indicated under (b).
　　　　　　(b) Not including undergarments (Cl. 02-01), or garments to be placed in Cl. 02-03, Cl. 02-04, Cl. 02-05 or Cl. 02-06.
02-03　HEADWEAR　(76)
　　　Note: Including all kinds of headwear for men, women and children.
02-04　FOOTWEAR, SOCKS AND STOCKINGS　(77)
　　　Note: Including special boots for sports such as football, skiing and ice hockey,

orthopedic footwear and socks, as well as tights, gaiters and other legwear.

02-05　　NECKTIES, SCARVES, NECKERCHIEFS AND HANDKERCHIEFS ·············· (78)

　　　　　Note: Including all "flat" clothing accessories.

02-06　　GLOVES ··· (79)

　　　　　Note: Including surgical gloves and rubber or plastic protective gloves for household use or for various occupations or sports.

02-07　　HABERDASHERY AND CLOTHING ACCESSORIES ······························ (79)

　　　　　Notes: (a) Including buttons, for garments, for headwear and for footwear, laces, pins, hand sewing, knitting and embroidery equipment and clothing accessories such as belts, straps for suspender belts, braces.

　　　　　　　　(b) Not including yarns or other threads (Cl. 05-01), decorative trimmings (Cl. 05-04), sewing, knitting and embroidery machines (Cl. 15-06) or sewing kits (containers) (Cl. 03-01).

02-99　　MISCELLANEOUS ·· (82)

CLASS 3

Travel goods, cases, parasols and personal belongings, not elsewhere specified

03-01　　TRUNKS, SUITCASES, BRIEFCASES, HANDBAGS, KEYHOLDERS, CASES SPECIALLY DESIGNED FOR THEIR CONTENTS, WALLETS AND SIMILAR ARTICLES ·· (83)

　　　　　Note: Not including articles for the transport of goods (Cl. 09) or cigar cases and cigarette cases (Cl. 27-06).

03-02　　[VACANT] ·· (86)

03-03　　UMBRELLAS, PARASOLS, SUNSHADES AND WALKING STICKS ·············· (86)

03-04　　FANS ··· (87)

03-05　　DEVICES FOR CARRYING AND WALKING WITH BABIES AND CHILDREN ············ (87)

　　　　　Note: Not including baby carriers in Cl. 06 and Cl. 12.

03-99　　MISCELLANEOUS ·· (88)

CLASS 4

Brushware

04-01　　BRUSHES AND BROOMS FOR CLEANING ······································· (89)

　　　　　Note: Not including clothes brushes (Cl. 04-02).

04-02　　TOILET BRUSHES, CLOTHES BRUSHES AND SHOE BRUSHES ············ (89)

Notes: (a) "Toilet brushes" means brushes for corporal use, for example, for the hair, nails or teeth.

(b) Not including electric toothbrushes [appliances] (Cl. 28-03).

04-03　BRUSHES FOR MACHINES .... (90)

Note: "Brushes for machines" means brushes incorporated in machines or in special vehicles.

04-04　PAINTBRUSHES, BRUSHES FOR USE IN COOKING .... (90)

04-99　MISCELLANEOUS .... (90)

CLASS 5

Textile piece goods, artificial and natural sheet material

Notes: (a) Including all textile or similar articles, sold by the yarn and not made up.

(b) Not including ready-made articles (Cl. 02 or 06).

05-01　SPUN ARTICLES .... (91)

Notes: (a) Including yarn and thread.

(b) Not including, for instance, rope, wire rope, string, twine (Cl. 09-06).

05-02　LACE .... (91)

05-03　EMBROIDERY .... (91)

05-04　RIBBONS, BRAIDS AND OTHER DECORATIVE TRIMMINGS .... (91)

05-05　TEXTILE FABRICS .... (92)

Note: Including textile fabrics, woven, knitted or otherwise manufactured, tarpaulins, felt and loden.

05-06　ARTIFICIAL OR NATURAL SHEET MATERIAL .... (93)

Notes: (a) Including sheets whose only characteristic features are their surface ornamentation or their texture, in particular, covering sheets such as wallpaper, linoleum, self-adhesive plastic sheets, wrapping sheets and rolls of paper, subject to the exceptions indicated under (b).

(b) Not including writing paper, even in rolls (Cl. 19-01), or sheets used as building components, such as wall panels and wainscoting (Cl. 25-01).

05-99　MISCELLANEOUS .... (94)

CLASS 6

Furnishing

Notes: (a) Composite furniture articles embodying components included in several subclasses are classified in Cl. 06-05.

(b) Sets of furniture, as far as they can be looked upon as one design, are classified in Cl. 06-05.

(c) Not including textile piecegoods (Cl. 05).

06-01　　SEATS ··· (95)

　　　　　Notes: (a) Including all seats even if they are suitable for laying, such as benches, couches, divans [sofas], ottomans, benches for saunas and sofas.

　　　　　　　　(b) Including vehicle seats.

06-02　　BEDS ··· (96)

　　　　　Notes: (a) Including mattress supports.

　　　　　　　　(b) Not including seats suitable for laying (Cl. 06-01), such as benches, couches, divans [sofas], ottomans, benches for saunas and sofas.

06-03　　TABLES AND SIMILAR FURNITURE ·· (97)

06-04　　STORAGE FURNITURE ·· (98)

　　　　　Notes: (a) Including cupboards, furniture with drawers or compartments, and shelves.

　　　　　　　　(b) Including coffins, coffin linings and crematory urns.

06-05　　COMPOSITE FURNITURE ···(100)

06-06　　OTHER FURNITURE AND FURNITURE PARTS ···(100)

06-07　　MIRRORS AND FRAMES ··(102)

　　　　　Note: Not including mirrors included in other classes (see Alphabetical List).

06-08　　CLOTHES HANGERS ···(102)

06-09　　MATTRESSES AND CUSHIONS ··(102)

06-10　　CURTAINS AND INDOOR BLINDS ···(103)

06-11　　CARPETS, MATS AND RUGS ··(103)

06-12　　TAPESTRIES ···(104)

06-13　　BLANKETS AND OTHER COVERING MATERIALS, HOUSEHOLD LINEN AND NAPERY ··(104)

　　　　　Note: Including furniture covers, bedspreads and table covers.

06-99　　MISCELLANEOUS ···(105)

CLASS 7

Household goods, not elsewhere specified

Notes: (a) Including household appliances and utensils operated by hand, even if motor driven.

　　　　(b) Not including machines and appliances for preparing food and drink (Cl. 31).

07-01　　CHINA, GLASSWARE, DISHES AND OTHER ARTICLES OF A SIMILAR NATURE ··· (106)

　　　　Notes: (a) Including dishes and crockery in all materials, in particular, paper and cardboard dishes.

　　　　　　　(b) Not including cooking utensils and containers, such as glass and earthenware pots (Cl. 07-02), or flower vases, flower pots and china and glassware of a purely ornamental nature (Cl. 11-02).

07-02　　COOKING APPLIANCES, UTENSILS AND CONTAINERS ·················· (108)

07-03　　TABLE CUTLERY ·· (110)

07-04　　APPLIANCES AND UTENSILS, HAND-OPERATED, FOR PREPARING FOOD OR DRINK ····················· (111)

　　　　Notes: (a) Not including appliances and utensils classified in Cl. 07-02 and in Cl. 31.

　　　　　　　(b) Not including kitchen knives, knives for boning meat (Cl. 08-03).

07-05　　FLAT-IRONS AND WASHING, CLEANING AND DRYING EQUIPMENT ·········· (113)

　　　　Note: Not including electric household appliances for washing, cleaning or drying (Cl. 15-05).

07-06　　OTHER TABLE UTENSILS ·· (114)

07-07　　OTHER HOUSEHOLD RECEPTACLES ·· (115)

07-08　　FIREPLACE IMPLEMENTS ·· (116)

07-09　　STANDS AND HOLDERS FOR HOUSEHOLD APPLIANCES AND UTENSILS ·········· (116)

07-10　　COOLING AND FREEZING DEVICES AND ISOTHERMAL CONTAINERS ·········· (117)

07-99　　MISCELLANEOUS ·· (117)

CLASS 8

Tools and hardware

Notes: (a) Including hand-operated tools, even if mechanical power takes the place of muscular force, for example, electric saws and drills.

　　　　(b) Not including machines or machine tools (Cl. 15 or 31).

08-01　　TOOLS AND IMPLEMENTS FOR DRILLING, MILLING OR DIGGING ·········· (119)

08-02　　HAMMERS AND OTHER SIMILAR TOOLS AND IMPLEMENTS ················ (120)

08-03　　CUTTING TOOLS AND IMPLEMENTS ·· (120)

　　　　Notes: (a) Including tools and instruments for sawing.

　　　　　　　(b) Not including table knives (Cl. 07-03), cutting tools and implements for kitchen use (Cl. 31), or knives used in surgery (Cl. 24-02).

08-04　　SCREWDRIVERS AND OTHER SIMILAR TOOLS AND IMPLEMENTS ·········· (122)

08-05　　OTHER TOOLS AND IMPLEMENTS ·· (122)

Notes: (a) Including tools which are not classified, or not to be placed, in other subclasses or classes.

(b) Including sanding blocks and discs for sanding machines.

(c) Not including sandpaper (Cl. 05-06).

08-06 HANDLES, KNOBS AND HINGES ·· (126)

08-07 LOCKING OR CLOSING DEVICES ··· (127)

Note: Not including buckles [haberdashery] (Cl. 02-07) and key rings (Cl. 03-01).

08-08 FASTENING, SUPPORTING OR MOUNTING DEVICES NOT INCLUDED IN OTHER CLASSES ··· (128)

Notes: (a) Including nails, screws, nuts and bolts.

(b) Not including fastening devices for clothing (Cl. 02-07), for adornment (Cl. 11-01), or for office use (Cl. 19-02).

08-09 METAL FITTINGS AND MOUNTINGS FOR DOORS, WINDOWS AND FURNITURE, AND SIMILAR ARTICLES, NOT INCLUDED IN OTHER CLASSES OR SUBCLASSES ··· (130)

08-10 BICYCLE AND MOTORCYCLE RACKS ··· (131)

Notes: (a) Including repair stands or stands for parking cycles.

(b) Not including retractable stands that are parts of cycles (Cl. 12-11).

08-11 HARDWARE FOR CURTAINS ·· (131)

08-99 MISCELLANEOUS ·· (132)

Note: Including non-electric cables, regardless of the material of which they are made.

CLASS 9

Packaging and containers for the transport or handling of goods

09-01 BOTTLES, FLASKS, POTS, CARBOYS, DEMIJOHNS, AND PRESSURIZED CONTAINERS ·· (133)

Notes: (a) "Pots" means those serving as containers.

(b) Not including pots regarded as crockery (Cl. 07-01), or flower pots (Cl. 11-02).

09-02 STORAGE CANS, DRUMS AND CASKS ·· (134)

09-03 BOXES, CASES, CONTAINERS, TIN CANS ·· (134)

Note: Including freight containers.

09-04 HAMPERS, CRATES AND BASKETS ··· (135)

09-05 BAGS, SACHETS, TUBES AND CAPSULES ·· (136)

Notes: (a) Including plastic bags or sachets, with or without handle or means of closing.

(b) "Capsules" means those used for packaging.

09-06	ROPES AND HOOPING MATERIALS	(137)
09-07	CLOSING MEANS AND ATTACHMENTS	(137)

        Notes: (a) Including only closing means for packaging.

                (b) "Attachments" means, for example, dispensing and dosing devices incorporated in containers and detachable atomizers.

09-08	PALLETS AND PLATFORMS FOR FORKLIFTS	(138)
09-09	REFUSE AND TRASH CONTAINERS AND STANDS THEREFOR	(138)
09-10	HANDLES AND GRIPS FOR THE TRANSPORT OR HANDLING OF PACKAGES AND CONTAINERS	(139)
09-99	MISCELLANEOUS	(139)

CLASS 10

Clocks and watches and other measuring instruments, checking and signalling instruments

Note: Including electrically-driven instruments.

10-01	CLOCKS AND ALARM CLOCKS	(140)
10-02	WATCHES AND WRIST WATCHES	(140)
10-03	OTHER TIME-MEASURING INSTRUMENTS	(140)

        Note: Including time-measuring apparatus such as parking meters, timers for kitchen use and similar instruments.

10-04	OTHER MEASURING INSTRUMENTS, APPARATUS AND DEVICES	(141)

        Notes: (a) Including instruments, apparatus and devices for measuring temperature, pressure, weight, length, volume and electricity.

                (b) Not including exposure meters (Cl. 16-05).

10-05	INSTRUMENTS, APPARATUS AND DEVICES FOR CHECKING, SECURITY OR TESTING	(145)

        Note: Including fire and burglar alarms, and detectors of various types.

10-06	SIGNALLING APPARATUS AND DEVICES	(146)

        Note: Not including lighting or signalling devices for vehicles (Cl. 26-06).

10-07	CASINGS, CASES, DIALS, HANDS AND ALL OTHER PARTS AND ACCESSORIES OF INSTRUMENTS FOR MEASURING, CHECKING AND SIGNALLING	(147)

        Note: "Casings" means watch and clock casings and all casings being integral parts of instruments of which they protect the mechanism, with the exception of cases specially designed for their contents (Cl. 03-01) or for packaging (Cl. 09-03).

10-99	MISCELLANEOUS	(148)

CLASS 11

Articles of adornment

11-01	JEWELLERY	(149)

        Notes: (a) Including costume and imitation jewellery.
                 (b) Not including watches (Cl. 10-02).

11-02	TRINKETS, TABLE, MANTEL AND WALL ORNAMENTS, FLOWER VASES AND POTS	(150)

        Note: Including sculptures, mobiles and statues.

11-03	MEDALS AND BADGES	(151)
11-04	ARTIFICIAL FLOWERS, FRUIT AND PLANTS	(151)
11-05	FLAGS, FESTIVE DECORATIONS	(152)

        Notes: (a) Including garlands, streamers and Christmas tree decorations.
                 (b) Not including candles (Cl. 26-04).

11-99	MISCELLANEOUS	(152)

CLASS 12

Means of transport or hoisting

Notes: (a) Including all vehicles: land, sea, air, space and others.

        (b) Including parts, components and accessories which exist only in connection with a vehicle and cannot be placed in another class; these parts, components and accessories of vehicles are to be placed in the subclass of the vehicle in question, or in Cl. 12-16 if they are common to several vehicles included in different subclasses.

        (c) Not including, in principle, parts, components and accessories of vehicles which can be placed in another class; these parts, components and accessories are to be placed in the same class as articles of the same type, in other words, having the same function. Thus, carpets or mats for automobiles are to be placed with carpets (Cl. 06-11); electric motors for vehicles are to be placed in Cl. 13-01, and non-electric motors for vehicles in Cl. 15-01 (the same applies to the components of such motors); automobile headlamps are to be placed with lighting apparatus (Cl. 26-06).

        (d) Not including scale models of vehicles (Cl. 21-01).

12-01	VEHICLES DRAWN BY ANIMALS	(153)
12-02	HANDCARTS, WHEELBARROWS	(153)
12-03	LOCOMOTIVES AND ROLLING STOCK FOR RAILWAYS AND ALL OTHER RAIL VEHICLES	(154)

12-04	TELPHER CARRIERS, CHAIR LIFTS AND SKI LIFTS	(155)
12-05	ELEVATORS AND HOISTS FOR LOADING OR CONVEYING	(155)

Note: Including passenger lifts, goods lifts, cranes, forklift trucks and conveyor belts.

12-06	SHIPS AND BOATS	(157)
12-07	AIRCRAFT AND SPACE VEHICLES	(158)
12-08	MOTOR CARS, BUSES AND LORRIES	(158)

Note: Including ambulances and refrigerator vans (road).

12-09	TRACTORS	(159)
12-10	ROAD VEHICLE TRAILERS	(159)

Note: Including caravans.

12-11	CYCLES AND MOTORCYCLES	(159)
12-12	PERAMBULATORS, INVALID CHAIRS, STRETCHERS	(161)

Notes: (a) "Perambulators" means hand carriages for infants.
(b) Not including toy perambulators (Cl. 21-01).

12-13	SPECIAL-PURPOSE VEHICLES	(162)

Notes: (a) Including only vehicles not specifically intended for transport, such as street cleaning vehicles, watering lorries, fire engines, snow ploughs and breakdown lorries.
(b) Not including mixed-purpose agricultural machines (Cl. 15-03), or self-propelled machines for use in construction and civil engineering (Cl. 15-04).

12-14	OTHER VEHICLES	(162)

Note: Including sleighs and air-cushion vehicles.

12-15	TYRES AND ANTI-SKID CHAINS FOR VEHICLES	(163)
12-16	PARTS, EQUIPMENT AND ACCESSORIES FOR VEHICLES, NOT INCLUDED IN OTHER CLASSES OR SUBCLASSES	(163)

Notes: (a) Not including safety belts for the seats of vehicles (Cl. 29-02), door handles for vehicles (Cl. 08-06).
(b) Not including pantographs for electric locomotives or trams (Cl. 13-03).

12-17	RAILWAY INFRASTRUCTURE COMPONENTS	(166)

Note: Not including railway rails and sleepers (Cl. 25-01), buffers for railway terminals (Cl. 25-99) and railway signals (Cl. 10-06).

12-99	MISCELLANEOUS	(166)

CLASS 13

Equipment for production, distribution or transformation of electricity

Notes: (a) Including only apparatus which produces, distributes or transforms electric current.
(b) Including electric motors, however.
(c) Not including electrically-driven apparatus, such as electric watches (Cl. 10-02), or apparatus for the measurement of electric current (Cl. 10-04).

13-01	GENERATORS AND MOTORS	(167)
	Note: Including electric motors for vehicles.	
13-02	POWER TRANSFORMERS, RECTIFIERS, BATTERIES AND ACCUMULATORS	(167)
13-03	EQUIPMENT FOR DISTRIBUTION OR CONTROL OF ELECTRIC POWER	(168)
	Note: Including conductors, switches and switchboards.	
13-04	SOLAR EQUIPMENT	(170)
	Note: Not including solar heat collectors (Cl. 23-03).	
13-99	MISCELLANEOUS	(170)

CLASS 14

Recording, telecommunication or data processing equipment

14-01	EQUIPMENT FOR THE RECORDING OR REPRODUCTION OF SOUNDS OR PICTURES	(171)
	Note: Not including photographic or cinematographic apparatus (Cl. 16).	
14-02	DATA PROCESSING EQUIPMENT AS WELL AS PERIPHERAL APPARATUS AND DEVICES	(172)
14-03	TELECOMMUNICATIONS EQUIPMENT, WIRELESS REMOTE CONTROLS AND RADIO AMPLIFIERS	(174)
	Note: Including telephone and television apparatus, as well as radio sets.	
14-04	SCREEN DISPLAYS AND ICONS	(176)
	Note: Including those for goods belonging to other classes.	
14-05	RECORDING AND DATA STORAGE MEDIA	(176)
14-06	HOLDERS, STANDS AND SUPPORTS FOR ELECTRONIC EQUIPMENT, NOT INCLUDED IN OTHER CLASSES	(176)
14-99	MISCELLANEOUS	(177)

CLASS 15

Machines, not elsewhere specified

15-01	ENGINES	(178)

Notes: (a) Including non-electric engines for vehicles.

(b) Not including electric motors (Cl. 13).

15-02	PUMPS AND COMPRESSORS	(178)

Note: Not including hand or foot pumps (Cl. 08-05), or fire extinguishing pumps (Cl. 29-01).

15-03	AGRICULTURAL AND FORESTRY MACHINERY	(179)

Notes: (a) Including ploughs and combined machinery, i.e., both machines and vehicles, for example, reaping and binding machines.

(b) Not including hand tools (Cl. 08).

15-04	CONSTRUCTION AND MINING MACHINERY	(181)

Notes: (a) Including machines used in civil engineering and self-propelled machines such as excavators, concrete mixers and dredgers.

(b) Not including hoists and cranes (Cl. 12-05).

15-05	WASHING, CLEANING AND DRYING MACHINES	(181)

Notes: (a) Including appliances and machines for treating linen and clothes, such as ironing machines and wringers.

(b) Including dishwashing machines and industrial drying equipment.

15-06	TEXTILE, SEWING, KNITTING AND EMBROIDERING MACHINES, INCLUDING THEIR INTEGRAL PARTS	(183)
15-07	REFRIGERATION MACHINERY AND APPARATUS	(184)

Notes: (a) Including household refrigeration apparatus.

(b) Not including refrigerator wagons (rail) (Cl. 12-03) or refrigerator vans (road) (Cl. 12-08).

15-08	[VACANT]	(184)
15-09	MACHINE TOOLS, ABRADING AND FOUNDING MACHINERY	(184)

Note: Including 3D printers.

15-10	MACHINERY FOR FILLING, PACKING OR PACKAGING	(187)
15-99	MISCELLANEOUS	(187)

CLASS 16

Photographic, cinematographic and optical apparatus

Note: Not including lamps for photography or filming (Cl. 26-05).

16-01	PHOTOGRAPHIC CAMERAS AND FILM CAMERAS	(189)
16-02	PROJECTORS AND VIEWERS	(189)
16-03	PHOTOCOPYING APPARATUS AND ENLARGERS	(190)

Note: Including microfilming equipment and apparatus for viewing microfilms, as well as office machines known as "photocopying" apparatus which use other than photographic processes (in particular, thermal or magnetic processes).

16-04	DEVELOPING APPARATUS AND EQUIPMENT	(190)
16-05	ACCESSORIES	(190)

Note: Including filters for photographic cameras, exposure meters, tripods and photographic flash apparatus.

16-06	OPTICAL ARTICLES	(191)

Notes: (a) Including spectacles and microscopes.

(b) Not including measuring instruments embodying optical devices (Cl. 10-04).

16-99	MISCELLANEOUS	(192)

CLASS 17

Musical instruments

Note: Not including cases for musical instruments (Cl. 03-01), or equipment for the recording or reproduction of sounds (Cl. 14-01).

17-01	KEYBOARD INSTRUMENTS	(193)

Note: Including electronic and other organs, accordions, and mechanical and other pianos.

17-02	WIND INSTRUMENTS	(193)

Note: Not including organs, harmoniums and accordions (Cl. 17-01).

17-03	STRINGED INSTRUMENTS	(194)
17-04	PERCUSSION INSTRUMENTS	(195)
17-05	MECHANICAL INSTRUMENTS	(195)

Notes: (a) Including music boxes.

(b) Not including mechanical keyboard instruments (Cl. 17-01).

17-99	MISCELLANEOUS	(195)

CLASS 18

Printing and office machinery

18-01　　TYPEWRITERS AND CALCULATING MACHINES ·· (197)

Note：Not including computers and other apparatus to be placed in Cl. 14-02.

18-02　　PRINTING MACHINES ··· (197)

Notes：（a）Including typesetting machines, stereotype machines and apparatus, typographic machines and other reproducing machines such as duplicators and offset equipment, as well as addressing machines, franking and cancelling machines.

（b）Not including computer printers（Cl. 14-02）and photocopying machinery（Cl. 16-03）.

18-03　　TYPE AND TYPE FACES ··· (198)

18-04　　BOOKBINDING MACHINES, PRINTERS' STAPLING MACHINES, GUILLOTINES AND TRIMMERS（FOR BOOKBINDING）·· (199)

Note：Including machines and similar devices for cutting paper, analogous to guillotines and trimmers.

18-99　　MISCELLANEOUS ··· (199)

CLASS 19

Stationery and office equipment, artists' and teaching materials

19-01　　WRITING PAPER, CARDS FOR CORRESPONDENCE AND ANNOUNCEMENTS ····· (200)

Note：Including all paper, in the widest sense of the term, which is used for writing, drawing, painting or printing, such as tracing paper, carbon paper, newsprint, envelopes, greetings cards and illustrated postcards, even if they embody a sound recording.

19-02　　OFFICE EQUIPMENT ··· (201)

Notes：（a）Including equipment used at cash desks, such as change sorters.

（b）Some office equipment is to be placed in other subclasses or classes, for example, office furniture in Cl. 06, office machines and equipment in Cl. 14-02, Cl. 16-03, Cl. 18-01, Cl. 18-02 or Cl. 18-04, and writing materials in Cl. 19-01 or Cl. 19-06（see Alphabetical List）.

19-03　　CALENDARS ··· (203)

Note：Not including diaries（Cl. 19-04）.

19-04　　BOOKS AND OTHER OBJECTS OF SIMILAR OUTWARD APPEARANCE ················ (203)

Note：Including covers of books, bindings, albums, diaries and similar objects.

LOCARNO CLASSIFICATION (13th EDITION) —LIST OF CLASSES AND SUBCLASSES, WITH EXPLANATORY NOTES

19-05 [VACANT] (204)

19-06 MATERIALS AND INSTRUMENTS FOR WRITING BY HAND, FOR DRAWING, FOR PAINTING, FOR SCULPTURE, FOR ENGRAVING AND FOR OTHER ARTISTIC TECHNIQUES (204)

    Note: Not including paintbrushes (Cl. 04-04), drawing tables and attached equipment (Cl. 06-03), or writing paper (Cl. 19-01).

19-07 TEACHING MATERIALS AND APPARATUS (206)

    Notes: (a) Including maps of all kinds, globes and planetariums.

           (b) Not including audio-visual teaching aids (Cl. 14-01).

19-08 OTHER PRINTED MATTER (207)

    Note: Including printed advertising materials.

19-99 MISCELLANEOUS (208)

CLASS 20

Sales and advertising equipment, signs

20-01 AUTOMATIC VENDING MACHINES (210)

20-02 DISPLAY AND SALES EQUIPMENT (210)

    Note: Not including articles of furniture (Cl. 06).

20-03 SIGNS, SIGNBOARDS AND ADVERTISING DEVICES (211)

    Notes: (a) Including luminous advertising devices and mobile advertising devices.

           (b) Not including packaging (Cl. 09), or signalling devices (Cl. 10-06).

20-99 MISCELLANEOUS (212)

CLASS 21

Games, toys, tents and sports goods

21-01 GAMES AND TOYS (213)

    Notes: (a) Including scale models.

           (b) Not including toys for animals (Cl. 30-12)[1].

21-02 GYMNASTICS AND SPORTS APPARATUS AND EQUIPMENT (215)

    Notes: (a) Including sports apparatus and equipment that are necessary for the practice of various sports and which normally have no other specific purpose, such as footballs, skis and tennis rackets, excluding all other sporting objects classified in other classes and subclasses according to other functions (for example, canoes, boats(Cl. 12-06), air guns(Cl. 22-01), mats for sports(Cl. 06-11)).

---

1 原英文注释为 (Cl. 30-99),由于第 12 版中产品项"动物用玩具"由 30-99 类转移至新增的 30-12 类,编译时进行了修改。

46

(b) Including, subject to the reservation mentioned under (a), training equipment, and apparatus and equipment necessary for outdoor games.

(c) Not including sports clothing (Cl. 02), toboggans or sleighs (Cl. 12-14).

21-03 OTHER AMUSEMENT AND ENTERTAINMENT ARTICLES ·········· (218)

Notes: (a) Including fairground roundabouts and automatic machines for games of chance.

(b) Not including games and toys (Cl. 21-01), or other articles to be placed in Cl. 21-01 or Cl. 21-02.

21-04 TENTS AND ACCESSORIES THEREOF ·········· (219)

Notes: (a) Including poles, pegs and other similar articles.

(b) Not including other camping articles to be placed in other classes according to their nature, such as chairs (Cl. 06-01), tables (Cl 06-03), plates (Cl. Cl. 07-01), and caravans (Cl. 12-10).

21-99 MISCELLANEOUS ·········· (219)

CLASS 22

Arms, pyrotechnic articles, articles for hunting, fishing and pest killing

22-01	PROJECTILE WEAPONS ··········	(220)
22-02	OTHER WEAPONS ··········	(221)
22-03	AMMUNITION, ROCKETS AND PYROTECHNIC ARTICLES ··········	(221)
22-04	TARGETS AND ACCESSORIES ··········	(222)

Note: Including the special device for actuating mobile targets.

22-05 HUNTING AND FISHING EQUIPMENT ·········· (222)

Note: Not including articles of clothing (Cl. 02), or weapons (Cl. 22-01 or Cl. 22-02).

22-06 TRAPS, ARTICLES FOR PEST KILLING ·········· (223)

22-99 MISCELLANEOUS ·········· (224)

CLASS 23

Fluid distribution equipment, sanitary, heating, ventilation and air-conditioning equipment, solid fuel

23-01 FLUID DISTRIBUTION EQUIPMENT ·········· (225)

Note: Including pipes and pipe fittings.

23-02 [VACANT] ·········· (227)

23-03 HEATING EQUIPMENT ·········· (227)

23-04 VENTILATION AND AIR-CONDITIONING EQUIPMENT ·········· (228)

23-05	SOLID FUEL	(229)
23-06	SANITARY APPLIANCES FOR PERSONAL HYGIENE	(229)
23-07	EQUIPMENT FOR URINATION AND DEFECATION	(230)
23-08	OTHER SANITARY EQUIPMENT AND ACCESSORIES, NOT INCLUDED IN OTHER CLASSES OR SUBCLASSES	(230)
23-99	MISCELLANEOUS	(231)

CLASS 24

Medical and laboratory equipment

Note: The term "medical equipment" covers also surgical, dental and veterinary equipment.

24-01	APPARATUS AND EQUIPMENT FOR DOCTORS, HOSPITALS AND LABORATORIES	(232)
24-02	MEDICAL INSTRUMENTS, INSTRUMENTS AND TOOLS FOR LABORATORY USE	(233)

Note: Including only hand-operated instruments.

24-03	PROSTHETIC ARTICLES	(236)
24-04	MATERIALS FOR DRESSING WOUNDS, NURSING AND MEDICAL CARE	(236)

Note: Including absorbent dressings.

24-99	MISCELLANEOUS	(238)

CLASS 25

Building units and construction elements

25-01	BUILDING MATERIALS	(239)

Note: Including bricks, beams, pre-shaped strips, tiles, slates and panels.

25-02	PREFABRICATED OR PRE-ASSEMBLED BUILDING PARTS	(240)

Notes: (a) Including windows, doors, outdoor shutters, partition walls and gratings.
(b) Not including staircases (Cl. 25-04).

25-03	HOUSES, GARAGES AND OTHER BUILDINGS	(243)
25-04	STEPS, LADDERS AND SCAFFOLDS	(245)
25-99	MISCELLANEOUS	(246)

CLASS 26

Lighting apparatus

26-01	CANDLESTICKS AND CANDELABRA	(247)
26-02	TORCHES AND HAND LAMPS AND LANTERNS	(247)
26-03	PUBLIC LIGHTING FIXTURES	(247)

Note: Including outside lamps, stage lighting and searchlight projectors.

26-04	LUMINOUS SOURCES, ELECTRICAL OR NOT	(248)

Note: Including bulbs for electric lamps, luminous plaques and tubes, and candles.

26-05	LAMPS, STANDARD LAMPS, CHANDELIERS, WALL AND CEILING FIXTURES, LAMPSHADES, REFLECTORS, PHOTOGRAPHIC AND CINEMATOGRAPHIC PROJECTOR LAMPS	(249)
26-06	LUMINOUS DEVICES FOR VEHICLES	(250)
26-99	MISCELLANEOUS	(250)

CLASS 27

Tobacco and smokers' supplies

27-01	TOBACCO, CIGARS AND CIGARETTES	(251)
27-02	PIPES, CIGAR AND CIGARETTE HOLDERS	(251)
27-03	ASHTRAYS	(251)
27-04	MATCHES	(251)
27-05	LIGHTERS	(251)
27-06	CIGAR CASES, CIGARETTE CASES, TOBACCO JARS AND POUCHES	(252)

Notes: (a) Not including packaging (Cl. 09).
(b) Including cases for electronic smoking supplies.

27-07	ELECTRONIC CIGARETTES AND OTHER ELECTRONIC SMOKING SUPPLIES	(252)
27-99	MISCELLANEOUS	(252)

CLASS 28

Pharmaceutical and cosmetic products, toilet articles and apparatus

Note: Not including packaging (Cl. 09).

28-01	PHARMACEUTICAL PRODUCTS	(254)

Notes: (a) Including for animals.

(b) Including chemicals in cachet, capsule, lozenge, pill and tablet forms, also for plants.

(c) Not including materials for dressing wounds and nursing (Cl. 24-04).

28-02 COSMETIC PRODUCTS (254)
Note: Including for animals.

28-03 TOILET ARTICLES AND BEAUTY PARLOR EQUIPMENT (255)
Notes: (a) Including razors, apparatus and appliances for massaging, hair removing or hair dressing.

(b) Not including toilet and make-up brushes (Cl. 04-02), or grooming articles for animals (Cl. 30-10).

28-04 WIGS AND FALSE BEAUTY ARTICLES (257)
28-05 AIR FRESHENERS (258)
28-99 MISCELLANEOUS (258)

CLASS 29

Devices and equipment against fire hazards, for accident prevention and for rescue

29-01 DEVICES AND EQUIPMENT AGAINST FIRE HAZARDS (259)
Notes: (a) Including fire extinguishers.

(b) Not including fire engines (vehicles) (Cl. 12-13), fire-hoses and nozzles for fire-hoses (Cl. 23-01).

29-02 DEVICES AND EQUIPMENT FOR ACCIDENT PREVENTION AND FOR RESCUE, NOT ELSEWHERE SPECIFIED (259)
Notes: (a) Including devices and equipment for animals.

(b) Not including helmets (Cl. 02-03) and garments for protection against accidents (Cl. 02-02, Cl. 02-04 or Cl. 02-06).

29-99 MISCELLANEOUS (260)

CLASS 30

Articles for the care and handling of animals

Note: Not including animal foodstuffs (Cl. 01), or pharmaceutical and cosmetic products for animals (Cl. 28-01 or Cl. 28-02).

30-01 ANIMAL CLOTHING (261)
30-02 PENS, CAGES, KENNELS AND SIMILAR SHELTERS (261)
Note: Not including buildings (Cl. 25).

30-03 FEEDERS AND WATERERS (262)

30-04	SADDLERY	(262)
	Note: Including collars for animals.	
30-05	WHIPS AND PRODS	(263)
30-06	BEDS, NESTS AND FURNITURE FOR ANIMALS	(264)
	Note: Including scratching posts for cats.	
30-07	PERCHES AND OTHER CAGE ATTACHMENTS	(264)
30-08	MARKERS, MARKS AND SHACKLES	(264)
30-09	HITCHING POSTS	(264)
30-10	GROOMING ARTICLES FOR ANIMALS	(265)
30-11	LITTER BOXES AND DEVICES FOR REMOVING ANIMAL EXCREMENT	(265)
30-12	TOYS FOR ANIMALS	(265)
30-99	MISCELLANEOUS	(265)

CLASS 31

Machines and appliances for preparing food or drink, not elsewhere specified

Note: Not including hand-operated utensils, instruments and appliances for serving or preparing food or drink (Cl. 07), or kitchen knives, knives for boning meat (Cl. 08-03).

31-00	MACHINES AND APPLIANCES FOR PREPARING FOOD OR DRINK, NOT ELSEWHERE SPECIFIED	(266)

CLASS 32

Graphic symbols and logos, surface patterns, ornamentation

32-00	GRAPHIC SYMBOLS AND LOGOS, SURFACE PATTERNS, ORNAMENTATION	(269)

大类和小类表（含注释）

01类　食品

注：（a）包括人类食品、动物食品和食疗食品。
　　（b）不包括包装（09类）。

01-01	烘制食品、饼干、点心、意大利面制品及其他谷类食品，巧克力，糖果类，冰冻食品	（69）
01-02	水果、蔬菜和水果蔬菜制品	（70）
01-03	奶酪、黄油及其代用品、其他奶制品	（70）
01-04	肉制品（包括猪肉制品）、鱼肉制品	（71）
01-05	豆腐和豆腐制品	（71）
01-06	动物食品	（71）
01-99	其他杂项	（71）

02类　服装、服饰用品和缝纫用品

注：不包括玩偶服装（21-01类），防火灾、防事故和救援用的专用装备（29类），以及动物服装（30-01类）。

02-01　内衣、女内衣、妇女紧身胸衣、乳罩和睡衣 ……（72）

　　注：（a）包括矫形用妇女紧身胸衣和亚麻内衣。
　　　　（b）不包括家用亚麻制品（06-13类）。

02-02　服装 ……（73）

　　注：（a）包括各种服装，皮衣、游泳衣、运动衣和矫形用服装，受（b）所列排除项的限制。
　　　　（b）不包括内衣（02-01类）或分入02-03类、02-04类、02-05类、02-06类中的服装。

02-03　帽子、头部遮盖物 ……（76）

　　注：包括男用、女用及儿童用的各种帽子和头部遮盖物。

02-04　鞋、短袜和长袜 ……（77）

　　注：包括足球、滑雪和冰球等专用运动鞋，矫形鞋，矫形短袜，紧身裤袜，绑腿及其他袜类。

02-05　领带、围巾、颈巾和手帕 ……（78）

　　注：包括所有"平面的"服装附件。

02-06　手套 ……（79）

　　注：包括外科手套，家用、各种职业用、运动用橡胶或塑料防护手套。

02-07　缝纫用品、服饰用品和服装附件 ……（79）

　　注：（a）包括服装用、帽类用及鞋类用纽扣、鞋带、别针，手工缝制、编织、刺绣的工具，服装附件如腰带、吊袜带、背带。
　　　　（b）不包括纱线或其他细线（05-01类），装饰边（05-04类），缝纫、编织和刺绣机械（15-06

类）或缝纫用具包（容器）（03-01类）。

02-99　其他杂项 ··· （82）

03类　其他类未列入的旅行用品、箱包、阳伞和个人用品

03-01　大衣箱、手提箱、公文包、手提包、钥匙袋、钱夹、专门为内容物设计的箱包和

类似物品 ··· （83）

注：不包括商品运输用容器（09类）、雪茄盒和香烟盒（27-06类）。

03-02　［空缺］ ·· （86）

03-03　雨伞、阳伞、遮阳篷和手杖 ·· （86）

03-04　扇子 ·· （87）

03-05　用于婴儿、儿童的携带及辅助行走装置 ··· （87）

注：不包括06类和12类中的婴儿携带装置。

03-99　其他杂项 ··· （88）

04类　刷子

04-01　清洁刷和扫帚 ·· （89）

注：不包括服装刷（04-02类）。

04-02　梳妆刷、服装刷和鞋刷 ·· （89）

注：（a）"梳妆刷"指身体用刷，例如用于头发、指甲或牙齿。

（b）不包括电动牙刷［器具］（28-03类）。

04-03　机器用刷 ··· （90）

注："机器用刷"指与机器或专用车辆相结合的刷子。

04-04　油漆刷和烹饪用刷 ··· （90）

04-99　其他杂项 ··· （90）

05类　纺织品，人造或天然材料片材

注：（a）包括所有以纱线和非成品形式出售的纺织品或类似物品。

（b）不包括成品（02或06类）。

05-01　纺纱制品 ··· （91）

注：（a）包括纱和线。

（b）不包括如绳索、金属绳、细绳、合股绳等（09-06类）。

05-02　花边 ·· （91）

05-03　刺绣品 ··· （91）

05-04　缎带、编带和其他缀饰品 ·· （91）

05-05	纺织纤维制品	（92）

    注：包括机织的、编织的或其他人造的纺织纤维制品，防水布，毛毡和罗登呢。

05-06	人造或天然材料片材	（93）

    注：(a) 包括其特征仅在于表面装饰性和纹理质地的片材，特别是覆盖片材如墙纸、油毡、自黏性塑料片材、包装片材和卷纸，受 (b) 所列排除项的限制。
    (b) 不包括书写用纸和卷状书写用纸（19-01类），不包括用于建筑构件的片材，如墙板和壁板（25-01类）。

05-99	其他杂项	（94）

06类　家具和家居用品

    注：(a) 组成部分包含于不同小类的组合家具分入 06-05 类。
    (b) 被视为一项设计的成套家具分入06-05类。
    (c) 不包括纺织品（05类）。

06-01	座椅	（95）

    注：(a) 包括所有座椅，即使其适于躺卧，如长凳、长沙发、长榻、无扶手无靠背的长沙发椅[沙发]、有垫矮凳、桑拿浴用长凳和沙发。
    (b) 包括交通工具上的座椅。

06-02	床	（96）

    注：(a) 包括床垫架。
    (b) 不包括适于躺卧的座椅（06-01类），如长凳、长沙发、长榻、无扶手无靠背的长沙发椅[沙发]、有垫矮凳、桑拿浴用长凳和沙发。

06-03	桌子及类似家具	（97）
06-04	存放物品用家具	（98）

    注：(a) 包括橱柜、架子、带抽屉或间隔的家具。
    (b) 包括棺材、棺材衬套和骨灰盒。

06-05	组合家具	（100）
06-06	其他家具和家具零部件	（100）
06-07	镜子和框架	（102）

    注：不包括包含在其他类的镜子（见字母顺序表）。

06-08	挂衣架	（102）
06-09	床垫和垫子	（102）
06-10	窗帘、门帘和室内百叶帘	（103）
06-11	地毯、地席、地垫和小地毯	（103）
06-12	挂毯	（104）
06-13	毯子及其他覆盖物，家用亚麻制品和餐桌用布	（104）

    注：包括家具覆盖物、床单床罩和桌面覆盖物。

06-99	其他杂项	（105）

07类　其他类未列入的家用物品

注：(a) 包括手动或者电动的家用用具和器具。
(b) 不包括食物和饮料的制备机械和设备（31类）。

07-01　瓷器、玻璃器皿、餐用盘碟和其他类似物品 ·················· (106)

注：(a) 包括各种材料的盘子、碟子和罐子，特别是纸盘和纸板盘。
(b) 不包括烹调器具和容器，如玻璃锅和陶制锅（07-02类）；也不包括花瓶、花盆以及纯装饰性的瓷器和玻璃器皿（11-02类）。

07-02　烹调用具、器具和容器 ·················· (108)

07-03　桌上用刀、叉、匙等餐具 ·················· (110)

07-04　用于制备食物或饮料的手动操作用具和器具 ·················· (111)

注：(a) 不包括07-02类和31类中的设备和器具。
(b) 不包括菜刀和剔骨刀（08-03类）。

07-05　熨烫用具、洗涤用具、清洁用具和干燥用具 ·················· (113)

注：不包括用于洗涤、清洁或干燥的家用电动设备（15-05类）。

07-06　其他桌上用品 ·················· (114)

07-07　其他家用容器 ·················· (115)

07-08　壁炉用具 ·················· (116)

07-09　家用器具和用具的立架及支架 ·················· (116)

07-10　用于冷却、冷冻的器具和保温容器 ·················· (117)

07-99　其他杂项 ·················· (117)

08类　工具和五金器具

注：(a) 包括手动操作工具，即机械力代替了人力，如电锯和电钻。
(b) 不包括机械或机床（15或31类）。

08-01　钻孔、铣削或挖掘的工具和器具 ·················· (119)

08-02　锤及其他类似工具和器具 ·················· (120)

08-03　切削工具和器具 ·················· (120)

注：(a) 包括锯切工具和器具。
(b) 不包括餐刀（07-03类），厨房用切削工具和器具（31类），外科手术用刀（24-02类）。

08-04　螺丝起子及其他类似工具和器具 ·················· (122)

08-05　其他工具和器具 ·················· (122)

注：(a) 包括未分类或者不能放在其他大类或小类的工具。
(b) 包括打磨墩、砂磨块和砂轮打磨机盘。
(c) 不包括砂纸（05-06类）。

08-06　把手，球形捏手，铰链、合页 ·················· (126)

| 08-07 | 锁紧或关闭装置 | （127） |

注：不包括扣环，皮带扣［服饰用品］（02-07类）和钥匙环（03-01类）。

| 08-08 | 其他类未包括的夹紧、支撑或安装装置 | （128） |

注：(a) 包括钉子、螺丝钉、螺母和螺栓。

(b) 不包括用于服装（02-07类）、装饰品（11-01类）或办公（19-02类）的夹紧装置。

| 08-09 | 其他大类或小类未包括的用于门、窗、家具的金属配件、金属装配件及类似物品 | （130） |
| 08-10 | 自行车和摩托车支架 | （131） |

注：(a) 包括修理支架或停车支架。

(b) 不包括作为自行车部件的可收放脚撑（12-11类）。

| 08-11 | 窗帘用五金件 | （131） |
| 08-99 | 其他杂项 | （132） |

注：包括非电力线缆，不考虑其制作材料。

09类　用于商品运输或装卸的包装和容器

| 09-01 | 瓶、长颈瓶、鼓形瓶、盛装腐蚀性液体的大玻璃瓶、细颈瓶和压力容器 | （133） |

注：(a)"鼓形瓶"仅指包装容器。

(b) 不包括家用壶、鼓形瓶（07-01类）或花盆（11-02类）。

| 09-02 | 储藏用罐、鼓形圆桶和木桶 | （134） |
| 09-03 | 盒、箱、集装箱和罐 | （134） |

注：包括货运集装箱。

| 09-04 | 有盖篮子、柳条筐和篮子 | （135） |
| 09-05 | 袋、小袋、管和囊 | （136） |

注：(a) 包括采用各种封口方式的有提手或无提手的塑料袋和小袋。

(b) "囊"指包装物。

| 09-06 | 绳索和捆箍用品 | （137） |
| 09-07 | 封口装置和封口附件 | （137） |

注：(a) 仅包括用于包装的封口装置。

(b) "封口附件"，例如可拆卸的喷嘴、与容器一体的分配装置和定量给料装置。

09-08	叉车的货盘和装卸台	（138）
09-09	废物和垃圾的容器及其座架	（138）
09-10	运输或搬运包装物及容器用提手和握柄	（139）
09-99	其他杂项	（139）

10类　钟、表及其他测量仪器，检测仪器，信号仪器

注：包括电子仪器。

10-01	钟和闹钟	(140)
10-02	表和手表	(140)
10-03	其他计时仪器	(140)

注：包括如停车计时器、厨房用定时器和类似仪器的计时装置。

10-04	其他测量仪器、设备和装置	(141)

注：（a）包括测量温度、压力、重量、长度、体积和电流等的仪器、设备和装置。
（b）不包括曝光计（16-05类）。

10-05	检测、安全和测试用仪器、设备和装置	(145)

注：包括防火及防盗警铃和各种类型的探测器。

10-06	信号设备和装置	(146)

注：不包括交通工具上的照明或信号装置（26-06类）。

10-07	测量仪器、检测仪器和信号仪器的外壳、盘面、指针和所有其他零部件及附件	(147)

注："外壳"指手表及钟表外壳和保护机械装置并作为仪器组成部分的所有外壳，为了其内装物（03-01类）或包装（09-03类）而专门设计的容器除外。

10-99	其他杂项	(148)

11类　装饰品

11-01	珠宝和首饰	(149)

注：（a）包括人造和仿制珠宝首饰。
（b）不包括表（10-02类）。

11-02	小装饰品，桌子、壁炉台和墙的装饰物，花瓶和花盆	(150)

注：包括雕塑、风铃和雕像。

11-03	纪念章和徽章	(151)
11-04	人造的花、水果和植物	(151)
11-05	旗帜、节日装饰物	(152)

注：（a）包括花环、彩带和圣诞树装饰物。
（b）不包括蜡烛（26-04类）。

11-99	其他杂项	(152)

12类　运输或提升工具

注：（a）包括陆、海、空、太空等所有交通工具。
（b）包括仅用于交通工具且其他大类未包含的零件、部件和附件；该零件、部件和附件应分入其所涉及的交通工具的小类，若其可通用于多个不同小类的交通工具，则分入

12-16类。

（c）原则上，不包括其他类已含有的交通工具零件、部件和附件。这些零件、部件和附件应与其同类型或同用途的产品分入一类。因此，车辆用地毯或地垫应与地毯（06-11类）分入一类；交通工具的电动马达分入13-01类，交通工具的非电动马达分入15-01类（上述两类马达的零件同理）；车辆前灯应与照明设备（26-06类）分入一类。

（d）不包括交通工具的比例模型（21-01类）。

12-01	畜力车辆	（153）
12-02	手推车、独轮手推车	（153）
12-03	机车、铁路车辆及其他有轨车辆	（154）
12-04	高架索车、缆椅和滑雪索车	（155）
12-05	装载或输送用的升降机和提升机	（155）

注：包括载客升降机、货物升降机、起重机、铲车和传送带。

12-06	船和艇	（157）
12-07	航空器和太空运载工具	（158）
12-08	汽车、公共汽车和货车	（158）

注：包括救护车和冷藏货车（公路）。

12-09	拖拉机	（159）
12-10	公路车辆的挂车	（159）

注：包括篷车。

12-11	自行车和摩托车	（159）
12-12	婴儿车、病人用轮椅、担架	（161）

注：（a）"婴儿车"指婴儿的手推车。
（b）不包括玩具婴儿车（21-01类）。

12-13	专用车辆	（162）

注：（a）仅包括不特定用于运输的车辆，如街道清洁车、洒水车、消防车、除雪犁车和救援车辆。
（b）不包括复合用途农业机械（15-03类）或用于建筑和土木工程的自驱动式机械（15-04类）。

12-14	其他交通工具	（162）

注：包括雪橇、气垫车和气垫船。

12-15	交通工具的轮胎和防滑链	（163）
12-16	其他大类或小类未包括的交通工具零部件、装置和附件	（163）

注：（a）不包括交通工具座位安全带（29-02类）和交通工具门把手（08-06类）。
（b）不包括电力机车和有轨电车用集电弓（13-03类）。

12-17	铁路基础设施零件	（166）

注：不包括铁轨和铁路轨枕（25-01类）、铁轨终端缓冲垫（25-99类）和铁路信号设备（10-06类）。

12-99	其他杂项	（166）

13类　发电、配电或变电设备

注：(a) 仅包括发电、配电或变电的设备。
　　(b) 也包括电动机。
　　(c) 不包括电动设备，例如电子表（10-02类）或电流测量仪（10-04类）。

13-01	发电机和电动机	(167)

注：包括交通工具的电动机。

13-02	电力变压器、整流器、电池和蓄电池	(167)
13-03	配电或电力控制设备	(168)

注：包括导线、导电体、开关、电闸和配电盘。

13-04	太阳能设备	(170)

注：不包括太阳能集热器（23-03类）。

13-99	其他杂项	(170)

14类　记录、电信或数据处理设备

14-01	声音或图像的记录或再现设备	(171)

注：不包括照相或电影摄影设备（16类）。

14-02	数据处理设备及其外围设备和装置	(172)
14-03	电信设备、无线遥控设备和无线电放大器	(174)

注：包括电话和电视设备，以及无线电设备。

14-04	显示界面和图标	(176)

注：包括属于其他大类的产品的显示界面和图标。

14-05	记录数据和存储数据的介质	(176)
14-06	其他类未列入的电子设备用支架、立架和支撑装置	(176)
14-99	其他杂项	(177)

15类　其他类未列入的机械

15-01	发动机	(178)

注：(a) 包括交通工具的非电力发动机。
　　(b) 不包括电动机（13类）。

15-02	泵和压缩机	(178)

注：不包括手动、脚动的泵（08-05类），或消防泵（29-01类）。

15-03	农业和林业机械	(179)

注：(a) 包括犁和既是机器又是交通工具的联合机械，例如收割捆扎机。
　　(b) 不包括手动工具（08类）。

15-04	建筑机械、采矿机械、选矿机械	(181)

注：(a) 包括土木工程用的机械、自驱动式机械，例如挖掘机、混凝土搅拌机和挖泥机。
(b) 不包括提升机和起重机（12-05类）。

15-05 洗涤、清洁和干燥机械 (181)

注：(a) 包括亚麻制品、服装的处理设备和机械，例如熨平机、绞干机。
(b) 包括碗盘清洗机和工业干燥设备。

15-06 纺织、缝纫、针织和绣花机械及其零部件 (183)

15-07 制冷机械和冷藏设备 (184)

注：(a) 包括家用冷藏设备。
(b) 不包括冷藏车（铁路用）（12-03类）或冷藏车（公路用）（12-08类）。

15-08 ［空缺］ (184)

15-09 机床、研磨和铸造机械 (184)

注：包括3D打印机。

15-10 填装、打包和包装机械 (187)

15-99 其他杂项 (187)

16类 照相设备、电影摄影设备和光学设备

注：不包括照相和摄影用灯（26-05类）。

16-01 照相机和电影摄影机 (189)

16-02 放映机、投影仪和看片器 (189)

16-03 影印设备和放大机 (190)

注：包括缩微设备、观看缩微胶片的设备和被通称为"影印机"的办公设备，该设备不采用照相工艺（特别是热工艺或磁工艺）。

16-04 显影器械和设备 (190)

16-05 附件 (190)

注：包括照相机用滤镜、曝光计、三脚架和照相闪光设备。

16-06 光学制品 (191)

注：(a) 包括眼镜和显微镜。
(b) 不包括含有光学器件的测量仪器（10-04类）。

16-99 其他杂项 (192)

17类 乐器

注：不包括乐器盒（03-01类）、声音的记录或再现设备（14-01类）。

17-01 键盘乐器 (193)

注：包括电子式和其他类型的风琴、手风琴、机械式和其他类型的钢琴。

17-02 管乐器 (193)

注：不包括风琴、脚踏式风琴和手风琴（17-01类）。

17-03	弦乐器	（194）
17-04	打击乐器	（195）
17-05	机械乐器	（195）

    注：（a）包括音乐盒、八音盒。
      （b）不包括机械式键盘乐器（17-01类）。

17-99	其他杂项	（195）

18类　印刷和办公机械

18-01	打字机和运算机器	（197）

    注：不包括属于14-02类的计算机及其他设备。

18-02	印刷机械	（197）

    注：（a）包括排版机、铅版印刷机、活版印刷机和其他复制机，例如复制机、胶印机、印地址机、邮资盖戳机和盖销机。
      （b）不包括计算机打印机（14-02类）和影印设备（16-03类）。

18-03	活字和字体	（198）
18-04	装订机、印刷工用订书机、切纸机和修边机（装订用）	（199）

    注：包括类似切纸机、修边机的切纸机械和类似装置。

18-99	其他杂项	（199）

19类　文具、办公用品、美术用品和教学用品

19-01	书写用纸、通信用卡片和通知用卡片	（200）

    注：包括广义而言的纸张，即用于书写、绘图、绘画或印刷的所有纸张，即使其中记录有声音，例如描图纸、复写纸、新闻用纸、信封、贺卡和插图明信片。

19-02	办公用品	（201）

    注：（a）包括收款台上用的设备，如零钱拣选机。
      （b）不包括办公家具（06类）、办公机械和设备（14-02、16-03、18-01、18-02 或者 18-04类）和书写用具（19-01 或者19-06类）。

19-03	日历	（203）

    注：不包括日记簿（19-04类）。

19-04	书本及与其外观相似的其他物品	（203）

    注：包括封面、书籍装帧、剪贴簿、日记簿和其他类似物品。

19-05	［空缺］	（204）
19-06	用于书写、绘图、绘画、雕塑、雕刻和其他艺术技法的用品和工具	（204）

    注：不包括油漆刷（04-04类）、绘图桌及其附属设备（06-03类）或者书写用纸（19-01类）。

19-07	教学用具和教学设备	（206）

    注：（a）包括各种地图、地球仪和天象仪。

(b) 不包括音视频教学辅助设备（14-01类）。

19-08　其他印刷品 (207)

　　　　　注：包括印刷的广告品。

19-99　其他杂项 (208)

20类　销售设备、广告设备和标志物

20-01　自动售货机 (210)

20-02　陈列设备和销售设备 (210)

　　　　　注：不包括家具和家居用品（06类）。

20-03　标志物，招牌、布告牌和广告设备 (211)

　　　　　注：(a) 包括发光和可动的广告设备。

　　　　　　　(b) 不包括包装物（09类）或者信号装置（10-06类）。

20-99　其他杂项 (212)

21类　游戏器具、玩具、帐篷和体育用品

21-01　游戏器具和玩具 (213)

　　　　　注：(a) 包括比例模型。

　　　　　　　(b) 不包括动物用玩具（30-12类）。

21-02　体育和运动的器械及设备 (215)

　　　　　注：(a) 包括用于各种运动锻炼所必需且通常无其他特定用途的运动器械和设备，例如足球、滑雪板、网球拍。不包括根据其他功能可以分入其他大类或小类的运动用品，例如独木舟、小艇（12-06类）、气枪（22-01类）、运动用地垫（06-11类）。

　　　　　　　(b) 在 (a) 所限定的条件下，包括训练设备和器械，以及户外运动所必需的设备。

　　　　　　　(c) 不包括运动服装（02类），雪橇或雪地车（12-14类）。

21-03　其他娱乐和游艺用品 (218)

　　　　　注：(a) 包括露天旋转木马和碰运气游戏的自动机器。

　　　　　　　(b) 不包括游戏器具和玩具（21-01类），或者其他列入21-01或21-02类中的物品。

21-04　帐篷及其附件 (219)

　　　　　注：(a) 包括撑杆、拴柱和其他类似物品。

　　　　　　　(b) 不包括根据其用途分在其他类中的露营物品，如椅子（06-01类）、桌子（06-03类）、盘子（07-01类）、旅行用大篷车（12-10类）。

21-99　其他杂项 (219)

22类　武器，烟火用品，用于狩猎、捕鱼及捕杀有害动物的用具

22-01　射击武器 (220)

22-02　其他武器 (221)

22-03	弹药、火箭和烟火用品	(221)
22-04	靶及附件	(222)
	注：包括驱动活动靶子的专用装置。	
22-05	狩猎和捕鱼器械	(222)
	注：不包括服装（02类）或武器（22-01或22-02类）。	
22-06	捕捉器、捕杀有害动物的用具	(223)
22-99	其他杂项	(224)

23类 流体分配设备、卫生设备、加热设备、通风和空气调节设备、固体燃料

23-01	流体分配设备	(225)
	注：包括管和管配件。	
23-02	[空缺]	(227)
23-03	加热设备	(227)
23-04	通风和空气调节设备	(228)
23-05	固体燃料	(229)
23-06	个人卫生用卫生设备	(229)
23-07	便溺设备	(230)
23-08	其他大类或小类未包括的卫生设备及附件	(230)
23-99	其他杂项	(231)

24类 医疗设备和实验室设备

注：术语"医疗设备"还包括外科、牙科和兽医用设备。

24-01	医生、医院和实验室用的仪器和设备	(232)
24-02	医疗器械、实验室用器械和实验室用工具	(233)
	注：仅包括手动操作的器械。	
24-03	修复假体及其用具	(236)
24-04	用于包扎伤口、护理和医疗处理的用品	(236)
	注：包括吸水性敷料剂。	
24-99	其他杂项	(238)

25类 建筑构件和施工元件

25-01	建筑材料	(239)
	注：包括砖、梁、未成形板、瓦、瓷砖、石板和镶板。	

25-02	预制或预装建筑构件	（240）

注：（a）包括窗户、门、户外百叶窗、隔断墙和栅栏。
　　（b）不包括楼梯（25-04类）。

25-03	房屋、车库和其他建筑	（243）
25-04	台阶、梯子和脚手架	（245）
25-99	其他杂项	（246）

26类　照明设备

26-01	烛台和烛架	（247）
26-02	手电筒、手提灯和灯笼	（247）
26-03	公共场所照明装置	（247）

注：包括户外灯、舞台照明设备和探照灯。

26-04	电或非电的光源	（248）

注：包括电灯泡、发光板、发光管和蜡烛。

26-05	灯，落地灯，枝形吊灯，墙壁和天花板装置，灯罩，反光罩，摄影和电影投光灯	（249）
26-06	交通工具发光装置	（250）
26-99	其他杂项	（250）

27类　烟草和吸烟用具

27-01	烟草、雪茄和香烟	（251）
27-02	烟斗、雪茄和香烟烟嘴	（251）
27-03	烟灰缸	（251）
27-04	火柴	（251）
27-05	打火机	（251）
27-06	雪茄盒、香烟盒、烟草罐和烟草袋	（252）

注：（a）不包括包装（09类）。
　　（b）包括电子烟用品盒。

27-07	电子烟和其他电子吸烟用具	（252）
27-99	其他杂项	（252）

28类　药品，化妆品，梳妆用品和设备

注：不包括包装（09类）。

28-01	药品	（254）

　　　　注：（a）包括动物用药品。
　　　　　　（b）包括扁囊剂、胶囊剂、锭剂、丸剂、片剂形状的化学药品，也可用于植物。
　　　　　　（c）不包括包扎伤口和护理用品（24-04类）。

28-02	化妆品	（254）

　　　　注：包括动物用化妆品。

28-03	梳妆用品和美容院设备	（255）

　　　　注：（a）包括剃须刀，按摩、剪发、美发用器械和设备。
　　　　　　（b）不包括梳妆刷和化妆刷（04-02类）或者动物梳洗用品（30-10类）。

28-04	假发和人造美妆用品	（257）
28-05	空气清新剂	（258）
28-99	其他杂项	（258）

29类　防火灾、防事故、救援用的装置及设备

29-01	防火灾装置和设备	（259）

　　　　注：（a）包括灭火器。
　　　　　　（b）不包括消防车（交通工具）（12-13类）、消防水带和消防水带喷嘴（23-01类）。

29-02	其他类未列入的防事故和救援用装置及设备	（259）

　　　　注：（a）包括动物用的装置和设备。
　　　　　　（b）不包括头盔（02-03类）和避免意外伤害的保护服装（02-02、02-04、02-06类）。

29-99	其他杂项	（260）

30类　动物照管与驯养用品

　　　　注：不包括动物食品（01类），或者动物用药品和化妆用品（28-01或28-02类）。

30-01	动物服装	（261）
30-02	围栏、笼、舍及类似居所	（261）

　　　　注：不包括建筑物（25类）。

30-03	喂食器和饮水器	（262）
30-04	鞍具	（262）

　　　　注：包括动物颈圈。

30-05	鞭子和刺棒	（263）
30-06	动物用床、窝和家具	（264）

　　　　注：包括猫抓柱。

30-07	栖木和其他笼子配件	(264)
30-08	标记用具、标记和脚镣	(264)
30-09	拴柱	(264)
30-10	动物梳洗用品	(265)
30-11	动物排泄盒和排泄物清除装置	(265)
30-12	动物用玩具	(265)
30-99	其他杂项	(265)

31类　其他类未列入的食品或饮料制备机械和设备

注：不包括用于分发或制备食品或饮料的手动操作器具、工具和用具（07 类）或者菜刀、剔骨刀（08-03 类）。

| 31-00 | 其他类未列入的食品或饮料制备机械和设备 | (266) |

32类　图形符号、标识、表面图案、纹饰

| 32-00 | 图形符号、标识、表面图案、纹饰 | (269) |

LIST OF GOODS IN CLASS ORDER

按类别顺序排列
产品项列表

Class 01
Foodstuffs

Notes：(a) Including foodstuffs for human beings, foodstuffs for animals and dietetic foods.
(b) Not including packaging (Cl. 09).

01-01
Bakers' products, biscuits, pastry, pasta and other cereal products, chocolates, confectionery, ices

100004	Bakers' products	烘制食品	
100002	Biscuits	饼干	
100015	Bread	面包	
100008	Cakes	蛋糕	
100005	Caramels [candy]	牛奶硬糖，软糖，焦糖[糖果]	
100027	Cereal preparations	谷制食品	
100011	Chewing gum	口香糖	
104839	Chocolate figurines	造型巧克力	【12】
100006	Chocolates	巧克力	
100007	Confectionery	糖果	
100002	Cookies	饼干	【11】
100017	Farinaceous food pastes	谷制食品糊	
104608	Fruit gums	果胶糖，果味橡皮糖	【10】
100016	Gingerbread	姜饼	
100010	Ice cream	冰激凌	
100009	Ice cream cornets [edible]	圆锥形冰激凌蛋卷[可食用]	
100023	Lollipops	棒棒糖	
100012	Macaroni	通心粉	
100013	Meringues	蛋白酥皮卷	
100014	Noodles	面条，粉条	
100017	Pasta	意大利面制品，意大利面食	
100018	Pastries	点心	
100019	Petits fours [cakes]	花色小蛋糕[蛋糕]	
100028	Pizzas	比萨饼	

---

1 由"macaroni 通心粉"修改为"pasta 意大利面制品"。

100020	Pralines	果仁糖	
100001	Rusks	面包干，脆饼干	
104696	Shaped tortillas	成形的玉米饼	【11】
100021	Sherbets［ices］	雪酪［冰冻食品］	
100021	Sorbets［ices］	冰沙［冰冻食品］	
100022	Spaghetti	意大利式细面条	
100003	Sweetmeats［candy］	甜食，蜜饯［糖果］	
100024	Tarts	果馅饼	
100025	Vermicelli	细面条，粉丝，挂面	
104679	Wafers	威化，薄脆饼	【10】
104680	Waffles	华夫饼	【10】
100026	Zwiebacks	烤面包片	

01-02
Fruit, vegetables and products made from fruits and vegetables

01-02
水果、蔬菜和水果蔬菜制品 【11】[1]

100029	Fruit	水果	
104840	Fruit chips	水果脆片，水果干	【12】
104840	Fruit crisps	水果脆片，水果干	【12】
104598	Vegetable chips	蔬菜脆片，蔬菜干	【12】[2]
104598	Vegetable crisps	蔬菜脆片，蔬菜干	【12】[3]
100030	Vegetables	蔬菜	

01-03
Cheeses, butter and butter substitutes, other dairy produce

01-03
奶酪、黄油及其代用品、其他奶制品

100031	Butter and butter substitutes	黄油及其代用品
100032	Cheeses	奶酪
100033	Dairy produce	奶制品
100034	Margarine	人造黄油

---

1 由"Fruit and vegetables 水果和蔬菜"修改为"Fruit，vegetables and products made from fruits and vegetables 水果、蔬菜和水果蔬菜制品"。
2 第10版新增的"Potato chips"修改为"Vegetable chips"。
3 第10版新增的"Crisps 薯片、脆片"，第11版修改为"Potato crisps 马铃薯薯片"，第12版修改为"Vegetable crisps 蔬菜脆片，蔬菜干"。

01-04
Butchers' meat (Including pork products), fish

01-04
肉制品（包括猪肉制品）、鱼肉制品

104841	Dried meat strips	肉干、肉脯	【12】
100035	Fish cakes	鱼饼	
104697	Meatballs	肉丸	【11】
100036	Sausages	香肠	

01-05
Tofu and tofu products

01-05
豆腐和豆腐制品 【12】[1]

104844	Dried tofu	豆腐干	【12】
104842	Tofu	豆腐	【12】
104843	Tofu skin	豆腐皮	【12】

01-06
Animal foodstuffs

01-06
动物食品 【5】[2]

100038	Bread for birds	禽类食用面包	
100037	Dog biscuits	狗食饼干	
104845	Dry pet food	宠物干粮	【12】
100040	Oil cake for animals	兽类食用油渣饼	
100039	Salt licks for cattle and game	牲畜和野生动物用盐舔块	

01-99
Miscellaneous

01-99
其他杂项

100042	Stock [bouillon] cubes	调味汤块［肉汤］	
100041	Sugar cubes	方糖	
104698	Sushi	寿司	【11】
100043	Tea	茶	

---

1 第 5 版增加 01-05 空缺小类，第 12 版将其修改为 "Tofu and tofu products 豆腐和豆腐制品" 小类。
2 新增加 01-06 类。

Class 02
Articles of clothing and haberdashery

Notes: Not including articles of clothing for dolls (Cl.21-01), special equipment for protection against fire hazards, for accident prevention and for rescue (Cl.29), and animal clothing (Cl. 30-01).

02-01
Undergarments, lingerie, corsets, brassieres, nightwear

Notes: (a) Including orthopedic corsets and body linen. (b) Not including household linen (Cl. 06-13).

100066	Abdominal belts	腹带	
104846	Adhesive articles for breast support	用于支撑乳房的自黏性物品，乳贴	【12】
100062	Babies' diaper covers	婴儿尿布套	【13】
100052	Babies' diapers	婴儿尿布	
100062	Babies' nappy covers	婴儿尿布套	
100052	Babies' nappies	婴儿尿布	
100044	Boxer shorts	男式平角裤	
100065	Brassieres	乳罩	
100050	Corsets	妇女紧身胸衣	
100055	Detachable collars	活衣领	
100070	Diaper-pants	尿布裤	【13】
100050	Girdles [underwear]	腹带[内衣]	
100069	Hip protectors for sports	运动护臀内裤	
100053	Knickers	女式内裤	
100059	Lingerie	女内衣	
104927	Maternity underwear	孕妇内衣	【13】
104927	Maternity lingerie	孕妇内衣	【13】
100070	Nappy-pants	尿布裤	
100046	Nightdresses	妇女或儿童的睡衣	
100046	Nightshirts	衬衫式长睡衣	
100067	Nightwear	睡衣	
104928	Nursing underwear	哺乳内衣	【13】

02 类
服装、服饰用品和缝纫用品

注：不包括玩偶服装（21-01类），防火灾、防事故和救援用的专用装备（29类），以及动物服装（30-01类）。

02-01
内衣、女内衣、妇女紧身胸衣、乳罩和睡衣

注：（a）包括矫形用妇女紧身胸衣和亚麻内衣。（b）不包括家用亚麻制品（06-13类）。

104928	Nursing lingerie	哺乳内衣	【13】
100051	Orthopaedic corsets	矫形用妇女紧身胸衣	
100051	Orthopedic corsets	矫形用妇女紧身胸衣	
100063	Pajamas	睡衣裤	
100053	Panties	短内裤，内裤	
100048	Petticoats	衬裙	
100058	Petticoats［underskirts］	衬裙［贴身内衣］	
100063	Pyjamas	睡衣裤	
100049	Reducing garments	瘦身内衣	
100054	Rubber pants for babies	婴儿用橡胶衬裤	
100057	Singlets［underwear］	背心［内衣］	
100068	Sleeved vests for infants	婴儿有袖内衣	
100048	Slips［petticoats］	女式内衣［衬裙］	
104699	Underpants	衬裤	【11】
100059	Underwear	内衣裤	

02-02
Garments

Notes:（a）Including all sorts of garments, and furs, bathing costumes, sports clothing and orthopedic garments, subject to the exceptions indicated under（b）.（b）Not including undergarments（Cl. 02-01）, or garments to be placed in Cl. 02-03, Cl. 02-04, Cl. 02-05 or Cl. 02-06.

02-02
服装

注：（a）包括各种服装，皮衣、游泳衣、运动衣和矫形用服装，受（b）所列排除项的限制。（b）不包括内衣（02-01 类）或分入 02-03 类、02-04 类、02-05 类、02-06 类中的服装。

100071	Anoraks	带风帽的夹克
100114	Aprons［clothing］	围裙［服装］
100117	Ballet skirts	芭蕾舞裙
100099	Bathing costumes	游泳衣
100078	Bathing trunks	游泳裤
100132	Bathrobes	浴衣
100133	Bikinis	比基尼，三点式女泳装
100072	Blazers	休闲上衣
100073	Blouses	女式宽松上衣
100076	Boas［necklets］	披肩［皮围巾］
100077	Boleros	女式短上衣
100088	Breeches	马裤
100081	Cardigans	开襟羊毛衫
100084	Chasubles	十字褡

100080	Cloaks	斗篷	
100101	Coats	外衣	
100129	Decontamination clothing	消毒服	
100056	Dickies [false shirtfronts]	衬胸[衬衫的假衬胸]	【10】¹
100124	Diving suits	潜水服	
100111	Dresses	礼服，连衣裙	
100105	Dressing gowns	晨衣	
100056	False shirtfronts [dickies]	衬衫的假衬胸[衬胸]	【10】¹
100127	Fireproof garments	防火服	
100119	Fishermen's jerseys	捕鱼人穿运动衫	
104701	Football jerseys	足球服	【11】
100093	Furs [garments]	毛皮衣服[服装]	
104621	Hooded jackets	连帽夹克，连帽上衣，风雪衣	【10】
104850	Hooded sweatshirts	连帽运动衫	【12】
100089	Housecoats	（女式家常）宽松长袍，家常女便服	
100122	Isothermic garments for underwater fishing	水下捕鱼用恒温服	
100120	Jackets	夹克	
100096	Jeans	牛仔裤	
100083	Jerseys	运动衫，针织衫	
100082	Jumper-blouses	女套衫	
104700	Jumpsuits	连衣裤	【11】
100098	Kimonos	和服	
100126	Ladies' suits	女式套装	
100128	Lifesaving clothing [nautical]	救生服[航海]	
104848	Masquerade costumes	化妆舞会服装	【12】
104929	Maternity clothing	孕妇服	【13】
100102	Middy blouses	水手衫	
100125	Morning coats	晨礼服，大礼服	
100089	Negligees	女便服	
104930	Nursing clothing	哺乳服	【13】
100087	Nursing uniforms	护理服	
100074	Overalls	工装裤，工装服	
100104	Overcoats	外套大衣	
100103	Pants	裤子，短裤	
100106	Pelerines [capes]	衣式披肩[披风]	
100107	Pelisses	皮制上衣	

1　由02-01类转移至02-02类。

100108	Pockets for clothing	服装口袋	
104851	Polo shirts	马球衫	【12】
100109	Ponchos	披风，斗篷，雨衣	
100110	Pullovers	套衫	
104650	Reflective clothing	反光服装	【10】
100123	Religious apparel	宗教服	
100116	Robes	长袍	
100102	Sailor blouses [for women]	水手衫[女用]	
100112	Scapulars	无袖外衣	
100061	Shirt cuffs	衬衫袖口	【10】[1]
100060	Shirt sleeves	衬衫袖子	【10】[1]
100047	Shirt-collars	衬衫衣领	【10】[1]
100045	Shirts	衬衫，衬衣	【10】[1]
100113	Shorts	短裤，婴儿短装	
100100	Singlets for gymnastics	体操背心	
100130	Ski suits	滑雪服	
100097	Skirts	裙子	
104847	Sleeveless sweaters	无袖毛衣，毛背心	【12】
100092	Stoles	圣带，祭衣	
100079	Strait jackets	紧身夹克衫	
100086	Suits of clothes for men	男式套装	
100115	Surgery apparel	外科手术服	
100083	Sweaters	毛线衫，毛衣	
100106	Tippets	女用披肩，法官、教士的黑色长披肩	
100116	Togas	宽外袍	
104673	Tops [clothing]	上衣，无袖上衣[服装]	【10】
100091	Tracksuits	田径服	
104849	Traditional dresses or costumes	民族服装或者戏服	【12】
100091	Training clothes	训练服	
100103	Trousers	裤子	
100131	T-shirts	T恤衫	
100117	Tutus	芭蕾舞短裙	
100118	Uniforms	制服	
100094	Vests	马甲	
100094	Waistcoats	西服背心，马甲	
100121	Warming garments	保暖服	
100095	Waterproof coats	防水外衣	
100075	Wind jackets	挡风夹克	

1　由02-01类转移至02-02类。

100085	Working clothes	工作服	
100085	Workmen's overalls	工装服	

02-03
Headwear

Note: Including all kinds of headwear for men, women and children.

02-03
帽子、头部遮盖物

注：包括男用、女用及儿童用的各种帽子和头部遮盖物。

100149	Anti-dazzle shades for fixing to headgear	用来固定在帽子上的遮光帽檐	
100137	Bathing caps	游泳帽	
100135	Berets	贝雷帽	
104932	Bicycle helmets	自行车头盔	【13】
100134	Birettas	四角帽，法冠	
100136	Bonnets	无边圆软帽	
100142	Carnival hats	游艺表演帽	
100151	Divers' helmets	潜水头盔	
100146	Ear muffs	耳套	
100144	Eye shades	遮光眼罩	
100155	Hats	帽子	
100154	Headbands	头带，束发带	
100153	Headgear for protection against insect bites	防虫叮咬的防护帽	
100143	Headwear	帽子，头部遮盖物	
100152	Hoods [headwear]	兜帽[帽子，头部遮盖物]	
100145	Kepis	法式军用平顶帽	
104852	Knitted caps	针织帽	【12】
100140	Military helmets	军用头盔	
104931	Motorcycle helmets	摩托车头盔	【13】
100150	Peaks for headgear	帽子的帽舌	
100138	Protective helmets	安全防护头盔	
100156	Spoilers for motorcycle crash helmets	摩托车防护头盔的扰流板	
100147	Toques	无边女帽，羽饰丝绒帽	
100148	Turbans	缠头巾式帽	
100141	Vizored caps	带帽檐的帽	
100139	Welders' helmets	焊工头盔	

02-04

Footwear, socks and stockings

Note: Including special boots for sports such as football, skiing and ice hockey, orthopedic footwear and socks, as well as tights, gaiters and other legwear.

02-04

鞋、短袜和长袜

注：包括足球、滑雪和冰球等专用运动鞋，矫形鞋，矫形短袜，紧身裤袜，绑腿及其他袜类。

100157	Ballet shoes	芭蕾舞鞋	
100160	Boots	长筒靴，靴子	
100167	Boots for sports [special]	运动靴[专用]	
100195	Climbing boots	登山靴	
100185	Clogs	木底鞋	
100173	Dancing shoes	舞蹈鞋	
100196	Downhill skiing boots	滑雪靴	
100174	Espadrilles	帆布鞋	
100175	Football boots	足球鞋	
100166	Footwear	鞋	
100178	Gaiters	高帮松紧靴，绑腿式长筒靴	
100176	Galoshes	橡胶套鞋，雨鞋	
100194	Golf shoes	高尔夫球鞋	
100161	Half-boots	半高筒靴	
100188	Heel protectors for footwear	鞋跟保护物	
100186	Heels	鞋后跟	
100165	Infants' bootees	婴儿毛线鞋	
100169	Infants' leggings	婴儿筒袜	
100180	Inner soles	鞋内底	
100180	Insoles	鞋垫	
100177	Knee pads	护膝	
100179	Leggings	绑腿，护胫	
104933	Maternity tights	孕妇紧身裤袜	【13】
100187	Medical stockings	医用长袜	
100181	Moccasins	鹿皮软鞋	
100189	Non-slip protectors for shoes [except crampons]	鞋的防滑保护件[冰爪除外]	
100190	Orthopaedic footwear	矫形鞋	
100191	Orthopaedic socks	矫形短袜	
100192	Orthopaedic soles	矫形鞋鞋底	

100190	Orthopedic footwear	矫形鞋	
100191	Orthopedic socks	矫形短袜	
100192	Orthopedic soles	矫形鞋鞋底	
100170	Overshoes	套鞋	
100159	Panty hose	女用连裤袜	
100173	Pumps	舞鞋，无带有跟女鞋	
100182	Puttees	绑腿	
100168	Safety footwear	安全防护鞋	
100183	Sandals	凉鞋	
100172	Shoe and boot uppers	鞋和靴的面、帮	
100162	Shoes	鞋	
100193	Shoes for mountaineering	登山鞋	
100164	Slippers	拖鞋	
100200	Snow boots［après-ski boots］	雪地靴［雪屐］	
100198	Snowboard boots	单板滑雪靴	
100163	Socks	短袜	
100184	Soles for footwear	鞋底	
100171	Spats	鞋罩	
100167	Special boots for sports	运动专用靴	
100158	Stockings	长袜	
104703	Surf shoes	冲浪鞋	【11】
100197	Telemark boots	滑雪回转鞋	
100159	Tights	紧身裤袜	
100199	Trekking boots	徒步鞋	
104702	Water shoes	涉水鞋	【11】

02-05

Neckties, scarves, neckerchiefs and handkerchiefs

Note：Including all "flat" clothing accessories.

02-05

领带、围巾、颈巾和手帕

注：包括所有"平面的"服装附件。

100201	Bibs	围涎，围嘴	
100257	Bow-ties	领结	【13】[1]
104704	Cravats	男士领巾，（系在衣领里的）男士围巾	【11】
100210	Fancy handkerchiefs	花式手帕	

---

1 由02-07类转移至02-05类。

100209	Handkerchiefs	手帕
100207	Neckerchiefs	围巾，颈巾
100204	Neckties	领带
100206	Sashes for wear	绶带
100205	Scarves ［long］	围巾［长］
100208	Scarves	围巾
100203	Shawls	片式披肩
100202	Squares ［scarves］	方巾［围巾］

02-06
Gloves

Note: Including surgical gloves and rubber or plastic protective gloves for household use or for various occupations or sports.

02-06
手套

注：包括外科手套，家用、各种职业用、运动用橡胶或塑料防护手套。

100213	Boxing gloves	拳击手套	
100211	Finger-stalls ［for household, medical or other purposes］	指套，护指套［家用、医用或其他用途］	
104854	Gardening gloves	园艺手套	【12】
100212	Gloves	手套	
100214	Gloves for protection ［for household, medical or other purposes］	防护手套［家用、医用或其他用途］	
100216	Mittens	连指手套	
100215	Signalling gloves	信号手套	
104853	Work gloves	工作手套	【12】
100217	X-ray operators' gloves	X光操作人员用手套	

02-07
Haberdashery and clothing accessories

Notes: (a) Including buttons, for garments, for headwear and for footwear, laces, pins, hand sewing, knitting and embroidery equipment and clothing accessories such as belts, straps for suspender belts, braces. (b) Not including yarns or other threads (Cl. 05-01), decorative trimmings (Cl. 05-04), sewing, knitting and embroidery machines (Cl. 15-06) or sewing kits (containers) (Cl. 03-01).

02-07
缝纫用品、服饰用品和服装附件

注：(a) 包括服装用、帽类用及鞋类用纽扣、鞋带、别针，手工缝制、编织、刺绣的工具，服装附件如腰带、吊袜带、背带。(b) 不包括纱线或其他细线（05-01类），装饰边（05-04类），缝纫、编织和刺绣机械（15-06类）或缝纫用具包（容器）（03-01类）。

| 100260 | Belt trimmings | 带的装饰物 |

100234	Belts［clothing］	腰带［服装］	
100251	Bobbins for embroidery	刺绣用线轴	
100233	Braces for trousers	裤子背带	
100232	Brassards	臂章，袖章	
100229	Buckles［haberdashery］	扣环，皮带扣［服饰用品］	
100230	Buttons［haberdashery］	纽扣［服饰用品］	
104855	Cord stoppers	抽绳伸缩扣	【12】
100238	Crochet hooks	编织钩针	
100221	Crochet needles	钩针	
100231	Cuff links	袖口的链扣，袖扣	
100231	Cufflinks	袖口的链扣，袖扣	【11】
100267	Darning balls	织补用球形工具	
100267	Darning balls or mushrooms	织补用球形或蘑菇形工具	
100268	Darning needles	织补针	
100237	Embroidering crochet hooks	刺绣编织用钩针	
100245	Epaulets	肩章，肩饰	
100259	Eyelets for shoes	鞋上的眼孔	
100258	Eyelets［haberdashery］	眼孔［服饰用品］	
100226	Fasteners for footwear	鞋扣	
100218	Fasteners［haberdashery］	扣件［服饰用品］	
100278	Fastenings for babies' diapers	婴儿尿布紧扣件	
100277	Fastenings for babies' nappies	婴儿尿布紧扣件	【13】
100264	Feathers for adornment	装饰用羽毛	【13】[1]
100274	Fluorescent belts［clothing］	荧光带［服装］	
100270	Frames for darning or embroidery	织补或刺绣用框架	
100270	Frames for embroidery or darning	刺绣或织补用框架	
100252	Frills	褶边，褶边饰	
100254	Garters	吊袜带	
100269	Hat bands	帽圈，帽边上的圈丝带	
100243	Hat linings	帽子衬里	
100276	Hat pins	帽针	
100272	Hat veils	帽子的面纱	
100265	Holders for balls of wool［for knitting］	毛线球固定架［编织用］	
104622	Hook-and-loop fasteners	拉链黏贴带，尼龙搭扣	【10】
100218	Hooks［haberdashery］	钩针［缝纫用品］	
100223	Knitting needles	编织针	
100255	Laces	系带，鞋带	

---

[1] 由"Feathers for dress ornament 服饰羽毛"修改为"Feathers for adornment 装饰用羽毛"。

100250	Necktie holders	领带扣
100222	Needles for unpicking	拆线针
100219	Needles［haberdashery］	针［缝纫用品］
100244	Needle-threaders	穿针器
100281	Perspiration-absorbing pads for clothing	吸汗排汗用服装衬垫
100263	Pin cushions	插针垫
100246	Pins［haberdashery］	别针［服饰用品］
100271	Pulls for slide fasteners［zippers］	拉链拉手［拉链］
100277	Reels for thread	线轴
100277	Reels for yarn	纱线轴
100277	Reels for yarn and thread	纱线轴、线轴
100248	Safety pins	安全别针
100227	Scarf clips	围巾夹
100261	Sequins, spangles［haberdashery］	发光金属小圆片［服饰用品］
100220	Sewing needles	缝衣针
100241	Shoe decorations	鞋的装饰物
100226	Shoe fasteners	鞋扣
100239	Shoe hooks	鞋钩
100236	Shoe trimmings	鞋的装饰物
100224	Shoemakers' needles	缝鞋针
100228	Shoulder belts	肩带
100245	Shoulder pads	肩垫
100256	Shuttles for making fishing nets	织渔网的梭
100249	Slide fasteners［zippers］	拉锁［拉链］
100240	Sliders of slide fasteners［zippers］	拉链的滑扣［拉链］
100240	Sliders of zip fasteners	拉链滑扣
100279	Sock suspenders	吊袜带
100261	Spangles, sequins［haberdashery］	发光金属小圆片［服饰用品］
100266	Stiffened cloth for clothing	服装的硬衬
104705	Straps for brassieres	乳罩肩带　【11】
100253	Straps for suspender belts	吊袜带
100235	Suspender belts	吊袜腰带
100233	Suspenders for trousers	裤子背带
100242	Thimbles	针箍，顶针
100262	Threaders	穿线器
100250	Tie clips	领带夹
100247	Tie pins	领带别针
100273	Veil holders	面纱撑架

100275	Veils	面纱，面罩
100225	Wires for brassieres	乳罩金属托
100280	Wristbands [clothing]	袖口 [服装]
100249	Zip fasteners	拉链

02-99
Miscellaneous

02-99
其他杂项

100284	Elbow protectors for sports	运动护肘
100283	Muffs [clothing]	暖手筒 [服装]
100282	Yokes [apparel]	上衣的抵肩，裙子的腰 [服饰]

Class 03
Travel goods, cases, parasols and personal belongings, not elsewhere specified

03 类
其他类未列入的旅行用品、箱包、阳伞和个人用品

03-01
Trunks, suitcases, briefcases, handbags, keyholders, cases specially designed for their contents, wallets and similar articles

Note: Not including articles for the transport of goods (Cl. 09) or cigar cases and cigarette cases (Cl. 27-06).

03-01 【3】[1]
大衣箱、手提箱、公文包、手提包、钥匙袋、钱夹、专门为内容物设计的箱包和类似物品

注：不包括商品运输用容器（09类）、雪茄盒和香烟盒（27-06类）。

100399	Address holders for luggages	行李箱用地址牌夹	【13】[2]
104569	Armbands for mobile telephones	臂带式移动电话套	【10】
100316	Attaché cases	公文包	
100311	Backpacks	背包	【12】
100373	Bags for storage of spruce trees	云杉树储藏袋	
100285	Ball cases [for games]	球盒，球套，球包［游艺用］	
100367	Belt bags	腰包	
100369	Bicycle and motorcycle panniers [bags]	自行车和摩托车的挂篮［包］	
100343	Billfolds	钱夹	
100296	Binocular cases	望远镜盒	
100349	Bowling ball carrying cases	保龄球携带箱	
100327	Briefcases	公文包	
100299	Camera cases	照相机盒，照相机包	
100366	Card cases	名片夹，名片盒	
100336	Cartridge pouches	弹药袋	
100360	Cases for bandaging materials [except packaging]	包扎用品箱［包装除外］	
100361	Cases for brushes	刷子盒	
100353	Cases for computer discs	光盘盒，光盘包	
100375	Cases for electronic organizers	电子记事簿套，电子记事簿包	
100354	Cases for lenses	镜头盒，镜头包	
100376	Cases for mobile telephones	手机套，手机包	

---

[1] 原 03-02 类的类别标题和所有产品项合并入此类。
[2] 由 03-99 类转移至 03-01 类。

100298	Cases for playing cards	纸牌盒	
100304	Cases for pocket combs	小梳子的套、包	
100370	Cases for portable computers	笔记本电脑包	
100355	Cases for radios	收音机盒	
100357	Cases for razors or shavers	刮胡刀或剃须刀盒、包	
104588	Cases for sharpening stones	磨石盒，磨石包	【10】
100356	Cases for skis［bags］	雪屐雪橇箱［包］	
100292	Caskets	首饰盒	
100338	Chains for key rings	钥匙环的链	
100342	Check book covers	支票夹	
100342	Cheque book covers	支票本套	
100300	Cine-camera cases	电影摄影机箱	
100351	Coin holders	硬币盒	
100309	Covers for fishing rods	鱼杆套	
100350	Covers for telephones	电话机套	
100332	Doctors' instrument cases［containers］	医疗器械箱［容器］	
100324	First aid kits［containers］	急救箱，急救包［容器］	
100288	Game bags	狩猎袋	
100329	Golf club bags	高尔夫球杆包	
100305	Gun holsters	枪套	
100347	Handbags	手提包	
101343	Handles for briefcases	公文包提手	【13】[1]
100291	Hat boxes［except packaging］	帽盒［包装除外］	
100341	Identity card cases	身份证卡片盒、套、包和夹	
100340	Jewel boxes	珠宝箱	
100295	Jewel cases	珠宝盒	
100339	Key cases	钥匙包	
100344	Key fobs	带饰物的钥匙链	
100344	Key rings	钥匙环	
104935	Lanyards	挂绳	【13】
104936	Lipstick cases	唇膏盒，口红盒	【13】
100371	Luggage cases for motorcycles	摩托车行李箱包	
100402	Luggage wheels	行李箱轮	【13】[2]
100318	Manicure cases［containers］	修指甲剪盒［容器］	
100303	Measuring instrument cases	测量仪器箱	
100337	Money belts	钱带	

---

[1] 由 08-06 类转移至 03-01 类。
[2] 由 03-99 类转移至 03-01 类。

100377	Money boxes [piggy banks]	钱盒[存钱罐]	【10】
100320	Music bags	乐谱袋	
100302	Musical instrument cases	乐器箱	
100307	Net bags for shopping	购物网兜	
100343	Notecases	钱包，皮夹子	
100341	Passport or identity card cases	护照或身份证卡片盒、套、包和夹	
100306	Pen cases	钢笔盒	
100317	Phonograph record cases	唱片盒	
100323	Picnic cases	野餐箱	
100377	Piggy banks	存钱罐	
104937	Pill organizer boxes	药丸分装盒	【13】
100362	Pillboxes	药盒	
100298	Playing card cases	纸牌盒	
100335	Portfolios for drawings	画夹	
100301	Projection screen cases	投影屏盒	
100374	Protective bags for car radios	汽车无线电设备保护袋	
104934	Protective covers for bags and luggage	包、行李箱的防护套	【13】
100333	Purses	钱包	
100289	Quivers	箭袋	
100357	Razor cases	剃须刀盒，剃须刀包	
100345	Reticules [handbags]	拉带手提包[手提包]	
100365	Rucksack frames	背包的骨架	
100311	Rucksacks	背包	
100319	Satchels	挎包	
100308	Scabbards for weapons	武器套	
100290	School bags	书包	
100330	School pencil cases	笔袋	
100352	Security boxes for bicycle accessories	自行车附件箱	
100294	Sewing kits [containers]	缝纫用具箱[容器]	
100314	Sewing machine cases	缝纫机箱，缝纫机盒	
100357	Shaver cases	剃须刀盒，剃须刀包	
100308	Sheaths for arms	武器鞘	
100372	Sheaths for gardening tools	园艺工具护套	
100310	Sheaths for knives	刀鞘	
100312	Shoe bags	鞋袋	
100322	Shoe-cleaning kits [containers]	擦鞋用具箱[容器]	

100334	Shopping bags	购物袋，购物包	
104856	Shopping baskets	购物篮	【12】
100346	Shoulder bags	肩背包	
100363	Shoulder straps for bags	背包的肩带	
100364	Shoulder straps for rucksacks	背包的肩带	
100297	Spectacle cases	眼镜盒	
104706	Spectacle cords	眼镜挂绳	【11】
100368	Sport bags	运动用品包	
100307	String bags for shopping	购物网兜	
104857	Suitcases	手提箱	【12】
100313	Tennis racket covers	网球拍套，网球拍袋	
104707	Tissue box covers	纸巾盒	【11】
100325	Toilet cases	梳妆盒	
100358	Tool belts	工具带	
100286	Tool boxes	工具箱	
100331	Tool cases	工具盒，工具包	
100326	Travel kits [containers]	旅行用品包[容器]	
100328	Travelling bags	旅行袋，旅行包	
100315	Trunks [luggage]	大衣箱[行李箱]	
100293	Typewriter cases	打字机盒	
100348	Umbrella covers	伞套	
100359	Umbrella sheaths	伞护套	
100325	Vanity cases	化妆包	
100343	Wallets	钱夹	
100287	Work baskets	针线筐，针线篮	
104583	Wrist cases for mobile telephones	腕带式移动电话套	【10】
100321	Writing cases	文具箱	

03-02

[Vacant]

03-02

[空缺]

【3】[1]

03-03

Umbrellas, parasols, sunshades and walking sticks

03-03

雨伞、阳伞、遮阳篷和手杖

100396	Bases for parasols	阳伞支座	

---

[1] 原类别标题和所有产品项合并入03-01类，03-02类成为空缺。

100392	Beach windshields	海滨挡风篷	
100381	Canes	拐杖	
100378	Crutch armrests	拐杖扶手	
100388	Crutch tips	拐杖头	
100379	Crutches for invalids	残疾人拐杖	
100390	Ferrules for umbrella handles	伞把柄金属包头	
100384	Ferrules for umbrellas	雨伞金属包头	
100387	Garden or beach parasols	花园或海滨遮阳伞	
100391	Garden windshields	花园挡风篷	
104858	Guide sticks for the visually impaired	视障者用引导杖	【12】
100395	Holders for crutches or walking sticks	拐杖或手杖的握柄	
100394	Parasol stands	阳伞架	
100386	Parasols	阳伞	
100382	Shooting sticks	顶端可打开为座凳的手杖	
100383	Umbrella runners	伞的滑动束套	
100389	Umbrella handles	伞手持把柄	
100393	Umbrella shafts	伞杆	
100385	Umbrellas	伞	
100386	Umbrella-sunshades	遮阳伞篷	
100380	Walking-stick ferrules	手杖金属包头	
100381	Walking-sticks	手杖	

03-04
Fans

03-04
扇子

100397	Fans for personal use	个人使用的扇子	

03-05
Devices for carrying and walking with babies and children

03-05 【12】[1]
用于婴儿、儿童的携带及辅助行走装置

Note: Not including baby carriers in Cl. 06 and Cl. 12.

注：不包括06类和12类中的婴儿携带装置。

100401	Backpacks for carrying babies	婴儿背篓	
100400	Infant carriers worn on the body	穿戴式婴儿携带装置	
104938	Safety wrist straps for children	儿童安全牵引腕带	【13】
104939	Slings for carrying babies	婴儿背巾	【13】

---

1 新增加03-05类，产品项由03-99类转移至03-05类。

104708　　Toddler reins　　　　　　　　　　　婴儿学步带　　　　　　　　　　　　　　【11】

03-99　　　　　　　　　　　　　　　　　**03-99**
Miscellaneous　　　　　　　　　　　　　其他杂项

Class 04
Brushware

04 类
刷子

04-01
Brushes and brooms for cleaning

Note：Not including clothes brushes（Cl. 04-02）.

04-01
清洁刷和扫帚

注：不包括服装刷（04-02类）。

100408	Absorbent brushes	吸水刷
100407	Attachments for affixing brushes to their handles	板刷和刷柄的接合部件
100414	Broom handles	扫帚柄
100404	Brooms	扫帚
100410	Brushes for cleaning bottles	瓶刷
100409	Cleaning brushes	清洁刷
100416	Crumb brushes	扫碎屑用刷
100420	Devices with brushes for cleaning spectacles	清洗眼镜用刷洗装置
100419	Dishwashing brushes	洗盘刷
100411	Dusting brushes	除尘刷
100417	Feather dusters	羽毛掸子
100412	Furniture dusters with handle	带手柄的家具用掸子
100415	Handles for cleaning brushes	清洁刷刷柄
100418	Lavatory brushes	盥洗室用刷
100405	Mops	拖把
100413	Scouring brushes	擦洗用刷子
100403	Scrubbing brushes, long handled	长柄板刷
100406	Whisks	掸帚，小毛掸子

04-02
Toilet brushes，clothes brushes and shoe brushes

Notes：（a）"Toilet brushes" means brushes for corporal use，for example，for the hair，nails or teeth.（b）Not including electric toothbrushes [appliances]（Cl. 28-03）.

04-02
梳妆刷、服装刷和鞋刷

注：(a)"梳妆刷"指身体用刷，例如用于头发、指甲或牙齿。(b)不包括电动牙刷[器具]（28-03类）。 【11】[1]

100435	Bristles for toothbrushes	牙刷毛

---

1 增加注释内容："(b) Not including electric toothbrushes [appliances]（Cl. 28-03）.(b)不包括电动牙刷[器具]（28-03类）。"

100431	Brushes for electric toothbrushes	电动牙刷的刷头
100426	Clothes brushes	服装刷
100428	Cosmetic brushes	化妆刷
100422	Hair brushes	毛发刷
100430	Handles for clothes brushes	服装刷柄
100429	Handles for toilet brushes	梳妆刷柄
100432	Interdental brushes	牙齿缝隙刷
100434	Mascara brushes	睫毛刷
100427	Nail brushes	指甲刷
100421	Shaving brushes	修面刷，须膏刷
100425	Shoe brushes	鞋刷
100424	Toilet brushes	梳妆刷
100433	Toothbrush heads	牙刷头
100423	Toothbrushes	牙刷

04-03
Brushes for machines

Note: "Brushes for machines" means brushes incorporated in machines or in special vehicles.

04-03
机器用刷

注："机器用刷"指与机器或专用车辆相结合的刷子。

100436	Brushes for machines	机器用刷

04-04
Paintbrushes, brushes for use in cooking

04-04
油漆刷和烹饪用刷

100438	Brushes used in cooking	烹调用刷
100440	Handles for brushes used in cooking	烹饪用刷柄
100439	Paintbrush handles	油漆刷柄
100437	Paintbrushes	油漆刷

04-99
Miscellaneous

04-99
其他杂项

Class 05
Textile piece goods, artificial and natural sheet material

05 类
纺织品，人造或天然材料片材

Notes:（a）Including all textile or similar articles, sold by the yarn and not made up.（b）Not including ready-made articles（Cl. 02 or 06）.

注：（a）包括所有以纱线和非成品形式出售的纺织品或类似物品。（b）不包括成品（02或06类）。

05-01
Spun articles

05-01
纺纱制品

Notes:（a）Including yarn and thread.（b）Not including, for instance, rope, wire rope, string, twine（Cl. 09-06）.

注：（a）包括纱和线。（b）不包括如绳索、金属绳、细绳、合股绳等（09-06类）。

100441	Purls for embroidery	刺绣用丝线
100442	Textile threads	纺织线
100442	Yarns	纱线

05-02
Lace

05-02
花边

100444	Insertions [tulle, lace]	嵌饰 [薄纱，花边]
100443	Lace	花边

05-03
Embroidery

05-03
刺绣品

100445	Embroidery	刺绣品

05-04
Ribbons, braids and other decorative trimmings

05-04
缎带、编带和其他缀饰品

100455	Adhesive tapes	胶带
100451	Braids	编带，穗带
100448	Braids [decorative trimmings]	编带 [缀饰品]
100453	Decorative trimmings	缀饰品
100458	Detachable trimmings for clothing	服装可分离的饰品

100449	Elastic edgings	弹性饰边
100450	Elastic ribbons	弹性缎带
100446	Garment edgings	服装饰边
100456	Gummed tapes	胶带 【10】[1]
100447	Insulating tapes for cables	线缆绝缘胶带
100453	Passementerie	饰带，饰珠
100454	Pompons	绒球
104940	Ribbons [decorative trimmings]	缎带 [缀饰品]
100452	Tassels [haberdashery]	缨穗，流苏 [服饰用品]
100457	Textile labels for clothing	服装用纺织品标签

05-05
Textile fabrics

Note: Including textile fabrics, woven, knitted or otherwise manufactured, tarpaulins, felt and loden.

05-05
纺织纤维制品

注：包括机织的、编织的或其他人造的纺织纤维制品，防水布，毛毡和罗登呢。

100461	Brocades	织锦，锦缎
100462	Calico	印花布，白棉布
100481	Canvas for packaging	包装帆布
100466	Cloth	布
100486	Corduroy	灯芯绒
100464	Crepe [fabric]	绉纱，绉绸 [织物]
100478	Crocheted fabrics	钩编编织物
100465	Damask	锦缎
100460	Dimity	凸纹条格布
100479	Elastic fabrics	弹性织物
100467	Fabrics	织物
100468	Felt	毛毡
100469	Flannel	法兰绒
100470	Imitation fur	人造毛皮
100480	Insulating fabrics	绝缘织物
100471	Jacquard fabric	提花织物
100477	Mesh fabrics	网眼织物
100472	Moires [fabric]	波纹绸 [织物]
100473	Moquettes [fabric]	绒织物 [织物]
100477	Netting [mesh fabric]	网 [网眼织物]

---

1 由"Gummed tapes [stationery] 胶带 [文具]"修改为"Gummed tapes 胶带"。

100483	Oilcloths	油布	
100488	Plush	长毛绒	
100474	Poplin cloth	府绸	
100475	Silk fabrics	丝织物	
100459	Tarpaulins	防水布	
100489	Textile sheets for cutting out	可裁的纺织片材	
100482	Ticking	坚质条纹棉布	
100484	Tulle	薄纱	
100463	Twill	斜纹布	
100490	Upholstery fabrics	装饰织物	
100485	Velvet	天鹅绒	
100476	Woven fabrics	机织织物	
100487	Zephyr [cloth]	轻薄织物［布］	

05-06

Artificial or natural sheet material

Notes: (a) Including sheets whose only characteristic features are their surface ornamentation or their texture, in particular, covering sheets such as wallpaper, linoleum, self-adhesive plastic sheets, wrapping sheets and rolls of paper, subject to the exceptions indicated under (b). (b) Not including writing paper, even in rolls (Cl. 19-01), or sheets used as building components, such as wall panels and wainscoting (Cl. 25-01).

05-06

人造或天然材料片材

注：（a）包括其特征仅在于表面装饰性和纹理质地的片材，特别是覆盖片材如墙纸、油毡、自黏性塑料片材、包装片材和卷纸，受（b）所列排除项的限制。（b）不包括书写用纸和卷状书写用纸（19-01类），不包括用于建筑构件的片材，如墙板和壁板（25-01类）。

100514	Absorbent paper for household purposes	家用吸水纸	
100500	Aluminium foil for household use	家用铝箔	
100512	Animal skins	兽皮	
104859	Baking paper	烘焙纸	【12】
100491	Cork paper	软木纸	
100504	Flint paper	蜡光纸，研光纸	
100513	Glass sheets	玻璃片材	
104627	Imitation leather	人造革	【10】
100511	Impregnated wipes	清洁湿巾	
100508	Kitchen paper rolls	厨房用卷纸	
100497	Laminates of paper, metal or plastic materials	纸、金属或塑料的薄片制品	
100498	Linoleum	油毡，漆布	
100499	Matting for artificial ski slopes	人造滑雪斜坡用铺垫	

100501	Packing paper	包装纸	
100509	Paper handkerchiefs	纸帕	
100506	Paper towels	纸巾	
104646	PVC floor coverings	PVC 地板，地板革	【10】
100507	Rolls or packs of paper [toilet paper or napkins]	卷纸或捆纸［卫生纸或餐巾纸］	
100515	Sandpaper	砂纸	
100496	Self-adhesive plastic foil	自黏塑料薄膜	
100494	Sheets of artificial or natural material	人造或天然材料片材	
100493	Sheets of wrapping material	包装片材	
100510	Toilet paper	卫生纸	
104671	Toilet seat paper covers	马桶座圈垫纸	【10】
100495	Veneer sheets	饰面片材	
100505	Vulcanized paper	硬化纸，硫化纸	
100503	Wallpaper	墙纸，壁纸	
100502	Wax paper	蜡纸	
100492	Wood ribbon	木板条	
100501	Wrapping paper	包装纸	

05-99
Miscellaneous

05-99
其他杂项

100516	Wadding	软填料，填絮

Class 06
Furnishing

Notes: (a) Composite furniture articles embodying components included in several subclasses are classified in Cl. 06-05. (b) Sets of furniture, as far as they can be looked upon as one design, are classified in Cl. 06-05. (c) Not including textile piecegoods (Cl. 05).

06-01
Seats

Notes: (a) Including all seats even if they are suitable for laying, such as benches, couches, divans [sofas], ottomans, benches for saunas and sofas. (b) Including vehicle seats.

06-01
座椅 【8】[1]

注：(a) 包括所有座椅，即使其适于躺卧，如长凳、长沙发、长榻、无扶手无靠背的长沙发椅［沙发］、有垫矮凳、桑拿浴用长凳和沙发。(b) 包括交通工具上的座椅。

100529	Armchairs	扶手椅	
100544	Babies' chairs	婴儿椅	
100546	Baby bouncer seats	婴儿摇椅，婴儿弹乐椅	
100522	Back supports for vehicle seats	交通工具座位用后撑座	
104941	Bath seats for babies	婴儿浴椅	【13】
100545	Benches for saunas	桑拿浴用长凳	
100524	Benches [furniture]	长凳［家具］	
100549	Booster cushions for children	儿童安全座椅	
100526	Chairs [seats]	椅子［座位］	
100517	Chaises longues	躺椅	
100548	Child seats for motor cars	摩托车儿童座椅	
100543	Children's seats, for fixing on cycles or motorcycles	安装于自行车或摩托车上的儿童座椅	
100518	Couches	长沙发，长榻	
100519	Couches for massage	按摩用长沙发	
100528	Dentists' armchairs	牙科用扶手椅	
100518	Divans [sofas]	无扶手无靠背的长沙发椅［沙发］	
100525	Easy chairs	安乐椅	
100521	Elbow rests for vehicle seats	交通工具座位用扶手肘靠座	
100527	Fireside chairs	炉边座椅	
104710	Floor chairs	地板椅	【11】

---

1 原06-01类中所有床类产品项移入06-02类，06-01类标题由"床和椅子"修改为"座椅"。

100538	Fold-down seats	折合椅	
100532	Folding seats	折叠椅	
100531	Garden chairs	庭院座椅	
100530	Hairdressers' chairs	理发椅	
104712	Massage chairs	按摩椅	【11】
104711	Massaging chairs	按摩椅	【11】
104709	Méridiennes	长躺椅，贵妃榻	【11】
100547	Office chairs	办公椅	
100520	Ottomans	有垫矮凳，垫脚凳	
100533	Pouffs [seats]	蒲团形矮凳［座椅］	
100534	Rocking-chairs	摇椅	
100540	School benches	教室长凳	
100543	Seats for children, for fixing on cycles or motorcycles	安装于自行车或摩托车上的儿童座椅	
100537	Seats for fishermen	钓鱼座	
100536	Seats for means of transport [except saddles]	运输工具上的座［鞍除外］	
100535	Seats [furniture]	座椅［家具］	
104661	Sofa-beds	沙发床	【10】
100541	Sofas	沙发	
100539	Stools [furniture]	凳子［家具］	
104713	Street benches [street furniture]	街边长椅［公共设施］	【11】
100542	Swinging seats [garden furniture]	秋千椅［庭院家具］	
104591	Theatre chairs	剧院椅	【10】
100538	Tip-up seats	翻椅	
104942	Vehicle seats	交通工具座椅	【13】

06-02
Beds

Notes: (a) Including mattress supports. (b) Not including seats suitable for laying (Cl. 06-01), such as benches, couches, divans [sofas], ottomans, benches for saunas and sofas.

06-02
床

注：(a) 包括床垫架。(b) 不包括适于躺卧的座椅（06-01类），如长凳、长沙发、长榻、无扶手无靠背的长沙发椅［沙发］、有垫矮凳、桑拿浴用长凳和沙发。

【8】[1]

100550	Basket cots	婴儿床	
100551	Beds	床	
104575	Beds for children	儿童床	【10】
104943	Bumper beds	缓冲防撞床	【13】

---

[1] 原06-01类中所有床类产品项移入本小类，06-02类由空缺修改为"床"。

100552	Bunk beds	双层床	
100553	Camp beds	行军床，折叠床	
100554	Carrycots for babies	手提式婴儿床	
100555	Cradles	摇篮	
100556	Hammocks	吊床	
100557	Hospital beds	医院用床	
100558	Invalid beds	病人用床	
104860	Loft beds	高架床	【12】
100559	Mattress supports	床垫架	

06-03
Tables and similar furniture

06-03
桌子及类似家具

100574	Altars	祭桌，圣餐台	
100565	Baby changing tables	婴儿护理台	
100568	Bed tables for the sick	病人床上用桌	
100580	Bedside tables	床头柜	
104595	Coffee tables	咖啡桌，茶几	【10】
100571	Console tables	螺形托脚桌	
100561	Counters［tables］	柜台［桌子］	
100560	Desks［furniture］	书桌［家具］	
104600	Dining tables	餐桌	【10】
100578	Drawing tables	绘图桌	
100581	Folding tables	折叠桌	
100579	Laboratory tables	实验台	
100583	Nests of tables	套几	
100585	Office tables	办公桌	
100563	Pedestal tables	独腿桌，台座式桌	
100575	School desks	课桌	
100570	School tables	学校用桌	
100562	Serving trolleys	送餐手推台桌	
104659	Side tables	边几，边桌	【10】
100564	Tables	桌子	
100582	Tables for computer terminals	计算机终端桌	
100577	Trestle tables	搁板桌	
100584	Wallpapering tables	贴墙纸用工作台	
100572	Work benches	工作台	
100576	Worktables［sewing tables］	工作台［缝纫台］	

100560	Writing desks	写字台	

06-04
Storage furniture

Notes：(a) Including cupboards, furniture with drawers or compartments, and shelves. (b) Including coffins, coffin linings and crematory urns.

06-04
存放物品用家具

注：(a) 包括橱柜、架子、带抽屉或间隔的家具。(b) 包括棺材、棺材衬套和骨灰盒。

100593	Bathroom cabinets	浴室柜	
100637	Billiard cue racks	台球球杆架	
100596	Bookcases	书柜	
100606	Bookshelves	书架	
100624	Bottle racks [for storage]	瓶架[储藏用]	
100644	Cabinets for audio and video apparatus	视听设备柜	
100625	Cabinets for phonograph records	唱片柜	
100628	Cabinets for telecommunication apparatus	电信设备柜	
100609	Card index cabinets [furniture]	索引卡片柜[家具]	
100595	Chests	箱，柜	
100603	Chests of drawers	五斗橱，多屉柜	
100615	Clothes racks	隔层衣架	
100641	Coffin linings	棺材衬套	
100642	Coffins	棺材	
100603	Commodes	有抽屉的小柜	
100643	Crematory urns	骨灰盒	
104945	Drinks cabinets	饮料柜	【13】
100599	File cabinets [furniture]	文件柜[家具]	
100647	Furniture for bathrooms [without sanitary apparatus and equipment]	盥洗室用家具[不包括卫生设备]	
100612	Furniture with compartments	带隔层的家具	
100613	Furniture with drawers	带抽屉的家具	
100621	Glass cabinets	玻璃柜	
100631	Gun racks	枪架	
104616	Hat racks	帽架	【10】
104944	Intelligent delivery lockers	智能快递柜	【13】
100591	Kitchen cabinets	橱柜	
100620	Kitchen dressers [furniture]	厨房碗橱[家具]	
100635	Knife display racks	刀陈列架	
104946	Left-luggage lockers	行李寄存柜	【13】

104714	Lockers	寄存柜，储物柜	【11】
100638	Magazine racks［furniture］	杂志架［家具］	
100610	Meat chests	食品柜	
100610	Meat safes	食品橱	
100589	Medicine cabinets	药柜	
100598	Music cabinets	乐谱柜	
100590	Office cabinets	办公用柜	
100618	Plate racks［furniture］	盘碟架［家具］	
100597	Racks for fruit and vegetables［except for display stands］	水果蔬菜架［非陈列用］	
100636	Racks for hanging tools	悬挂工具用架	
100627	Racks for test tubes	试管架	
100623	Religious cabinets	宗教用柜	
100639	Rotating file cabinets	旋转式文件柜	
100600	Safes	保险箱，保险柜	
100629	Saucepan racks	长柄平底锅架	
100622	Shelves for flowers	隔层花架	
100608	Shelves for newspaper kiosks	报亭用架	
100607	Shelves for prospectuses	内容说明书或样张摆放架	
100586	Shelves［furniture］	架［家具］	
100619	Shelving	排架，组架	
100626	Shoe chests	鞋柜	
100617	Shoe racks	鞋架	
100605	Shoe stands［furniture］	鞋立架［家具］	
100621	Showcases［furniture］	陈设柜［家具］	
100604	Sideboards	餐具柜，餐边柜	
100587	Silver cabinets	银器柜	
104947	Ski racks, freestanding	独立式雪橇架	【13】
100646	Stands for discs［furniture］	磁盘架［家具］	
100602	Stationery cabinets［furniture］	文具柜［家具］	
100640	Storage cabinets	储藏柜	
100645	Storage cabinets with wheels	带轮子的储藏柜	
100592	Storage closets	储藏柜橱	
100614	Storage furniture	储藏用家具	
100632	Storage furniture for discs	磁盘用储藏家具	
100633	Storage racks for discs	光盘存储架	
100623	Tabernacles	神龛，壁龛，做弥撒用的圣体盒	
100588	Tool cupboards	工具柜	

100630	Umbrella stands	伞立架	
100616	Walking stick racks	手杖架	
100594	Wall cupboards	壁橱，吊柜	
100601	Wall safes	嵌墙式保险箱	
100611	Wardrobes	衣柜，衣橱	

06-05
Composite furniture
06-05
组合家具

100650	Composite furniture	组合家具	
100649	Dressing tables	梳妆台，镜台	
104715	Picnic tables with attached seats	连有座位的野餐桌	【11】
100648	School desks with attached seats	连有座位的课桌	

06-06
Other furniture and furniture parts
06-06
其他家具和家具零部件

100654	Aquarium stands	鱼缸立架	
104718	Back rests for chairs [parts of chairs]	椅背［座椅零部件］	【11】
100670	Bases for clocks	钟支撑座	
100662	Bed surrounds [furniture]	床四周框架［家具］	
100678	Book ends	书挡，书立，书靠	
104720	Book rests	阅书架	【11】
100652	Booths for teaching	教学用的小隔间	
100656	Cashiers' booths for shops	收银台	
100679	Cask stands	桶立架	
100693	Catafalques	灵柩台	
100651	Chair or seat footrests	椅子或座位的搁脚板	
100684	Chiropodists' footrests	脚病治疗用搁脚板	
100663	Clothes stands [valets]	衣服立架［衣物架］	
100683	Coat stands [furniture]	外衣立架［家具］	
100658	Confessional boxes	忏悔室	
100657	Corn or hay bins	谷物或干草储藏槽	
104719	Cubicle walls	隔间用壁板	【11】
100655	Decorative edgings for furniture	家具装饰边	
100685	Drawer casters	抽屉脚轮	
100686	Drawer rails	抽屉导轨	
100674	Extension table leaves	伸缩桌面的活动桌板	

100664	Flower stands [furniture]	花立架 [家具]	
100675	Furniture casters	家具脚轮	
100672	Furniture doors	家具门	
100677	Furniture drawers	家具抽屉	
100687	Furniture feet	家具支脚	
104610	Furniture fronts	家具前板	【10】
100671	Furniture legs	家具腿	
100691	Furniture tops	家具顶盖	
100680	Hat stands	帽子立架	
104716	Headboards	床头板	【11】
104688	Headrests for seats	座位头枕	【11】[1]
100652	Instruction booths	教学隔间	
100665	Lecterns	教堂诵经台，演讲台	
100688	Moldings for furniture	家具用模压件	
100688	Mouldings for furniture	家具用模压件	
100666	Music easels	乐谱架	
100666	Music stands	乐谱立架	
100669	Playpens for babies	供婴儿在内玩耍的围栏	
104948	Podiums [furniture]	领奖台，讲台，指挥台 [家具]	【13】
100653	Prayer stools	祷告者跪凳	
100681	Racks for hanging bags for filling	悬挂装袋架	
100659	Radiator covers	暖气罩板	
100682	Reading stands	阅览立架	
100668	Safety gates for babies	婴儿安全门	
100667	Screens [furniture]	屏风 [家具]	
104717	Seats [parts of chairs]	椅面 [座椅零部件]	【11】
100692	Sections for furniture	家具型材	
100676	Shoe stands with polisher guides	带抛光导向器的鞋架	
100660	Stepladders [furniture]	梯子 [家具]	
100661	Tips for furniture legs	家具腿的包头	
100689	Trestles	台架，叉架	
100663	Valets [clothes stands]	衣物架 [衣服立架]	
100690	Wrist supports	腕支撑架，扶手	

---

1 由06-01类转移至06-06类。

06-07
Mirrors and frames

Note: Not including mirrors included in other classes (see Alphabetical List).

100697	Anti-theft mirrors	防盗镜	
100695	Frames for pictures or mirrors	画框，镜框	
100702	Frames for posters	海报框架	
100696	Mirrors [furniture]	镜子[家具]	
100699	Moldings for picture frames	画框用模压件	
100699	Mouldings for picture frames	画框用模压件	【13】
100700	Paper mounts	纸衬板	
100701	Photograph stands	照片架	
100694	Picture-frame rods	画框杆	
104949	Smart mirrors	智能镜子	【13】
100698	Wall mirrors	壁镜	

06-08
Clothes hangers

100703	Clothes hangers	衣服挂架	【12】
100706	Clothes hangers with clips	带夹子的挂衣架	
100703	Coat hangers	外衣挂架	
100709	Shoe racks [hangers]	鞋架[悬挂]	
100704	Skirt hangers with clips	带夹子的裙架	
100708	Spacers for clothes hangers	衣架的限位隔挡	
100708	Spacers for coat hangers	衣架的限位隔挡	【12】
100705	Trouser hangers with clips	带夹子的裤架	
100707	Trouser stretchers	裤子撑架	

06-09
Mattresses and cushions

100713	Air cushions	气垫
100716	Air mattresses	充气床垫
100722	Anatomical cushions	符合人体工程学的垫
100718	Bolsters	软垫
100720	Camping mattresses	野营垫

100721	Changing mats for babies	可更换婴儿垫
100712	Cushions	垫子，靠垫
100714	Cushions for vehicle seats	交通工具座椅用垫
100710	Footmuffs ［electric or non-electric］	暖脚垫［电或非电的］
100719	Heating cushions	加热垫
100715	Mattresses	床垫
100717	Pillows	枕头
100711	Toilet seat pads	马桶坐垫

06-10
Curtains and indoor blinds

06-10
窗帘、门帘和室内百叶帘

100729	Blinds ［indoor］	百叶帘［室内］
100725	Curtain tiebacks	窗帘束带
100728	Curtains	窗帘
100727	Door curtains	门帘
100731	Mosquito nets ［furnishing］	蚊帐［家居用品］
100723	Pelmets	短幔
100730	Shower curtains	浴帘
100724	Valances	帷幔，装饰窗帘
100726	Venetian blinds	软百叶窗，百叶窗帘

06-11
Carpets，mats and rugs

06-11
地毯、地席、地垫和小地毯

100740	Anti-slip carpets	防滑地毯
100739	Anti-slip mats for bathtubs and shower trays	浴缸和沐浴房底盘用防滑垫
100742	Bathroom mats	浴室垫
100733	Bedside rugs	床边毯
100737	Carpets	地毯
100738	Carpets for automobiles	车辆用地毯
100735	Doormats	门垫
100732	Floor rugs	地面小地毯
100734	Mats for automobiles	车辆用脚垫
100741	Mats for sports	运动用地垫
100736	Rugs	小地毯

06-12
Tapestries

100743	Tapestries [embroidered or woven]	挂毯 [刺绣或编织的]	

06-13
Blankets and other covering materials, household linen and napery

Note: Including furniture covers, bedspreads and table covers.

06-12
挂毯

06-13
毯子及其他覆盖物，家用亚麻制品和餐桌用布

注：包括家具覆盖物、床单床罩和桌面覆盖物。

104723	Baby sleeping bags	婴儿睡袋	【11】
100761	Bath mitts	沐浴手套	
100750	Bed sheets	床单	
100749	Bedspreads	床罩	
100748	Blankets	毯子	
100745	Counterpanes	床单，床罩	
100754	Covers for clothes	衣服罩	
100770	Covers for vehicle seats	交通工具座位套	
100753	Covers [loose] for furniture	家具罩 [非固定的]	
104724	Crib bumpers	婴儿床围	【11】
100771	Cushion covers	坐垫套	
100762	Divan covers	长沙发罩	
100757	Doilies	垫碗碟或小摆设等的小布巾、装饰垫布	
100744	Drawsheets [for sick beds]	抽单，垫单 [病床用]	
104722	Duvet covers	羽绒被套	【11】
104721	Duvets	羽绒被	【11】
100751	Eiderdowns	鸭绒被	
100746	Electric blankets	电热毯	
100763	Gaming cloths [for tables]	游戏桌布 [桌用]	
100774	Head protection towels for massage couches	按摩长沙发椅用保护头巾	
100755	Household linen	家用亚麻制品	
100766	Mattress covers	床垫罩	
100759	Napkins [table linen]	餐巾 [餐桌用布]	
100765	Pillowcases	枕套	
100772	Place mats	餐具垫	
100769	Pot holders	壶垫	

100747	Quilts	被子	
100767	Sleeping bags	睡袋	
100764	Table covers	桌罩	
100756	Table linen	餐桌用布	
100768	Table mats [place mats]	餐垫[餐具垫]	
100758	Tablecloths	桌布	
104817	Toilet lid covers	马桶盖覆盖物，马桶盖罩	【12】[1]
100752	Towels	毛巾，手巾	

06-99
Miscellaneous

06-99
其他杂项

100776	Blanket supports [protective cradles for raising bedclothes]	毯子支架[撑起铺盖的护架]
100776	Protective cradles for raising bedclothes [blanket supports]	撑起铺盖的护架[毯子支架]
100775	Stands for Christmas trees	圣诞树支架
100777	Straps for securing bed sheets	床单固定带

---

1 第11版新增的产品项，由23-02类转移至06-03类。

Class 07
Household goods, not elsewhere specified

07 类
其他类未列入的家用物品

Notes：(a) Including household appliances and utensils operated by hand, even if motor driven. (b) Not including machines and appliances for preparing food and drink (Cl. 31).

注：(a) 包括手动或者电动的家用用具和器具。(b) 不包括食物和饮料的制备机械和设备（31类）。

07-01
China, glassware, dishes and other articles of a similar nature

07-01
瓷器、玻璃器皿、餐用盘碟和其他类似物品

Notes：(a) Including dishes and crockery in all materials, in particular, paper and cardboard dishes. (b) Not including cooking utensils and containers, such as glass and earthenware pots (Cl. 07-02), or flower vases, flower pots and china and glassware of a purely ornamental nature (Cl. 11-02).

注：(a) 包括各种材料的盘子、碟子和罐子，特别是纸盘和纸板盘。(b) 不包括烹调器具和容器，如玻璃锅和陶制锅（07-02类）；也不包括花瓶、花盆以及纯装饰性的瓷器和玻璃器皿（11-02类）。

104861	Baby feeding dummies	婴儿果蔬辅食器，果蔬咬咬袋	【12】
100829	Beakers	平底大口杯	
100790	Beer mugs	啤酒杯	
100785	Bowls	碗	
100830	Butter dish covers	黄油盘罩	
100782	Butter dishes	盛黄油用盘	
100835	Cabarets [trays]	酒具 [盘]	
100836	Carafes	餐桌上的玻璃水瓶	
100840	Champagne buckets	香槟冰桶	
100802	Cheese boards	干酪用盘	
100791	Cheese dish covers	干酪盘罩	
100802	Cheese platters	干酪用大浅盘	
100804	China [tableware]	瓷器 [餐具]	
100825	Coffee pots	咖啡壶	
100788	Coffee services	成套咖啡具	
100806	Coolers for butter	黄油冷却器	
100810	Coolers for caviar	鱼子酱冷却器	
100808	Coolers for wine	葡萄酒冷却器	
100807	Coolers [household]	冷却器 [家用]	

100795	Cream jugs	奶油罐，奶杯	
100817	Cups	杯子	
100803	Dishes	盘，碟	
100786	Dishes for sweetmeats	甜食盘	
104726	Disposable drinking cups	一次性水杯	【11】
104727	Disposable drinking glasses	一次性玻璃水杯	【11】
104728	Disposable plates［dishes］	一次性餐盘［餐具］	【11】
100841	Drinking bowls	饮用碗	
100828	Drinking cups	饮用杯	
100823	Drinking glasses	饮用玻璃杯	
100793	Egg-cups	蛋杯	
100783	Feeding bottles for infants	婴儿奶瓶	
100827	Finger bowls	洗指碗	
100838	Fruit bowls	水果钵	
100792	Fruit dishes	水果盘	
100824	Goblets	高脚杯	
100778	Goglets［water coolers］	陶制有气孔的长颈瓶［水冷却器］	
100809	Hors d'oeuvre dishes	餐前小吃盘	
100832	Ice buckets	冰桶	
100794	Ice cream goblets	冰激凌高脚杯	
100832	Ice pails	冰桶	
100784	Jars［except packaging］	广口瓶，坛子［包装除外］	
100796	Jugs	有柄的细口壶，罐	
100842	Lids for drinking vessels	酒器盖	
100831	Lids for jars	广口瓶盖，坛子盖	
100797	Mess tins	饭盒	
104725	Mugs	马克杯	【11】
100783	Nursing bottles	奶瓶	
100780	Oyster dishes	牡蛎碟	
100801	Pitchers	有嘴和柄的大水罐	
100822	Plates and dishes［except purely ornamental］	盘，碟［纯装饰性的除外］	
100779	Plates［dishes］	盘，碟［餐具］	
100805	Pots［household］	壶，鼓形瓶［家用］	
100834	Preserve jars	贮存用广口瓶，贮存用坛子	
100811	Salad bowls	色拉碗	
100812	Sauce boats	船形调料汁碟	
100815	Saucers	放茶杯的浅碟，茶碟	

100837	Services [tableware]	成套饮具［餐具］
100799	Shakers	摇杯，调酒器
100814	Siphons [for carbonated water]	苏打水瓶［苏打水用］
100816	Soup tureens	汤用盖碗
100790	Steins	啤酒杯
100824	Stemware	高脚器皿
101007	Sugar bowls	糖罐 【12】[1]
100843	Tea glasses	玻璃茶杯
100813	Tea services	成套茶具
100821	Teapots	茶壶
100833	Teats for feeding bottles	奶瓶用奶嘴
100820	Terrines [earthenware pots]	陶罐［陶器］
100829	Tumblers	平底无脚酒杯
100800	Vegetable dishes	菜盘
100781	Warming dishes	食品加温盘，食品加温碟
100798	Water coolers	水冷却器
100789	Water jugs	带柄水壶
100819	Wine-tasters [siphons]	品酒采样器［虹吸管］
100818	Wine-tasting glasses	品酒玻璃杯

07-02

Cooking appliances, utensils and containers

烹调用具、器具和容器

100844	Alcohol burners for cooking	烹调用酒精炉
100881	Baby-bottle warmers	奶瓶温热器
100858	Baking sheets	烤盘
100898	Barbecue toolsets	烧烤器具
100895	Barbecues	烧烤架
104950	Basting spoons [cooking utensils]	涂油勺［烹调用具］
100882	Bottle warmers	瓶温热器
100873	Casseroles	焙盘，砂锅，炖锅
100851	Cauldrons	大锅
100894	Coffee filters [except machine parts]	咖啡用过滤纸，咖啡用过滤网［机器零部件除外］
100893	Coffee makers	煮咖啡壶
100871	Coffee percolators	咖啡渗滤器，咖啡渗滤壶

1　由"Sugar bowls [holders] 糖罐［容器］"修改为"Sugar bowls 糖罐"，由07-06类转移至07-01类。

100848	Coffee roasters [household]	咖啡豆烘烤器[家用]	
100854	Cookers	灶具	【12】
100887	Cookery molds	烹饪用模具	
100856	Cooking appliances, utensils and containers	烹调用具、器具和容器	
104596	Cooking dishes	烹调盘，烹调器皿	【10】
100852	Cooking pans	平底锅	
100875	Cooking plates	炊事电炉	
100870	Cooking pots [including for camping]	蒸煮罐[包括野营用]	
100854	Cooking stoves	烹调炉灶	
100855	Cooking stoves for camping	野营用烹调炉灶	
100884	Deep fryers	深油炸锅	
100883	Discs to prevent milk boiling over	防止牛奶沸腾溢出的圆盘	
104951	Disposable coffee filters	一次性咖啡滤具	【13】
100867	Dripping pans	烤肉时用的油滴盘	
100899	Egg boilers	煮蛋器	
100865	Electric grills	电烤架	
100896	Electric teapots	电茶壶，电热水壶	
100849	Espresso coffee machines	蒸汽加压煮咖啡器	
100900	Fondue pots	干酪罐，火锅，热蘸锅	
100890	Food warmers for table use	桌用食物加热器	
100877	Frying pans	煎锅	
100866	Grills	烤肉用的铁架	
100879	Handles for saucepans [removable]	平底锅把手[可拆卸]	
100872	Heating plates of cooking stoves	烹调炉灶的加热盘	
100888	Immersion heaters	浸没式电热水棒，浸没式加热器	
100845	Kettles	烧水壶	
100860	Kitchen stoves	厨房用灶	
100868	Ladles for kitchen use	厨房用长柄勺	
100853	Lids for kitchen utensils	厨房器具的盖子	
100847	Meat skewers	烤肉叉，串肉扦	
100891	Micro-wave ovens	微波炉	
100859	Moulds for baking or confectionery	烘烤糕点或制作糖果用模具	
100863	Nut roasters	坚果烘烤器	
100861	Ovens [cooking]	烤箱[烹调]	
100874	Popcorn pans	爆玉米花锅	
100869	Pressure cookers [autoclaves]	压力锅，高压锅[高压炊具]	

104729	Rice cookers	电饭煲，电饭锅	【11】
100878	Roasting spits	烤肉用旋转铁叉	
100886	Saucepan handles	深平底锅的柄，有柄炖锅的柄	
100850	Saucepans	深平底锅，有柄炖锅	
100877	Sauté pans	单柄单耳煎盘，平底炒锅	
100876	Spit-roasting apparatus	旋转烧烤器	
100857	Stewpans	长柄炖锅	
100889	Tart pans	挞盘，派盘	
100892	Tea filters［except machine parts］	泡茶用滤网［机器零部件除外］	
100846	Tea infusers	茶叶浸煮器	
100864	Toasters	烤面包器，多士炉	
100855	Transparent doors for ovens	烤箱用透明门	
100862	Waffle irons	烘华夫饼的铁模	
100897	Woks	炒菜锅	

07-03

Table cutlery

07-03

桌上用刀、叉、匙等餐具 【12】[1]

100908	Butter knives	黄油刀
100904	Carving sets	成套切肉刀叉
100909	Cheese knives	奶酪刀
100911	Chopsticks	筷子
100910	Ferrules for table knives	餐刀用金属箍
100902	Forks［table］	餐叉［餐桌用］
100903	Handles for tableware	餐具柄
100905	Knives［table］	餐刀［餐桌用］
100906	Oyster openers	开牡蛎刀
100907	Salad servers	成套色拉叉匙
100901	Spoons	匙

---

[1] 小类名称由"Table knives, forks and spoons 餐刀、餐叉和匙"修改为"Table cutlery 桌上用刀、叉、匙等餐具"。

07-04

Appliances and utensils, hand-operated, for preparing food or drink

Notes: (a) Not including appliances and utensils classified in Cl. 07-02 and in Cl. 31. (b) Not including kitchen knives, knives for boning meat (Cl. 08-03).

07-04

用于制备食物或饮料的手动操作用具和器具

注：(a) 不包括07-02类和31类中的设备和器具。(b) 不包括菜刀和剔骨刀（08-03类）。 【12】[1]

100918	Appliances, hand-operated, for preparing drinks	制备饮料用手动操作器具	
100952	Baskets for washing vegetables	洗菜篮	
100917	Beaters for kitchen use, non-electric	非电动厨房用搅拌器	
100941	Bread boards	做面包用木板，切面包板	
100926	Bread slicers, non-electric	非电动面包切片器	
100916	Butter churns	黄油搅乳器	
100954	Cabbage shredders, hand-operated [household]	手动卷心菜切碎器［家用］	
100961	Cereal mills, non-electric	非电动谷物研磨器	
100957	Cheese slicers, non-electric	非电动干酪切片器	
100940	Chopping boards [household]	砧板，案板［家用］	
100934	Chopping devices, non-electric [household]	非电动切碎器［家用］	
100937	Coffee grinders, non-electric [household]	非电动咖啡豆研磨器［家用］	
104952	Coffee tampers	咖啡压粉器	【13】
100939	Colanders	过滤器	
100951	Cookie cutters	饼干成形切割具	
100927	Corers, hand-operated	手动水果去核器	
100938	Crushers for kitchen use, non-electric	非电动厨房用压碎器	
100947	Cutting boards [household]	砧板，案板［家用］	
101313	Decorating bags for confectioners	甜点师用裱花袋	【10】[2]
100956	Dough scrapers	削面器	
100924	Egg slicers	切蛋器	
100929	Emulsifiers, non-electric, for cream	非电动奶油乳化器	
100928	Fish scalers	鱼鳞刮除器	
100922	French-fry cutters, non-electric	非电动切薯条器	【13】
100932	Fruit juice extractors non-electric [household]	非电动榨果汁器［家用］	

---

1 增加注释"(b) Not including kitchen knives, knives for boning meat (Cl. 08-03). (b) 不包括菜刀和剔骨刀（08-03类）。"
2 由08-05类转移至07-04类。

100944	Fruit or vegetable juice extractors, hand-operated [household]	水果或蔬菜的手动榨汁器［家用］
100943	Fruit squeezers, hand-operated	手动榨果汁器
100920	Fruit stoners [household]	水果去核器［家用］
100962	Garlic presses	压蒜器
100945	Graters [household]	擦菜板［家用］
100936	Hammers for tenderizing meat	软化肉的锤子，嫩肉锤
100953	Icing syringes [confectionery]	注奶油器［甜点］
100919	Kitchen grinders, non-electric	非电动厨房用研磨器
100942	Lemon squeezers	柠檬榨汁器
100949	Meat chopping blocks	剁肉砧板，剁肉案板
100915	Meat tenderizers	肉软化器，嫩肉锤
100934	Mincing devices, non-electric [household]	非电动切碎器［家用］
100935	Mixers, hand-operated [household]	手动搅拌器［家用］
100959	Mortars [household]	研钵［家用］
100925	Onion choppers, non-electric	非电动洋葱切碎器
100930	Peelers, hand-operated [household]	手动剥皮器［家用］
101313	Piping bags	裱花袋 【13】
100922	Potato chippers, non-electric	非电动土豆切片器
100921	Poultry shears	鸡骨剪
100955	Rolling pins	擀面杖
100931	Salad spinners	色拉干燥器，色拉脱水器
100950	Sifters [household]	筛子［家用］
100913	Spatulas for cooking	厨房用刮铲
100912	Spice mills, non-electric	非电动调味料研磨器
100948	Strainers [household]	滤器，漏网，滤盆，滤网［家用］
100960	Tea strainers	茶过滤器
100923	Vegetable slicers, non-electric [household]	非电动切菜器［家用］
100946	Vessels for making ice cream, non-electric	非电动制冰激凌器皿
100933	Whisks [kitchen utensils]	打蛋器［厨房器具］
100914	Yoghurt makers [household]	酸奶制作器［家用］ 【13】
100914	Yogurt makers [household]	酸奶制作器［家用］

07-05

Flat-irons and washing, cleaning and drying equipment

Note: Not including electric household appliances for washing, cleaning or drying (Cl. 15-05).

07-05

熨烫用具、洗涤用具、清洁用具和干燥用具

注：不包括用于洗涤、清洁或干燥的家用电动设备（15-05类）。

100996	Absorbent cleaning cloths	吸水清洁布	
100981	Applicators of liquid wax [household]	液态蜡涂抹器［家用］	
100995	Carpet beaters [hand instruments]	地毯拍打器［手工工具］	
100978	Clothes horses	晒衣架	
100969	Clothes pegs	晒衣夹	
100969	Clothes pins	晒衣夹	
100994	Clothesline supports	晒衣绳支架	
100973	Comb cleaners	梳子清洁器	
100974	Combs for brooms	扫帚用清洁梳	
100989	Crumb trays	残屑盘	
100966	Dish draining racks	盘碟沥水架	
100997	Dosage containers for adding a washing agent	洗涤剂剂量容器	
100978	Drying racks for laundry	洗衣房用干燥架	
100964	Dusters for cleaning	清洁用除尘器	
101000	Dusting gloves	除尘手套，擦拭手套	
100985	Dustpans	簸箕	
100968	Flat-irons	熨斗，电熨斗	
100987	Flex holders for flat-irons	熨斗挂线架	
101001	Floor cloths	擦地布	
104730	Floor squeegees	地板刮水器	【11】
100991	Ironing board covers	熨衣板套	
100990	Ironing boards	熨衣板	
104862	Lint rollers	粘毛器，粘毛滚子	【12】
100981	Liquid wax applicators [household]	液态蜡涂抹器［家用］	
100983	Mats for dish draining racks	盘碟沥水架的垫子	
104731	Peg hangers	晒衣夹挂架，带有夹子的晒衣架	【11】
100992	Rinsing tubs	涮洗桶，漂洗桶	
100982	Rotary clothes driers	旋转式晒衣架	
100982	Rotary washing lines	旋转式晾衣绳	【12】
100963	Laundry balls	洗衣球	
100970	Sleeve ironing boards	熨袖板	

101002	Soleplates for flat-irons	熨斗的底板
100980	Sponges [household]	海绵［家用］
100998	Squeegees for removing waste from kitchen sinks	厨房水槽除垢用刮拭器
100976	Stands for flat-irons	熨斗支架
100999	Steam generators for flat-irons	熨斗用蒸汽发生器
100993	Tubs with incorporated wringers	有绞水器的桶
100975	Washing boards	洗衣板，搓衣板
100972	Washing tubs	洗涤盆
100965	Washtubs	洗涤盆
100984	Window cleaning appliances	窗户清洁用具
100988	Window squeegees	窗用刮拭器

07-06
Other table utensils

07-06
其他桌上用品

101011	Anti-drip devices for necks of containers	容器颈部的防滴装置
101008	Anti-drip rings for bottles	瓶用防滴环
101036	Beer foam scrapers	啤酒除沫器
101016	Bottle cap removers	瓶盖起子
101037	Bottle openers	开瓶器
101013	Bread baskets	面包篮
101034	Cake servers	蛋糕分配铲
101044	Cake slicers	蛋糕切片器
101032	Castors [table utensils]	调味瓶［桌上用品］
101038	Clips for tablecloths	桌布夹
101006	Coasters for glasses	玻璃杯杯托
101017	Coasters for jugs and bottles	壶托，罐托，瓶托
101035	Condiment holders and dispensers	调味品分格容器，调味品分撒器
101033	Corkscrews	开塞钻
101043	Corn ear holders [for corn on the cob]	玉米棒托［玉米棒用］
101004	Cruet stands for oil and vinegar	油、醋用瓶架
101009	Cruets	佐料瓶
101042	Drinking straws	饮料吸管
101015	Egg toppers	蛋壳开口器
101021	Egg-topping blades	蛋壳开口器的刀片
104733	Foil cutters for bottles	瓶用割箔器 【11】
101022	Ice tongs	冰块夹子

104953	Jar openers	开瓶器	【13】
101039	Knife, fork and spoon rests	餐刀托，餐叉托，汤匙托	
101005	Mustard pots	芥末罐，芥末瓶	
101030	Napkin rings	餐巾纸环	
101048	Napkin-holding devices worn round the neck	将餐巾围在脖子上的固定装置	
101010	Nutcrackers	核桃钳	
101023	Pastry tongs	糕点夹子	
101027	Pepper casters	胡椒粉调味瓶	
101027	Pepper pots	胡椒粉调味罐	
101012	Plate warmers	盘子温热器	
101031	Salt cellars	盐罐，盐瓶	
101026	Sandwich picks	三明治固定签	
101030	Serviette rings	餐巾环	
101024	Spaghetti tongs	意大利面条夹子	
101025	Sugar tongs	糖块夹子	
101020	Swizzle sticks for champagne	香槟用调酒棒	
101047	Table bins	餐桌容器	
101014	Tea cosies	茶壶保温套	
101046	Toast racks	烤面包片放置架	
104732	Tortilla warmers	玉米饼温热器	【11】
101018	Trivets [table utensils]	隔热架［桌上用品］	
104954	Wine stoppers [table utensils]	酒塞［桌上用品］	【13】

07-07
Other household receptacles

07-07
其他家用容器

101053	Bread bins	面包箱	
101057	Buckets [household]	水桶［家用］	
101059	Coal scuttles	煤斗，煤桶	
101060	Collapsible water carriers for camping	露营用可折叠储水器	
101062	Cutlery boxes	餐具盒	
104863	Food storage containers for household use	家用食品储藏容器	【12】
101055	Laundry baskets	洗衣篮	
104734	Lunch boxes	午餐箱	【11】
101058	Pails	提桶	
101050	Spice boxes	食用香料盒	
101051	Storage containers for use in refrigerators	冰箱用储藏容器	

101052	Tubs	桶，盆	

07-08
Fireplace implements

07-08
壁炉用具

101065	Andirons	柴火燃烧支架	
101065	Fire dogs	壁炉柴架	【12】[1]
101069	Fire tongs	火钳	
101061	Firewood holders	柴火托	【13】[2]
101071	Firewood stands [fireplace implements]	柴火架［壁炉用具］	
101066	Fireguards [household]	壁炉护栏［家用］	
101070	Fireplace bellows	壁炉风箱	
101064	Fireplace implements	壁炉用具	
101068	Fireplace screens	壁炉隔热屏	
101072	Firewood baskets	柴火篮	
101067	Pokers	拨火棒	

07-09
Stands and holders for household appliances and utensils

07-09
家用器具和用具的立架及支架

【12】[3]

101102	Beverage capsule holders	饮料胶囊架	
101028	Bottle holders [table utensils]	瓶座，瓶架［桌上用品］	
101041	Bottle stands [table utensils]	瓶立架［桌上用品］	
101090	Brush holders	刷架	
101104	Cup holder trays	置杯托盘	
101045	Holders for drinking cups [except for dispensers]	饮用杯用杯座、杯架［分配器除外］	
101045	Holders for drinking glasses [except for dispensers]	饮用玻璃杯的杯座、杯架［分配器除外］	
101094	Holders for lids for saucepans and jars	平底锅盖、坛盖用架	
101091	Holders for rolls of kitchen paper	厨房卷纸架	
101101	Knife holders	刀架，刀座	
101040	Menu card holders	菜单座，菜单架	
101029	Napkin holders	餐巾纸座，餐巾纸架	

1　由"Fire irons 火炉用具"修改为"Fire dogs 壁炉柴架"。
2　由 07-07 类转移至 07-08 类，并由"Firewood collectors 柴火收纳筐"修改为"Firewood holders 柴火托"。
3　新增加 07-09 类，产品项分别由 07-06 类和 07-99 类转移至 07-09 类。

101029	Serviette holders	餐巾纸座，餐巾纸架	【12】
101083	Stands or holders for tubes [household]	软管座，软管支架［家用］	
101049	Stands for wine boxes [table utensils]	葡萄酒盒架［桌上用品］	

07-10
Cooling and freezing devices and isothermal containers

07-10
用于冷却、冷冻的器具和保温容器 【12】[1]

101108	Cooling sticks	冷却棒
101105	Flexible cold packs	柔性冰袋，凝胶填充冰袋
101107	Freezer blocks	冷却块
101063	Ice cube trays	制冰格盘，制冰盒
100787	Insulating bottles	保温瓶
101054	Insulating boxes [household]	保温箱［家用］
100839	Insulating pots	保温壶，暖水壶
101056	Portable cool boxes	便携式冷却箱
101106	Reusable ice cubes	可重复使用的冰块
100787	Vacuum flasks	真空保温瓶

07-99
Miscellaneous

07-99
其他杂项

101092	Apparatus for drawing liquids and filling bottles, hand-operated	手动操作瓶装液体抽灌器	
101098	Apparatus for lighting fires	点火器	
101099	Appliances for sealing bags [household]	密封袋子的用具［家用］	
101075	Bed warmers, non-electric	非电动暖床器	
101086	Boot jacks	脱靴器	
101087	Buttonhooks	扣纽扣钩	
101089	Can openers	开罐器	
104955	Clips for lifting hot dishes	防烫夹	【13】
101103	Devices for pulling on socks	穿袜器	
101097	Dispensers for drinking cups	饮水杯分配器	
101093	Dispensers for packaging sachets [household]	包装小袋分配器［家用］	
104735	Food covers [domes]	食物罩［穹顶形］	【11】
101077	Funnels [household utensils]	漏斗［家用器具］	

---

1 新增加 07-10 类，产品项分别由 07-01 类、07-07 类和 07-99 类转移至 07-10 类。

101073	Gas lighters	煤气点火器
101080	Hand-operated appliances for winding balls of wool	绕线球用手动工具
101088	Hot water bottles	暖水袋
101100	Ladles for jars	坛子用长柄勺，坛子用长柄舀
101082	Scoops for ice cream	冰激凌挖球勺
101081	Serving trays [household]	服务托盘，上菜托盘［家用］
101076	Shoehorns	鞋拔
101078	Shoe-trees	鞋内撑
101085	Stretchers for boots and shoes	靴撑架，鞋撑架
101089	Tin openers	开罐器
101084	Tube squeezers	软管挤压器
101074	Warming pans for beds	暖床器
101079	Watering devices for plants	自动浇花器

Class 08
Tools and hardware

Notes: (a) Including hand-operated tools, even if mechanical power takes the place of muscular force, for example, electric saws and drills. (b) Not including machines or machine tools (Cl. 15 or 31).

08-01
Tools and implements for drilling, milling or digging

101125	Augers
101134	Awls
101122	Bits [tools]
101110	Borers
101131	Braces [tools]
101123	Combined countersink drills
101139	Counterbore boring heads
101138	Countersink reamers
101129	Dibbles
101115	Digging tools
101121	Draining-spades [tools]
101137	Drill bows
101117	Drilling tools
101125	Drills [tools]
101136	Garden forks
101133	Garden trowels
101132	Gimlets
101116	Hand drills
101135	Hoes
101113	Hoes [hand tools]
101128	Ice axes
101111	Jumpers [mining drills]
101127	Mattocks
101118	Milling apparatus, hand-operated
101120	Milling cutters [tools]
101119	Milling tools

08 类
工具和五金器具

注：(a) 包括手动操作工具，即机械力代替了人力，如电锯和电钻。(b) 不包括机械或机床（15或31类）。

08-01
钻孔、铣削或挖掘的工具和器具

	麻花钻，螺旋钻
	锥子
	机床用刀具 [工具]
	钻孔器
	手摇曲柄钻 [工具]
	组合埋头钻
	扩孔镗头
	埋头钻
	挖穴器
	挖掘工具
	排污铲 [工具]
	手钻弓柄
	钻孔工具
	钻 [工具]
	园艺叉
	园艺泥铲
	手钻，螺丝锥
	手钻
	锄头
	锄头 [手动工具]
	破冰斧
	穿孔凿 [矿用钻]
	鹤嘴锄
	手动操作铣削器具
	铣刀 [工具]
	铣削工具

101141	Percussion drills	冲击钻
101127	Pickaxes	手镐
101126	Picks [hand tools]	镐 [手动工具]
101114	Quarry picks	采石用镐
101109	Reamers	铰刀
101124	Shovels [tools]	铲，铁锹 [工具]
101140	Snow shovels	雪铲
101112	Spades [hand tools]	铁锹 [手动工具]
101130	Wall drills [tools]	墙钻 [工具]

08-02
Hammers and other similar tools and implements

锤及其他类似工具和器具

101142	Earth rammers [hand tools]	泥土夯具 [手动工具]
101145	Hammers [tools]	锤 [工具]
101144	Mallets	木锤
101148	Panel-beating hammers	钣金锤
101147	Pestles	杵
101146	Pneumatic hammers	气锤
101143	Rammers [hand tools]	夯具 [手动工具]
101150	Riveting hammers	铆锤
101148	Sheet metal dent removers	钣金锤
101149	Stonebreakers' hammers	碎石锤

08-03
Cutting tools and implements

切削工具和器具

Notes: (a) Including tools and instruments for sawing. (b) Not including table knives (Cl. 07-03), cutting tools and implements for kitchen use (Cl. 31), or knives used in surgery (Cl. 24-02).

注：(a) 包括锯切工具和器具。(b) 不包括餐刀（07-03类），厨房用切削工具和器具（31类），外科手术用刀（24-02类）。

101181	Adzes	扁斧
101179	Axes	斧子
101195	Billhooks	钩刀，钩镰
101191	Bone saws	骨锯
101193	Chain saws	链锯
104590	Chainsaw chains	链锯的链
101162	Chisels for grooving	开槽凿

【10】

101161	Chisels for stonework	石工凿	
101203	Chopping knives	斩骨刀，屠宰专用刀	【12】[1]
104736	Circular saws	圆盘锯	【11】
101176	Cleavers	屠刀，劈刀	
101201	Coachbuilders' chisels	车身制造厂用凿刀	
101204	Cutting nippers	剪钳	
101178	Dado cutters	开槽刀	
101184	Drawknives	拉刮刀	
101188	Fretsaws	钢丝锯，线锯	
101170	Glass cutters	玻璃刀	
101206	Glass-cutting tools	玻璃切割刀具	
101170	Glaziers' diamonds	金刚石玻璃刀	
101197	Gouges	圆凿	
101198	Grafting knives	嫁接刀	
101160	Grass shears	剪草用剪刀	【10】[2]
101166	Hacking knives	砍刀	
101190	Hacksaws	弓形锯，钢锯	
104956	Handles for kitchen knives	厨房用刀的刀柄	【13】
101180	Hatchets	短柄手斧	
101167	Hay choppers［tools］	干草切碎器［工具］	
101202	Hay cutters［hand knives］	铡草机，切草机［手动］	
101157	Hedge clippers	树篱剪	
101194	Hedge trimmers	树篱修剪器	
101199	Holders for electric knives	电刀固定器	
101168	Jackknives	折刀	
101209	Jig saws	竖线锯，镂花锯	
101153	Kitchen knives	菜刀	
101152	Knives for boning meat	剔骨刀	
101169	Knives，electric	电刀	
101183	Machetes	大砍刀，弯刀	
101192	Mechanical saws，hand-operated	手动操作机械锯	
101156	Mortise chisels	榫凿	
104957	Multi-tool knives	多工具组合刀	【13】
101151	Penknives	小刀	
101165	Pipe cutters	切管器	
101177	Plane blades［tools］	刨刀［工具］	

---

1 由"Butchers' mincers 屠户用碎肉器"修改为"Chopping knives 斩骨刀，屠宰专用刀"。
2 由"Lawn trimmers 草坪修剪器"修改为"Grass shears 剪草用剪刀"。

101185	Planes	刨
101168	Pocket knives	折叠式小刀
101173	Pruners for trees	树枝修剪刀
101196	Pruning hooks	修枝刀
101172	Pruning implements	修剪器具
101171	Pruning shears	修枝剪
101186	Root slicers, hand-operated	手动操作块根切片器
101182	Saw blades	锯条
101189	Saws [handsaws]	锯［手锯］
101159	Scissors	剪刀
101187	Scraping irons	刮铁屑刀
101175	Scythes	长柄大镰刀
101194	Secateurs	修整剪
101158	Shears	剪刀
101207	Sheath knives	鞘刀
101174	Sickles	镰刀
101205	Sod cutters [tools]	草皮切割器［工具］
101154	Tree felling machines, hand-operated	手动操作的伐木机
101155	Tree felling tools	伐木工具
101164	Tube cutters	截管器
101163	Twine cutters	切绳刀
101208	Vegetable knives [gardening tools]	割菜刀［园艺工具］
101200	Wood splitting wedges	劈木楔刀

08-04

Screwdrivers and other similar tools and implements

08-04

螺丝起子及其他类似工具和器具

101210	Screwdrivers	螺丝起子

08-05

Other tools and implements

Notes: (a) Including tools which are not classified, or not to be placed, in other subclasses or classes. (b) Including sanding blocks and discs for sanding machines. (c) Not including sandpaper (Cl. 05-06).

08-05

其他工具和器具

注：(a) 包括未分类或者不能放在其他大类或小类的工具。(b) 包括打磨墩、砂磨块和砂轮打磨机盘。(c) 不包括砂纸（05-06类）。 【11】[1]

101256	Abrasive files	方头锉

1　增加注释内容："(b) Including sanding blocks and discs for sanding machines. (c) Not including sandpaper (Cl. 05-06). (b) 包括打磨墩、砂磨块和砂轮打磨机盘。(c) 不包括砂纸（05-06类）。"

101307	Abrasive sheet holders	磨板架	
101308	Agricultural atomizers, hand-operated	手动操作农用喷雾器	
101312	Agricultural rollers, hand-operated	手动操作农用碾压滚筒	
101329	Angle grinders	角向磨光机	
101223	Anvil beaks for edging	轧边用砧角	
101243	Anvils	铁砧，砧座	
101220	Atomizers for varnish [except aerosol dispensers]	喷漆器 [气雾分配器除外]	
101295	Bakers' peels	面包师用送料铲	
101304	Beer pumps, hand-operated	手动操作啤酒唧筒、啤酒泵	
104576	Berry combs	浆果梳集器	【10】
104576	Berry scoops	浆果梳集器	【10】
101253	Blowlamps	喷灯，焊灯	
101250	Boat hooks	拖船钩，钩头篙	
101262	Bread molds for bakers	面包师用制作模具	
101221	Bricklayers' hods	泥瓦工用砂浆桶	
101212	Butchers' apparatus for slaughtering animals	屠夫的屠宰设备	
101260	Caulking implements	填隙工具	
101286	Cant hooks	钩杆	
101316	Carpenters' clamps	木工夹具	
101318	Cask scrapers	容器刮刀	
101234	Casting ladles	浇包，浇注包	
101260	Caulking implements	填隙工具	
101211	Caulking irons	填隙器	
101324	Chalk lines	粉线，墨线	
101298	Clock and watchmakers' pliers	钟表匠的手钳	
101299	Compressed air pistols for rust removal	气压除锈枪	
101263	Crowbars	撬棍，铁撬	
101259	Defrosting tools	除霜工具	
101238	Discs for sanding machines	砂轮打磨机盘	
101242	Drifts	冲头	
101297	Electricians' pliers	电工钳	
101293	Eyelet fixing tools [boots and shoes]	孔眼装钉工具 [靴和鞋]	
101309	Floor scrapers	地板刮刀，地板铲刀	
101248	Forks [tools] [except garden forks]	叉、耙类 [工具] [园艺叉除外]	
101233	Fruit gatherers [tools]	果实收集器 [工具]	
101250	Gaffs	手钩	

101265	Glassmakers' tongs	玻璃工用钳	
101266	Glaziers' point setters	玻璃工用定点器	
101315	Gluing clamps	黏贴夹	
101240	Grain separators［hand tools］	谷物脱粒器［手动工具］	
101251	Grapnels	抓钩，多爪锚	
101270	Grass-trap attachments for scythes	长柄镰刀的夹草附件	
101306	Grease guns, hand-operated	手动操作注油枪	
101325	Grilles for paint rollers	油漆滚筒格栅	
101274	Grinding tools	磨削工具，研磨工具	
101292	Grinding wheels for sharpening, trueing, adjusting［hand tools］	磨利、精修、调整用砂轮［手动工具］	
101225	Hat shaping apparatus	帽子定型器具	
101226	Hat shining apparatus	帽子轧光器具	
101275	Heat sealing tools	热封工具	
101216	Hones	磨石，磨孔器具	
101331	Ice scrapers	刮冰器	
104864	Inflatable lifting tools	充气式起重工具	【12】
101281	Inflators for dinghies and mattresses	橡皮艇和气垫充气机	
101257	Ingot molds	锭模	
101314	Joiners' cramps［tools］	工匠用夹具［工具］	
101213	Knife sharpeners	磨刀器	
101247	Lasts	楦	
101254	Levers［tools］	杠杆［工具］	
104737	Lug wrenches	棘轮扳手	【11】
101249	Manure forks	肥料叉	
101280	Marking gauges	划线规	
101321	Marking string for planting	栽培用标线	
101244	Marlinspikes	解缆针，穿索针	
101302	Masons' pointers	泥瓦工用指示器	
101319	Masons' trowels	泥瓦工用镘刀，泥铲	
101284	Miter boxes	轴锯箱	
101284	Mitre boxes	轴锯箱	
101217	Nail extractors	拔钉器	
104738	Nail tackers	射钉枪，钉枪	【11】
101285	Oil feeders	注油器，滴油器	
101285	Oilcans	机油壶	
101332	Paint removing scrapers	除漆刮刀	
101311	Paint rollers	油漆滚筒	

101268	Paint sprays for use in building	建筑用喷漆器	
104958	Paint trays	油漆滚筒刷托盘	【13】
101323	Pans for washing gold	淘金盘	
101296	Peavies	钩棍	
101218	Pin extractors	拔针器	
101236	Pipe clearing apparatus	管道清扫装置	
101276	Pipe crimping tools	管道卷边工具	
101229	Pipe wrenches	管扳手，管钳	
101317	Plasterers' floats	抹灰工的镘刀，抹子	
101277	Pliers	钳子	
101264	Pliers［tools］	钳子［工具］	
101255	Polishing appliances made of cork	软木制抛光器具	
101305	Pumps for inflating tires, hand-operated	手动操作轮胎充气泵、打气筒	
101305	Pumps for inflating tyres, hand-operated	手动操作轮胎充气泵、打气筒	【13】
101242	Punches［hand tools］	打孔器［手动工具］	
101272	Rakes［hand tools］	耙子［手动工具］	
101271	Rasps［tools］	锉［工具］	
101232	Riddles［tools］	粗筛［工具］	
101303	Roses for watering cans	洒水壶喷头	
101326	Sanders, hand-operated	手动操作打磨器	
101222	Sanding blocks	打磨墩，砂磨块	
101322	Sauna ladles	桑拿室用长柄勺	
101252	Saw table gauges	台锯推尺	
101228	Scaling tools for boilers	锅炉除垢、除锈工具	
101289	Screw plates	搓丝板，板牙，螺丝模	
101294	Screw thread cutting tools	螺纹切削工具	
101267	Scribers	划线器	
101246	Shapes for hats	帽坯	
101310	Sharpeners for razor blades	剃须刀刃磨具	
101215	Sharpening apparatus for bandsaws	带锯磨利器	
101288	Shoe lasts［shoemaking］	鞋楦［制鞋］	
101282	Sieves［tools］	筛［工具］	
104660	Ski wax scrapers	滑雪板用上蜡刮板	【10】
101227	Snowploughs［manual］	雪犁［手动］	
101227	Snowplows［manual］	雪犁［手动］	
101253	Soldering blow pipes	焊接喷气管	
101320	Soldering irons	烙铁，焊铁	
101230	Spanners	扳手	

101327	Spatulas［hand tools］	抹刀［手动工具］
101300	Spike guns	道钉枪
101269	Spokeshaves	辐刨
101290	Spray guns for paint	喷漆枪
101261	Stakes［leatherwork］	砧［皮革制品］
101239	Stalk separators	茎梗分离器
101214	Staple guns	打钉枪
101273	Straightedges	标尺，规板
101235	Strops	磨剃刀皮带
101217	Tack pullers	拔平头钉器
101278	Tap wrenches	丝锥扳手
101289	Threading dies	攻丝模具，螺纹板牙
101301	Ticket punches	票券打孔器，剪票铗
101237	Tire levers	轮胎杠杆，撬胎棒
101277	Tongs	钳子，夹具
101330	Tongs for lifting timber［tools］	起吊木料的夹钳［工具］
101258	Tools for cleaning metal pipes	清洁金属管道的工具
101228	Tools for scaling boilers	锅炉除垢、除锈工具
101279	Tracers	描图器
101241	Tube expanders	胀管器
101224	Tweezers	镊子
101237	Tyre levers	轮胎杠杆，撬胎棒
101291	Vice jaws	虎钳口
101245	Vices	老虎钳
101328	Wallpaper strippers	墙纸剥离器
101219	Watering cans	洒水壶
101231	Wedges	楔
101253	Welding torches	焊接喷灯
101216	Whetstones	磨刀石
101287	Wire insulation stripping tools	电线绝缘套剥除工具
101283	Wire stretchers［tools］	紧线钳［工具］
101217	Wrecking bars	拔钉撬棍

08-06

Handles, knobs and hinges

08-06

把手，球形捏手，铰链、合页

101342	Bell pulls	拉铃索
101340	Door handles	门把手

101341	Door handles for vehicles	交通工具门把手	
101334	Doorknobs	球形门把手	
101333	Drawer handles	抽屉把手	
101344	Handles for carrycots	手提式婴儿床提手	
101345	Handles for coffins	棺材把手	
101347	Handles for furniture	家具把手	
101346	Handles for windows	窗把手	
101338	Hinge pins for doors	门铰链轴	
101337	Hinges［hardware］	铰链，合页［五金器具］	
101335	Knobs for drawers	球形抽屉捏手	
101336	Push buttons	按钮	
101339	Strap hinges for doors or windows	门或窗的接合铰链	

08-07
Locking or closing devices

Note: Not including buckles［haberdashery］（Cl. 02-07）and key rings (Cl. 03-01).

08-07
锁紧或关闭装置

注：不包括扣环，皮带扣［服饰用品］（02-07类）和钥匙环（03-01类）。 【12】

101382	Anti-theft interlocking strips for doors	门用防盗联锁条	
101383	Anti-theft posts for motorcycles	摩托车防盗锁柱	
101373	Box fasteners	箱扣	
101380	Cable padlocks for motorcycles	摩托车钢丝挂锁	
101351	Cable-type padlocks for cycles	自行车钢丝挂锁	
101355	Casement bolts for windows or doors	门、窗插销	
101350	Catches for venetian blinds	软百叶窗帘扣	
101372	Clasps for cigarette cases	香烟盒钩扣	
101359	Clasps for leather goods	皮革制品钩扣	
101360	Clasps for purses and handbags	钱包、手提包用钩扣	
101358	Closing devices for doors and windows	门窗关闭装置	
104594	Code locks	密码锁	【10】
101368	Door bolts	门销	
101374	Door check brakes	门制动器	
101357	Door closers	闭门器	
101376	Door locks for vehicles	交通工具门锁	
101367	Door openers［electric］	开门器［电动］	
101356	Espagnolettes［window fasteners］	长插销［窗锁］	
101377	Fastenings for motor truck loading gates	卡车装卸门扣	
101370	Flat bolts［locks］	平板插销［锁］	

101364	Handbag frames	（带有搭扣部分的）手提包骨架	
101363	Handcuffs	手铐	
101365	Hasps	门、窗或箱子上的搭扣	
104739	Key card door locks	钥匙卡门锁	【11】
101353	Keys	钥匙	
101354	Keys for electric contacts	电感应钥匙	
104959	Keys for vehicles	交通工具钥匙	【13】
101362	Latches	门闩，插销	
101366	Lock bolts	插销的销，锁簧	
101371	Locking devices	锁闭装置	
101369	Locks	锁	
104632	Locks for safety belts	安全带用锁扣	【10】
101363	Manacles	镣铐	
101352	Padlocks	挂锁	
101378	Safety locks for bicycles	自行车安全锁	
101379	Shutter turnbuckles	百叶窗螺丝扣	
104960	Smart keys	智能钥匙	【13】
101361	Strike plates for locks	锁用销板	
101349	Theftproof locks	防盗锁	
104592	Tokens for shopping carts	购物车用代币	
104592	Tokens for shopping trolleys	购物车用代币	【12】
101375	Tumbler locks	杠杆锁	
101381	Wheel clamps［boots］	车轮锁［丹佛锁扣］	

08-08

Fastening, supporting or mounting devices not included in other classes

Notes: (a) Including nails, screws, nuts and bolts. (b) Not including fastening devices for clothing (Cl. 02-07), for adornment (Cl. 11-01), or for office use (Cl. 19-02).

08-08

其他类未包括的夹紧、支撑或安装装置

注：(a) 包括钉子、螺丝钉、螺母和螺栓。(b) 不包括用于服装（02-07类）、装饰品（11-01类）或办公（19-02类）的夹紧装置。

104742	Anchors for mining	矿用锚	【11】
104741	Bag hangers	挂包钩	【11】
101433	Bed angle irons	床角铁	
101435	Belleville washers	贝氏弹簧垫圈	
101410	Bolts	螺栓	
101443	Brackets	托架	
101392	Brackets for holding cleaning brushes	清扫刷托架	

101430	Brackets for showers	淋浴器托架	
101413	Brads	曲头钉	
101436	Cable clamps［cleats］［non-electric］	线缆箍［加固板］［非电动］	
101431	Chain swivels	锚链旋转环	
101391	Clamps for hoses and pipes	软管夹，管道夹	
101440	Cleats for docks	系索耳，系缆枕	
101452	Coat hooks	挂衣钩	
101403	Coat pegs	大衣挂钉	
101426	Collars for electric conductors	电导体套环	
101393	Collars for gas pipes	煤气管的套环	
101427	Collars for pipes	管套环	
101411	Cotter pins	开口销	
101444	Dowels	暗销，木榫钉	
101445	Eye-bolts	有眼螺栓，吊环螺栓	
101390	Fasteners for machine belts	机器传送带紧固件	
101429	Fastening clips for cables	线缆固定夹	
101441	Fittings for hanging cupboards	悬挂橱柜的配件	
101449	Fittings for shelving	搁架配件	
101432	Fittings for showers	淋浴器配件	
101400	Fixing devices for ceiling light fittings	顶棚灯固定装置	
101451	Flagpole holders	旗杆架，旗杆支撑物	
101424	Foundation bolts	地脚螺栓	
101395	Hooks for hanging	挂钩	
101407	Hosepipe supports	橡胶软管支座	
101414	Ice crampons for shoes［except for climbing］	鞋用冰爪［登山用除外］	
101450	Keyboards for hanging keys	挂钥匙盘	
101387	Lath staples	板条钉	
101418	Linchpins	保险销	
101417	Locknuts	防松螺母，锁紧螺母	
101388	Meat hooks	挂肉钩	
101396	Metal hooks［general］	金属钩［通用的］	
101401	Mirror fittings	镜子配件	
101453	Mooring buoys	系泊浮筒	
101412	Nails	钉	
101442	Picture frame fittings	画框配件	
101398	Pipe hangers［except for tobacco pipes］	管吊架［烟斗用除外］	
104743	Plant grafting clips	植物嫁接用夹	【11】

104740	Plant hangers	植物吊架	【11】
101384	Plate hangers	板托架	
101454	Poles [for supporting plants]	支柱[支撑植物用]	
101428	Railroad tie screws	铁路轨枕螺钉	
101428	Railway sleeper screws	铁路轨枕螺钉	
101422	Rivets	铆钉	
101415	Screw nuts	螺母，螺帽	
101425	Screws	螺钉	
101430	Shower holders	淋浴器架	
101402	Snap hooks	弹簧扣，弹簧钩	
101420	Spikes	长钉，道钉	
101456	Stakes for plants or flowers	植物或花卉的支柱	
101455	Stands for letter boxes	信箱支架	
101385	Staples for boxes	箱用卡钉	
101394	Staples for electric wires	电线钉	
101386	Staples for straps	带用卡钉	
101409	Suction cups for attachment	黏附吸盘	
101437	Supports for central heating radiators	集中供暖散热片托架	
101434	Tie holders [wardrobe]	领带架[衣柜]	
101446	Ties for plants	植物束缚带	
101419	Tin tacks	锡钉	
101438	Wall racks for canoes	墙置轻舟架	
101439	Wall racks for skis	墙置雪橇架	
101447	Wall slides [fastening devices]	墙壁滑轨[固定装置]	
101423	Washers for screws	螺钉用垫圈	
101416	Wing nuts	蝶形螺母	

08-09

Metal fittings and mountings for doors, windows and furniture, and similar articles, not included in other classes or subclasses.

08-09

其他大类或小类未包括的用于门、窗、家具的金属配件、金属装配件及类似物品 【12】[1]

101459	Coffin fittings	棺材配件
101458	Door stops	门挡，门吸
101463	Finger plates for doors	门推板
101471	Fittings for doors	门配件

1　注释中增加"not included in other classes or subclasses 其他大类或小类未包括的"。

101469	Fittings for furniture	家具配件
101465	Fittings for locks	锁配件
101470	Fittings for windows	窗配件
101461	Ironwork for gutters	沟槽铁制品
101466	Mountings for doors	门装配件
101467	Mountings for furniture	家具装配件
101468	Mountings for windows	窗装配件
101464	Rosettes for locks	锁孔环
101460	Squares [metalwork]	方钢［金属制品］
101462	Trunk fittings	箱子配件
101457	Window stops	窗用限位器

08-10
Bicycle and motorcycle racks 【2】[1]

Notes: (a) Including repair stands or stands for parking cycles. (b) Not including retractable stands that are parts of cycles (Cl. 12-11).

08-10
自行车和摩托车支架

注：（a）包括修理支架或停车支架。（b）不包括作为自行车部件的可收放脚撑(12-11类)。 【12】

101472	Bicycle racks	自行车支架
101473	Bicycle repair stands	自行车修理支架
101474	Motorcycle racks	摩托车支架
101475	Motorcycle repair stands	摩托车修理支架

08-11
Hardware for curtains

08-11
窗帘用五金件 【12】[2]

101408	Curtain hangers	窗帘吊架
101405	Curtain hooks	窗帘吊钩
101348	Curtain pulls	拉帘索
101488	Curtain rails	帘轨
101389	Curtain rings	帘环
101406	Curtain rod holders	帘杆托架
101491	Curtain rods	帘杆
101397	Curtain runners	帘转轮
101448	Finials for curtain poles	窗帘杆装饰头
101399	Fittings for curtains and blinds	帘帷和百叶窗配件

---

1 新增加 08-10 类。
2 新增加 08-11 类，产品项分别由 08-06 类、08-08 类和 08-99 类转移至 08-11 类。

08-99

Miscellaneous

Note: Including non-electric cables, regardless of the material of which they are made.

08-99

其他杂项

注：包括非电力线缆，不考虑其制作材料。

101477	Barbed wire	带刺金属丝
101493	Bowden cables	鲍登线
101478	Buffer stops for beds, trolleys and doors	床、手推车和门的止冲器
101504	Cables for tying down loads	拴货钢丝绳
101502	Carpet protectors for furniture	家具用地面保护物
101494	Chain links	链节
101479	Chains [metal]	链［金属］
101497	Chopping blocks for chopping wood	劈木墩
101489	Drums for electric cable	电缆卷盘
101502	Floor protectors for furniture	家具用地面保护物
101505	Handles for tools	工具手柄
101484	Hosepipe reels	软管卷轴
101499	Linemen's climbers	线路工用蹬杆脚扣
101476	Permanent magnets	磁体，磁铁
101500	Rails for sliding doors	推拉门轨
101483	Reels for electric wires	电线卷轴
101503	Reels for metal strips	钢带卷轴
101480	Sawhorses	锯木架
101485	Scarecrows [mobile strips]	稻草人［可移动板］
101482	Shoe scrapers	刮鞋器
101496	Ski-waxing racks	雪橇上蜡支架
101501	Storage reels for ropes	绳贮存卷轴
101498	Supports for boats ashore	岸上的船支架
101486	Tension links	张力调节器，拉环
101492	Tow ropes	拖拽索，牵引绳
101490	Trellis	格子架
101481	Trestles for building industry	建筑工业用支架
101495	Welding rods	焊条
101487	Wires of metal [not insulated]	金属线［非绝缘］

Class 09
Packaging and containers for the transport or handling of goods

09 类
用于商品运输或装卸的包装和容器

09-01

Bottles, flasks, pots, carboys, demi-johns, and pressurized containers

Notes: (a) "Pots" means those serving as containers. (b) Not including pots regarded as crockery (Cl. 07-01), or flower pots (Cl. 11-02).

09-01

瓶、长颈瓶、鼓形瓶、盛装腐蚀性液体的大玻璃瓶、细颈瓶和压力容器 【13】[1]

注：(a)"鼓形瓶"仅指包装容器。(b)不包括家用壶、鼓形瓶（07-01类）或花盆（11-02类）。

101506	Aerosol dispensers	喷雾分配容器	
101507	Aerosol dispensers for air fresheners	空气清新剂气雾分配器	
101508	Aerosol dispensers for insecticides	杀虫剂气雾分配器	
101521	Beakers used for packaging	包装用广口杯	
104577	Beverage bottles	饮料瓶	【10】
101519	Bottle coverings	瓶套	
101514	Bottle gourds	葫芦形容器	
101512	Bottles	瓶	
101522	Bottles for cosmetics [packaging]	化妆品瓶[包装]	
104581	Bottles for water dispensers	饮水机用桶	【10】
101509	Carboys	盛装腐蚀性液体的大玻璃瓶	
101513	Containers for liquid or solid gas	液化或固化气体容器	
101516	Cups for collecting resin	树脂收集杯	
101520	Cylinders of steel for compressed gas	压缩气体钢瓶	
101511	Demijohns	细颈瓶	
101523	Drink cans	饮料罐	
101514	Drinking flasks for travellers	旅行用饮料瓶	
101515	Jars [packaging]	广口瓶，坛[包装]	
101518	Liquid gas cartridges for cigarette lighters	打火机液化气筒	
104961	Pots [packaging]	罐，鼓形瓶[包装]	

---

1 第13版由"Bottles, flasks, pots, carboys, demi-johns, and containers with dynamic dispensing means 瓶、长颈瓶、罐、鼓形瓶、盛装腐蚀性液体的大玻璃瓶、细颈瓶和带有动力分配装置的容器"修改为"Bottles, flasks, pots, carboys, demijohns, and pressurized containers 瓶、长颈瓶、鼓形瓶、盛装腐蚀性液体的大玻璃瓶、细颈瓶和压力容器"。

09-02
Storage cans, drums and casks

09-02
储藏用罐、鼓形圆桶和木桶

101531	Barrels, casks, drums [containers]	桶，木桶，鼓形圆桶 [容器]
101531	Barrels, drums, casks [containers]	桶，鼓形圆桶，木桶 [容器]
101530	Canisters	桶
101533	Casks	木桶
101526	Casks, large barrels	木桶，大桶
101528	Herring barrels	青鱼桶
101532	Jerricans	油桶
101525	Kegs [small barrels]	小桶 [小桶]
104962	Paint buckets [packaging]	油漆桶 [包装] 【13】
101525	Small barrels [kegs]	小桶 [小桶]
101534	Small casks, kegs	小桶
101535	Storage cans	储藏罐
101533	Tuns	大酒桶
101524	Vats	缸，瓮
101529	Wine vats	葡萄酒桶

09-03
Boxes, cases, containers, tin cans
Note: Including freight containers.

09-03
盒、箱、集装箱和罐 【13】[1]
注：包括货运集装箱。

101569	Ballot boxes	投票箱
101548	Bottle carriers [for transport]	装瓶箱，装瓶容器 [运输用]
101549	Bottle racks [for transport]	瓶架 [运输用]
101560	Boxes for cosmetics [packaging]	化妆品盒 [包装]
101541	Boxes for gloves [packaging]	手套盒 [包装]
101561	Boxes for lozenges [packaging]	锭剂盒，含片盒 [包装]
104582	Boxes for paper tissues [packaging]	纸巾盒 [包装] 【10】
101554	Boxes for salt [packaging]	盐箱 [包装]
101543	Cardboard boxes [packaging]	纸板箱 [包装]
101553	Carriers for transporting tetrahedral cartons	运输四面体盒的容器
101568	Casings for radioactive products	放射性物品包装容器
101550	Cigarette packets [packaging]	烟盒 [包装]

---

[1] 第13版由"Boxes, cases, containers, (Preserve) tins or cans 盒子、箱子、集装箱和防腐罐头罐"修改为"Boxes, cases, containers, tin cans 盒、箱、集装箱和罐"。

101566	Collection boxes for religious purposes	宗教募捐箱	
101547	Comfit boxes	糖果盒	
101571	Disposable containers or pots for flowers or plants	包装花草的一次性容器或罐	
101557	Dividers for containers	容器隔板	
101546	Egg cartons	蛋盒	
101538	Freight containers	货运集装箱	
101564	Handlebar containers	周转箱，带把手的运送箱	
101545	Hat boxes [packaging]	帽盒 [包装]	
101537	Match boxes	火柴盒	
101552	Matchbooks	火柴纸夹	
101536	Motion picture storage cans	电影胶片储藏盒	
101540	Packaging boxes	包装盒，包装箱	
101551	Packaging boxes for pills	药品包装盒	
101562	Packaging boxes for storage	储藏用包装箱	
101555	Packaging cartons	包装盒，包装箱	
101563	Packaging for foodstuffs	食品包装盒	
101567	Packaging trays for plants	植物装运托盘	
101544	Packing cases	装运箱	
101556	Portable compost containers	便携式肥料容器	
101570	Seedling trays	育苗盘	
101557	Separators for containers	容器隔板	
101558	Shelves for use in freight containers	货运集装箱内架	
101558	Shelves for use in shipping containers	货运集装箱内架	【13】
101538	Shipping containers	货运集装箱	【13】
101539	Tetrahedral cartons [packaging]	四面体盒 [包装]	
101542	Tin cans	罐	
101565	Tins for packaging purposes	包装用罐头罐	
104963	Tote boxes	运送箱	【13】
104674	Transport frames for household appliances	家用电器用运输框架	【10】
101559	Trays for packaging foodstuffs	食品包装托盘	
101572	Trays for transporting flower pots or plants	装运花盆或植物用托盘	

09-04
Hampers, crates and baskets

09-04
有盖篮子、柳条筐和篮子

101576	Baskets [packaging]	篮，篓，筐 [包装]	
101574	Crates	柳条筐	

101575	Grape-picking baskets	葡萄采摘筐	
101573	Hampers	有盖篮子	
101577	Handlebar baskets	提篮	

09-05
Bags, sachets, tubes and capsules

Notes: (a) Including plastic bags or sachets, with or without handle or means of closing. (b) "Capsules" means those used for packaging.

09-05
袋、小袋、管和囊

注：(a) 包括采用各种封口方式的有提手或无提手的塑料袋和小袋。(b) "囊"指包装物。

101578	Ampules [packaging]	安瓿［包装］	
101590	Bags for making ice cubes	冰块制作袋	
101586	Bags of paper	纸袋	
101584	Bags for tea or coffee	茶包或咖啡包	
101585	Bags [packaging]	袋［包装］	
101595	Blister packs [packaging]	泡罩包装，罩板包装［包装］	
101580	Capsules for pharmaceutical products	药品用囊	
101579	Capsules [casings]	囊［包装］	
101597	Carrier bags	手提袋	
101591	Coin tubes [packaging]	硬币套管［包装］	
101596	Collection bags for religious purposes	宗教募捐袋	
101581	Cornets [packaging]	圆锥形纸袋［包装］	
104745	Disposable drip coffee bags [packaging]	一次性咖啡滤袋［包装］	【11】
101592	Garbage bags	垃圾袋	
101589	Mailbags	邮包	
101588	Packaging for ice cream cornets	冰激凌圆锥形纸袋包装	
104744	Packaging sleeves	包装套	【11】
101593	Pouches [packaging]	封口袋［包装］	
101592	Refuse bags	垃圾袋	【12】
101583	Sachets [packaging]	小袋，香袋［包装］	
101598	School cones [packaging]	学生用圆锥形纸袋［包装］	
101599	Sleeves for compact discs	光盘套	
101582	Sleeves for phonograph records	唱片套	
101587	Tubes [packaging containers]	软管［包装容器］	

09-06
Ropes and hooping materials

101607	Bands, straps, webbing	箍带，捆扎带，挽带
101603	Barrel hoops	桶箍
101601	Bundle carrier ties	禾捆输送器捆带
104964	Bungee cords for securing objects	用于固定物体的松紧绳　【13】
101605	Clothes lines	晒衣绳
101602	Hooping materials	捆箍用品
101611	Plant ties	植物捆扎带
101604	Ropes	绳索
101610	Straps for carrying or handling of loads	用于运输或搬运货物的带子
101601	Straps for luggage racks	行李架用捆扎带
101607	Straps, bands, webbing	捆扎带，箍带，挽带
101600	Straps [except driving belts or straps for saddlery]	捆扎带[驱动皮带或鞍具用捆扎带除外]
101606	String	细绳
101609	String for binders [agricultural equipment]	捆扎绳[农业设备]
104676	Twine	麻绳　【10】
101608	Twine for binding sheaves	捆扎绳
101607	Webbing, straps, bands	挽带，捆扎带，箍带

09-07
Closing means and attachments

Notes: (a) Including only closing means for packaging. (b) "Attachments" means, for example, dispensing and dosing devices incorporated in containers and detachable atomizers.

注：(a) 仅包括用于包装的封口装置。(b) "封口附件"，例如可拆卸的喷嘴、与容器一体的分配装置和定量给料装置。

101615	Bands for skeins of wool	毛线团的箍带
101625	Bottle caps incorporating brushes	带刷子的瓶盖
101628	Bottle fasteners	瓶扣
101617	Bottle stoppers	瓶塞
101623	Caps [for bottles]	盖[瓶用]
101633	Clips [closing means] for packaging	包装用夹子[封口装置]
101633	Closing means [Clips] for packaging	包装用封口装置[夹子]
101627	Closures for aerosol containers	气雾剂容器的封口
101624	Closures for containers	容器封口
101616	Coopers' bungs	桶匠用桶塞

101618	Cork stoppers	软木塞
101619	Dispensing stoppers	配料限量器，分配塞
104965	Fasteners for packaging	包装用扣件
101630	Lead stamps or seals for packaging containers	包装容器用铅印或铅封
101622	Measuring stoppers	计量塞
101629	Muselets［wire closures］for bottles	瓶用铁丝封口［线性封闭］
101626	Nozzles for aerosol containers	气雾剂容器的喷嘴
101632	Perfusion caps	灌注盖
101621	Pourer stoppers	浇口塞
101631	Sealing capsules for bottles	瓶用密封盖
101614	Sealing rings for packaging containers	包装容器用密封圈
101613	Spigots［cooperage］	孔塞［桶用］
101612	Spray caps for aerosol containers	喷雾容器的喷口盖
101620	Stoppers with built-in spraying device	内置喷雾装置的塞子

09-08

Pallets and platforms for forklifts

09-08

叉车的货盘和装卸台

101635	Pallets for forklifts	叉车货盘
101634	Pallets［fork truck platforms］	货盘［叉车装卸台］
101636	Stands for pallets	货盘支架

09-09

Refuse and trash containers and stands therefor

09-09

废物和垃圾的容器及其座架

101637	Ash bins	垃圾箱
101637	Ashpans	炉灰盘
101645	Collectors for returned papers	再生纸收集容器
101651	Compactors	垃圾捣碎机
101642	Cuspidors	痰盂
101639	Dustbins	垃圾箱
101639	Garbage cans	垃圾筒
101647	Garbage containers	垃圾容器
101643	Garbage disposal units	下水口垃圾处理器
101648	Garbage traversers	垃圾转台
101646	Holding stands for garbage sacks	垃圾袋支架

101644	Litter receptacles	废弃物容器	
104966	Organic waste composters	有机废物堆肥机	【13】
101639	Refuse receptacles	废物容器	
101642	Spittoons	痰盂	
101649	Stands for garbage containers	垃圾容器座	
101650	Stands for garbage traversers	垃圾转台座	
101638	Wastepaper baskets	废纸篓	

09-10　　　　　　　　　　　　　　　　　　　　　　　　　　　　**09-10**　　　　　　　　　　　　　　　　　　　　　　　　　　　　【12】[1]

Handles and grips for the transport or handling of packages and containers　　　**运输或搬运包装物及容器用提手和握柄**

101659	Gun handles for spray paint cans	喷漆罐用枪柄	
101654	Handles for buckets	桶提手	
101653	Handles for carrying parcels	运送包裹的提手	
101658	Handles for shopping bags	购物袋提手	

09-99　　　　　　　　　　　　　　　　　　　　　　　　　　　　**09-99**

Miscellaneous　　　　　　　　　　　　　　　　　　　　　　　**其他杂项**

101655	Corner protectors for packaging	包装护角	
101656	Devices for filling boxes of tablets	片剂盒填充装置	
101660	Ice cream drip guards	冰激凌防滴器	
104626	Ice cream sticks	冰激凌芯棒	【10】
101657	Shock absorbing material for packaging	包装用消震材料	

1　新增加 09-10 类，产品项由 09-99 类转移至 09-10 类。

Class 10
Clocks and watches and other measuring instruments, checking and signalling instruments

10 类
钟、表及其他测量仪器，检测仪器，信号仪器

Note: Including electrically-driven instruments.

注：包括电子仪器。

10-01
Clocks and alarm clocks

10-01
钟和闹钟

101663	Alarm clocks	闹钟
101664	Astronomical clocks	天文钟
101661	Clocks	钟
101666	Cuckoo clocks	布谷鸟钟
104746	Digital calendar clocks	数字日历钟 【11】
101665	Geographical clocks	地理钟
101667	Grandfather clocks	老爷钟，落地钟
101662	Regulators [clocks]	标准钟 [钟]
101668	Wall clocks	壁钟，挂钟

10-02
Watches and wrist watches

10-02
表和手表

101671	Alarm watches	闹表
101673	Chronograph watches	精密计时表
101672	Pendant watches	怀表
104747	Smartwatches	智能手表 【11】
101670	Watches	表
101669	Wrist watches	手表，腕表

10-03
Other time-measuring instruments

10-03
其他计时仪器

Note: Including time-measuring apparatus such as parking meters, timers for kitchen use and similar instruments.

注：包括如停车计时器、厨房用定时器和类似仪器的计时装置。

101674	Chronometers	计时计
101680	Chronometric counters	精密测时计量器

101678	Egg timers〔sand glasses〕	煮蛋计时器〔沙漏〕
101678	Hourglasses	沙漏
101676	Metronomes	节拍器
101675	Parking meters	停车计时器
101679	Sundials	日晷
101677	Timers〔automatic〕	定时器〔自动〕

10-04

Other measuring instruments, apparatus and devices

Notes:（a）Including instruments, apparatus and devices for measuring temperature, pressure, weight, length, volume and electricity.（b）Not including exposure meters（Cl. 16-05）.

10-04

其他测量仪器、设备和装置

注：（a）包括测量温度、压力、重量、长度、体积和电流等的仪器、设备和装置。（b）不包括曝光计（16-05类）。

101682	Accelerometers	加速计
101683	Acoumeters	听力计
101684	Acoustic measuring instruments	声学测量仪器
101685	Aerometers	气体比重计
101686	Alcoholometers	酒精比重计
101687	Altimeters	高度计
101688	Ammeters	电表
101689	Anemometers	风速计，风力计
101794	Appliances for dosing foodstuffs	粮食定量配料设备
101786	Apparatus for measuring the draft of ships	船舶吃水深度测量仪
101758	Assay balances	分析天平，试金天平
101692	Balances	天平
101693	Barometers	气压计
101695	Butyrometers	测脂仪
101696	Calipers	测径器，卡规
101698	Calorimeters	热量计
101774	Charge indicators for accumulators	蓄电池充电电量指示器
101699	Clinometers	测角器，倾斜仪
101700	Comparators	比较仪
101773	Compass cards	罗经刻度盘
101768	Compasses〔navigation〕	罗盘〔导航〕
101703	Content measuring apparatus for reservoirs	水库容量测量仪
101718	Cooking indicators〔kitchen〕	烹调指示器〔厨房〕

101776	Cross-staffs [surveying]	直角十字杆［测量］
101795	Cyclometers [bike computers]	记转器［自行车电脑，车速表］
101706	Densimeters	密度计
101708	Distance measuring apparatus	测距仪
101787	Droppers [except for medical or laboratory purposes]	滴量器［医疗或实验室用除外］
101709	Dynamometers	测力仪
101710	Ebulliometers	沸点测定器
101785	Echo sounders	回声测量仪
101702	Electricity meters	电量计，电表
101775	Fare recorders	计费器
101771	Fare registers	计费器
101704	Flowmeters	流量计
101707	Foot measuring devices	量脚装置
101717	Fuel-consumption indicators for vehicles	车辆燃料消耗指示器
101712	Galvanometers	电流计
101777	Gas meters	煤气表
101721	Gauges	计量器
101697	Gauges for agricultural products	农产品测量仪
101713	Geodetic apparatus and instruments	测地设备和仪器
101714	Goniometers	角度计
104751	Height gauges	高度计 【11】
101716	Hygrometers	湿度计
101699	Inclinometers	倾斜仪
101790	Kilometer recorders	里程表
101796	Kitchen scales	厨房秤
101737	Lactometers	乳比重计
101780	Letter scales	信件秤
101730	Levelling rods for surveyors	测量员用水准尺
101723	Luxmeters	照度计
101724	Manometers	压力计
101769	Marine compasses	航海罗盘
101783	Measuring cups	量杯
101726	Measuring instruments for tailors	剪裁用测量工具
101725	Measuring instruments [except for measuring time]	测量仪器［计时器除外］
101788	Measuring spoons	量匙
101727	Measuring tapes	卷尺，皮尺

101789	Measuring vessels [household]	量器［家用］	
101727	Meter tapes	米尺，卷尺，皮尺	
101735	Micrometer gauges	测微计，千分尺	
101728	Micrometers	千分尺	
101790	Mileage recorders	里程表	
101790	Mileometers	里程表	
101729	Milliammeters	毫安表	
101731	Octants	八分仪	
101732	Odometers	里程表	
101733	Ohmmeters	欧姆表	
104750	Pedometers	计步器	【11】
101739	Planimeters	测面器，面积仪	
101681	Plumb bobs	铅锤	
101681	Plumb lines	铅锤线，准绳	
101742	Polarimeters	偏振计	
101724	Pressure gauges	压力表	
104748	Pulse watches	脉搏手表	【11】
101743	Pyrometers	高温计	
101744	Radiometers	辐射计	
101740	Rain gauges	雨量仪	
101755	Range finders	测距仪	
101770	Recording meters for telephone charges	电话费记录器	
101791	Revolution counters	转数器，旋转计数器	
101793	Road marking apparatus	道路标线测量仪	
101705	Rules for measuring	测量尺	
101691	Scales	秤	
101738	Scales [for weighing people]	秤［测体重用］	
101747	Seismographs	地震仪	
101748	Seismometers	地震检波器	
101746	Sextants	六分仪	
101722	Ships' logs	船用测程仪	
101781	Slide measures	游标测量仪	
101792	Sonometers [measuring apparatus]	振动频率计［测量设备］	
101750	Sounding leads	测深锤	
101751	Spectrophotometers	分光光度计	
101720	Speedometers	速度表	
101778	Spirit levels	水平仪	
101784	Steelyards	杆秤	

101772	Surface plates	划线台，验平板	
101690	Surveying instruments	勘测仪器	
101767	Surveying rods	测杆	
101776	Surveyors' optical squares	测量员用光学角尺	
101752	Tacheometers	准距计	
101753	Tachometers	转速计	
101745	Tape measures	卷尺	
101711	Tape-measure cases	卷尺盒	
101754	Taximeters	出租汽车计程器	
101755	Telemeters	测距器	
101719	Temperature gauges	温度计	
101756	Theodolites	经纬仪	
101757	Thermometers [including medical thermometers]	温度计［包括医用体温计］	
101782	Tire pressure gauges	轮胎压力表	
101759	Typometers	印刷排版量尺	
101782	Tyre pressure gauges	轮胎压力表	
101749	Ultrasonic probes	超声测量器	
101762	Vacuum gauges	真空计	
101760	Variometers	磁力偏差计	
101761	Verniers	游标尺	
101763	Viscometers	黏度计	【12】
101763	Viscosimeters	黏度计	
101764	Voltmeters	电压表	
101715	Water hardness measuring instruments	水硬度测量仪	
101779	Water level gauges	水准仪	
101701	Water meters	水表	
101765	Wattmeters	瓦特计，功率计	
101734	Wavemeters	波长计	
104749	Wearable activity trackers	可穿戴式活动追踪器	【11】
104682	Weather stations	气象站用测量仪器	【10】
101736	Weighing apparatus and instruments	称量设备和仪器	
101694	Weighing machines	称重器，衡器	
101741	Weights [for scales]	砝码［天平用］	
101766	Yardsticks	码尺	

10-05

Instruments, apparatus and devices for checking, security or testing

Note: Including fire and burglar alarms, and detectors of various types.

10-05

检测、安全和测试用仪器、设备和装置

注：包括防火及防盗警铃和各种类型的探测器。

104752	Access control gates	通道控制闸机	【11】
101802	Alarms indicating water shortage in boilers	锅炉缺水信号报警器	
101835	Anti-theft alarms	防盗报警器	
101820	Apparatus for adjusting vehicle headlights	交通工具前灯校准仪	
101843	Baby monitoring apparatus	婴儿监控器	
101833	Boiler regulators	锅炉调控器	
101813	Brake-testing machines	制动试验用装置	
101799	Burglar alarms	防盗报警器	
101805	Checking apparatus	检验仪	
101840	Checking apparatus for lottery tickets and games of chance	用于彩票和运气游戏的核对仪器	【12】[1]
101803	Control photocells	控制性光电管，控制电眼	
101844	Counterfeit money detectors	伪钞检验器，验钞机	
101832	Crossroad mirrors	十字路口反光镜	
101839	Diagnostic testing apparatus [except for medical or laboratory purposes]	诊断测试设备［医疗或实验室用除外］	
101836	Divining rods	探矿杖	
101837	Dowsing pendulums	探测矿藏或水源的摆锤	
101806	Entry checking apparatus	入口检测仪	
101827	Fall controllers for parachutists	跳伞员降落控制器	
101800	Fire alarms	火警报警器	
101809	Fire detectors	火灾探测器	
101814	Firedamp detectors	沼气探测器	
101842	Flow checking apparatus	流量检验仪	
101798	Fluid analysis apparatus	流体分析仪	
101801	Frost indicators [electric]	霜冻指示仪［电动］	
101828	Gas detectors	气体探测器	
101804	Geiger-Muller counters	盖格－弥勒计数管	
101815	Gyroscopes [aviation, navigation]	陀螺仪［航空、航海］	
101808	Humidity detectors	湿度探测器	
101816	Hydrophones	水听器，水中测音器	

---

1 由"Pool coupon checking apparatus 贮油层切片检测仪器"修改为"Checking apparatus for lottery tickets and games of chance 用于彩票和运气游戏的核对仪器"。

101817	Hygrostats	湿度调节器，恒湿器	
104969	Inspection robots	巡检机器人	【13】
104968	Intelligent access control devices	智能门禁装置	【13】
101831	Lamps for candling eggs	验蛋灯	
101830	Lie detectors	测谎器	
101819	Lightning arresters	避雷器	
101819	Lightning conductors	避雷装置	
101819	Lightning rods	避雷针	
101845	Movement sensors	移动传感器	
101811	Ore detectors	矿藏探测器	
101841	Oscillographs	示波器	
101818	Oscilloscopes	示波镜	
101821	Photometers [checking apparatus]	光度计 [检测仪器]	
101823	Radar apparatus	雷达装置，电波探测器	
101810	Radiation detectors	辐射探测器	
101834	Regulators for heating installations	加热设备调节器	
104967	Sensor-driven baby rocking devices	传感器驱动的婴儿摇摆装置	【13】
101838	Smoke detectors	烟雾探测器	
101825	Sonometers [checking apparatus]	振动式频率计 [检测仪器]	
101829	Surveyors' staffs	测量员用标尺	
101797	Tacheometric poles	视距检测标杆	
101812	Testing instruments	测试仪器	
101826	Testing machines for woven fabrics	编织物检验机	
101807	Thermic flame controllers	火焰热控制器	
101824	Thermostats	恒温器，温度调节装置	
101822	Time clocks	打卡钟	

10-06
Signalling apparatus and devices

Note: Not including lighting or signalling devices for vehicles (Cl. 26-06).

10-06
信号设备和装置

注：不包括交通工具上的照明或信号装置（26-06类）。

101868	Accident signalling devices	事故信号装置	
101866	Beacons [aviation, navigation]	航标灯 [航空、航海]	
101860	Bells [electric]	电铃 [电动]	
101874	Breakdown triangles for motorists	司机用三角安全警示牌	
101876	Bus stop signposts	公共汽车站牌	
101849	Catadioptric reflectors	反射镜，反光饰条	
101873	Cycle bells	自行车铃	
101864	Dog whistles	犬笛	

101857	Door chimes	门铃	
101867	Door knockers	叩门环	
101856	Fog signals	尘雾信号装置	
101879	Gavels	议事槌，拍卖槌	
101853	Lighthouses	灯塔	
101877	Luminous road signs	夜光的道路标志，发光的道路标志	
101848	Marker buoys	浮标	
101871	Markers for ski slopes	滑雪坡度标志	
101847	Milestones	里程标	
104691	Pedestrian crossing signs	行人过街标志物	【11】[1]
101850	Railway signal discs	铁路信号盘	
101870	Railway signal [fixed]	铁路信号设备 [固定式]	
101870	Railway signals [fixed]	铁路信号设备 [固定式]	
101863	Reflecting bands for the feet	脚部用反光带	
101872	Road signals	道路信号设备	
101846	Road-marking devices	道路标记装置	
101855	Semaphores	信号机	
101861	Signal bells	信号铃	
101854	Signal gantries	信号桥，跨轨信号架	
101851	Signal lamps	信号灯	
101859	Sirens	汽笛，警报器	
101875	Swimming pool lane markers	泳道线	
101878	Tell-tale lights	警告信号灯	
101869	Traffic lights	交通信号灯	
101852	Traffic signs	交通标牌	
101862	Vehicle horns	交通工具喇叭	
101865	Warning horns	警示喇叭	
101880	Weathercocks	风标	
101858	Whistles	汽笛，哨子	

10-07

Casings, cases, dials, hands and all other parts and accessories of instruments for measuring, checking and signalling

Note："Casings" means watch and clock casings and all casings being integral parts of instruments of which they protect the mechanism, with the exception of cases specially designed for their contents (Cl. 03-01) or for packaging (Cl. 09-03).

10-07

测量仪器、检测仪器和信号仪器的外壳、盘面、指针和所有其他零部件及附件

注："外壳"指手表及钟表外壳和保护机械装置并作为仪器组成部分的所有外壳，为了其内装物（03-01类）或包装（09-03类）而专门设计的容器除外。

---

[1] 由 20-03 类转移至 10-06 类。

101886	Barrels [clocks and watches]	发条盒 [钟表]	
104753	Bracelets for smartwatches	智能手表表镯	【11】
101900	Clasps for watch bracelets	表带扣	
104593	Clock hands	钟针，钟表指针	【10】
101903	Clock striking mechanisms	时钟敲击装置	
101889	Dials for measuring, checking and signalling instruments	测量仪器、检测仪器和信号仪器的盘面	
101894	Escapements [clocks and watches]	摆轮机械 [钟表]	
101891	Frames for movements [clocks and watches]	机芯结构 [钟表]	
101881	Hairsprings for clocks and watches	钟表的游丝	
101882	Hands of dials	表盘指针	
101901	Hinge pins for watch cases	表壳铰链销	
101883	Indicating pointers	指针	
101892	Jewel settings [clocks and watches]	宝石轴承的嵌座 [钟表]	
101897	Jewels for clock and watch movements	钟表机芯用宝石	
101899	Links for watch bracelets	表带链扣	
101896	Movements for clocks and watches	钟表机芯	
101885	Pendulums for clocks	钟摆	
101898	Pivots for clocks and watches	钟表的枢轴	
101884	Pocket-watch bows	怀表环状柄	
101888	Watch bracelets	表镯	
101887	Watch casings	表壳	
101890	Watch chains	表链	
101905	Watch crystals	表镜	
101906	Watch dials	表盘	
101905	Watch glasses	表镜	
101895	Watch rims	表圈	
101904	Watch springs	表簧	
101900	Watch-strap clasps	表带扣	
101907	Watchstrap links	表带铰链	
104865	Watch winding apparatus	表的上弦机构	【12】
101902	Winders for watches	表的发条	
101893	Winding crowns for watches	表的发条柄头	
101888	Wrist watch straps	手表带	

10-99

Miscellaneous

10-99

其他杂项

Class 11
Articles of adornment

11 类
装饰品

11-01
Jewellery

Notes: (a) Including costume and imitation jewellery. (b) Not including watches (Cl. 10-02).

11-01
珠宝和首饰

注：(a) 包括人造和仿制珠宝首饰。(b) 不包括表（10-02类）。

101930	Bracelet links	手链
101911	Bracelets	手镯
101913	Brilliants	宝石
101914	Brooches [jewellery]	胸针，领针［首饰］
101933	Chain links [jewellery]	链节［首饰］
101915	Chains [jewellery]	链［首饰］
101912	Charms	小饰物
101917	Clips [jewellery]	夹［首饰］
104866	Cuff bracelets	开口手镯 【12】
101919	Diadems	王冠，冠冕形发饰
101920	Diamonds	钻石
101910	Ear pendants	耳坠
101910	Earrings	耳环
101909	Finger rings	戒指
101926	Gems	珠宝
101931	Hair fasteners [jewellery]	固定头发用饰品［首饰］
101922	Jewellery	首饰
101935	Jewellery for piercing	穿刺首饰
101934	Jewellery sets	成套首饰
101923	Lockets	盒式项链坠
101923	Medallions	圆盘形垂饰
101918	Necklaces [jewellery]	项链［首饰］
101925	Pearls	珍珠
101924	Pendants [jewellery]	垂饰，挂坠［首饰］
101921	Pins [jewellery]	饰针［首饰］
101926	Precious stones	宝石
101929	Religious objects [jewellery]	宗教物品［首饰］
101928	Rosaries	念珠
101932	Sautoirs [jewellery]	项饰［首饰］
101916	Signet rings	图章戒指，印戒

101927	Solitaire diamonds	独粒钻石
101908	Wedding rings	结婚戒指

11-02

Trinkets, table, mantel and wall ornaments, flower vases and pots

Note: Including sculptures, mobiles and statues.

11-02

小装饰品，桌子、壁炉台和墙的装饰物，花瓶和花盆

注：包括雕塑、风铃和雕像。

101937	Aquariums for flowers	玻璃花池
101964	Basins [decoration]	盆［装饰物］
101942	Baskets for holding flowerpots	装花盆的篮筐
101956	Baskets [ornamental]	篮筐［装饰性的］
101938	Bas-reliefs	浅浮雕
101964	Bowls [decoration]	碗，盆［装饰物］
101941	Ceramics	陶瓷工艺品
101954	Crucifixes	带耶稣像的十字架
101953	Epergnes	分隔层饰盘，餐桌中央饰品
101946	Figurines	小雕像
101943	Flower bowls	花盆
101963	Flower boxes [indoor]	花盆盒［室内］
101957	Flower holders	花束架
101961	Flower vases	花瓶
101940	Flowerpot covers	花盆罩
101958	Flowerpots	花盆
101968	Garden gnomes	花园守护神石像
101962	Glassware [purely ornamental]	玻璃器皿［纯装饰性的］
101959	Holders for flower arrangements	插花托架
101969	Holy-water stoups	圣水杯
101970	Incense burners	香炉
101971	Incense-smoking figurines	香薰小雕像
104754	Indoor propagators	室内培植箱 【11】
101967	Magnets	磁贴
101965	Magnets for magnetic boards	磁性板用磁贴
101955	Mantelpiece ornaments	壁炉装饰品
101947	Mobiles [decoration]	风动饰物，悬挂饰物［装饰物］
101948	Mosaics	镶嵌工艺品
101956	Ornamental baskets	装饰性篮筐
101950	Painted china [purely ornamental]	彩釉瓷器［纯装饰性的］

101960	Plates and dishes [purely ornamental]	盘和碟[纯装饰性的]	
101945	Pottery [artware]	陶器[工艺品]	
101951	Sculptures	雕塑	
104970	Snow globes	雪花水晶球	【13】
101959	Stands for flower arrangements	插花立架	
101952	Statuettes	小雕像	
101953	Table centerpieces	桌子中央饰品	
101949	Table ornaments	桌用装饰品	
101939	Trinkets	小装饰品	
101966	Trophies	奖杯	
101936	Wall ornaments	墙饰品	
104683	Wind chimes	风铃	【10】

11-03
Medals and badges

11-03
纪念章和徽章

101972	Badges	徽章	
101973	Campaign badges	军功章	
101975	Identification badges	证章	
101974	Medals	纪念章	
101976	Pins [badges]	带别针的徽章[徽章]	

11-04
Artificial flowers, fruit and plants

11-04
人造的花、水果和植物

101984	Artificial flowers	人造花	
101982	Artificial foliage	人造植物，人造树叶	
101987	Artificial plants	人造植物	
101979	Artificial wreaths	人造花环	
101978	Branches of artificial shrubs	人造灌木枝	
101977	Christmas trees [artificial]	圣诞树[人造]	
101981	Flower decorations	装饰花	
101985	Fruit [artificial]	水果[人造]	
101980	Funeral wreaths	葬礼用花圈	
101986	Garlands of artificial flowers or leaves	人造花或叶子做的花环	
101988	Imitation vegetation	仿真植物	
101983	Leaves of artificial plants	人造植物叶子	

11-05

Flags, festive decorations

Notes: (a) Including garlands, streamers and Christmas tree decorations. (b) Not including candles (Cl. 26-04).

101991	Banners	旗帜，横幅
102000	Burgees	小旗，燕尾旗，三角旗
101993	Candle holders for Christmas trees	圣诞树用的蜡烛架
101995	Christmas cribs	耶稣诞生马槽
101992	Christmas stockings	圣诞长袜
101989	Christmas tree decorations	圣诞树装饰物
101999	Coats of arms	盾形纹章，盾徽
102002	Decorative balls for car radio aerials	车辆无线电天线的装饰球
101999	Escutcheons	盾形装饰物
101996	Festive decorations	节日装饰物
104755	Festive dolls	节日装饰玩偶 【11】
101944	Figures for Christmas cribs	耶稣诞生马槽造型装饰 【10】[1]
101998	Flagpoles	旗杆
101997	Flags	旗帜
102001	Garlands	花环
104756	Non-illuminated Advent stars	非照明用基督降临星 【11】
104971	Ornamental Christmas trees	圣诞树形装饰品 【13】
101994	Rosettes [ornaments]	玫瑰花形饰物[装饰品]
101990	Streamers	横幅，长旗，幡，彩带

11-99

Miscellaneous

102004	Fountains for interior decoration	用于室内装饰的人造喷泉
102006	Ingots	金属锭，金属块，金属条
102003	Stage sets	舞台布景
102003	Theatre sets	剧场布景
104681	Waterfalls for interior decoration	用于室内装饰的人工瀑布 【10】
102005	Wedding bouquet sleeves	婚礼花束束套

---

[1] 由11-02类转移至11-05类。

Class 12
Means of transport or hoisting

Notes: (a) Including all vehicles: land, sea, air, space and others. (b) Including parts, components and accessories which exist only in connection with a vehicle and cannot be placed in another class; these parts, components and accessories of vehicles are to be placed in the subclass of the vehicle in question, or in Cl. 12-16 if they are common to several vehicles included in different subclasses. (c) Not including, in principle, parts, components and accessories of vehicles which can be placed in another class; these parts, components and accessories are to be placed in the same class as articles of the same type, in other words, having the same function. Thus, carpets or mats for automobiles are to be placed with carpets (Cl. 06-11); electric motors for vehicles are to be placed in Cl. 13-01, and non-electric motors for vehicles in Cl. 15-01 (the same applies to the components of such motors); automobile headlamps are to be placed with lighting apparatus (Cl. 26-06). (d) Not including scale models of vehicles (Cl. 21-01).

12类
运输或提升工具

注：（a）包括陆、海、空、太空等所有交通工具。（b）包括仅用于交通工具且其他大类未包含的零件、部件和附件；这些零件、部件和附件应分入其所涉及的交通工具的小类，若其可通用于多个不同小类的交通工具，则分入12-16类。（c）原则上，不包括其他类已含有的交通工具的零件、部件和附件。这些零件、部件和附件应与其同类型或同用途的产品分入一类。因此，车辆用地毯或地垫应与地毯（06-11类）分入一类；交通工具的电动马达分入13-01类，交通工具的非电动马达分入15-01类（上述两类马达的零件同理）；车辆前灯应与照明设备（26-06类）分入一类。（d）不包括交通工具的比例模型（21-01类）。

12-01
Vehicles drawn by animals

12-01
畜力车辆

102007	Carriage shafts	马车车辕
102010	Sulkies	单座两轮马车
102009	Tipcarts	翻斗小车，倾卸车
102008	Vehicles drawn by animals	畜力车辆

12-02
Handcarts, wheelbarrows

12-02
手推车、独轮手推车

102014	Barrows	手推车
102021	Boat launching trolleys	船舶下水用手推车
104757	Casters for transport purposes	运输用脚轮
102024	Cleaning trolleys	手推清洁车

【11】

102012	Dinner waggons [carriages]	装有脚轮的送菜车［带轮架子］	
102027	Dollies [wheeled platforms]	台车［有轮平板］	
102020	Dumpcarts	手推倾卸车	
102018	Garden carts	园艺手拖车	
102013	Golf carts	高尔夫球包车	
102014	Hand carts	手推车	
102016	Hand trolleys for handling goods	搬运货物的手推车	
104867	Hand trolleys for transporting guidance barriers	运输引导护栏用手推车	【12】
102015	Hand trucks	手推运输车	
102023	Itinerant vendors' carts	流动售货手推车	
102022	Platform trolleys	平板手推车	
102019	Sack-barrows	麻袋推车	
102017	Shopping carts	购物车	
102017	Shopping trolleys	购物车	【12】
102025	Trolleys for medical care	医护用手推车	
102026	Wheel carriers [trolleys]	轮架［手推车］	
102011	Wheelbarrows	独轮手推车	

12-03

Locomotives and rolling stock for railways and all other rail vehicles

12-03

机车、铁路车辆及其他有轨车辆

102029	Bogies for railway cars	铁路车厢转向架
102049	Buffers [railway wagon parts]	缓冲器［铁路货车零部件］
102052	Concertina vestibules for railway carriages	铁路客车的风箱式通廊
102047	Funicular railway carriages	缆索铁路客车
102034	Funicular railways	缆索铁路
102032	Funnels for locomotives	机车烟囱
102030	Grease boxes for railway carriages	铁路客车润滑油箱
102035	Locomotives	机车，火车头
102051	Luggage racks for railway carriages	铁路客车行李架
102028	Mine trucks	运矿车
102037	Monorails [transport]	单轨铁路［运输］
102038	Platforms for railway carriages	铁路客车连接平台
102048	Rail trolleys	铁路查道车
102053	Rail vehicles	有轨车辆
102031	Railway carriage bodies	铁路客车车体
102039	Railway carriage doors	铁路客车车门

102046	Railway carriages	铁路客车	
102054	Railway wagons	铁路货车	
102055	Refrigerator cars ［rail］	冷藏车［铁路］	
102055	Refrigerator wagons ［rail］	冷藏货车［铁路］	
102036	Running boards for railway carriages	铁路客车的脚踏板	
102042	Sandboxes of locomotives or trams	机车或有轨电车用的沙箱	
102050	Spark deflectors for locomotives	机车火花偏转器	
102040	Steam regulators for locomotives	机车蒸汽调节器	
102043	Suspensions for railway carriages	铁路客车用悬架	
102056	Tank cars ［rail］	油槽车［铁路］	
102056	Tank wagons ［rail］	油罐车［铁路］	
102044	Tenders	煤水车	
102045	Tramcars	矿山中的煤车，有轨电车	
102033	Trolleys for railway maintenance work	铁路养护用轨道车	
102041	Wheels for rail vehicles	有轨车辆车轮	

12-04

Telpher carriers, chair lifts and ski lifts

12-04

高架索车、缆椅和滑雪索车

102057	Cable cars	缆车
102059	Chair lifts	缆椅
102060	Ski lifts	滑雪索车
102058	Telpher cableways	缆车空中索道

12-05

Elevators and hoists for loading or conveying

Note: Including passenger lifts, goods lifts, cranes, forklift trucks and conveyor belts.

12-05

装载或输送用的升降机和提升机

注：包括载客升降机、货物升降机、起重机、铲车和传送带。

102074	Apparatus for handling	装卸设备	
102065	Bucket chains ［lifting apparatus］	铲斗链［升降设备］	
102064	Capstans	绞盘	
104868	Car parking lifts	停车提升设备，立体停车设备	【12】
102093	Control and indicator units for forklifts	铲车的控制操作单元	
102062	Conveyor belts	传送带	
102079	Conveyors ［machines］	输送机［机械］	
102078	Crane towers	起重机塔架	

102073	Cranes	起重机
102063	Davits for boats	吊艇杆，船舶用吊柱
102068	Derricks［drilling］	钻井架［钻井］
102086	Electro-magnetic cranes	电磁式起重机
102084	Elevator belts	升降机传送带
102085	Elevator buckets	提升斗，吊箱
102083	Elevator chains	升降机链
102061	Elevators	升降机，电梯
102071	Elevators for vehicles	交通工具用升降机
102069	Elevators, hoists, lifts	电梯，提升机，升降机
102062	Endless carriers	环形运送装置
102072	Escalators	自动扶梯
102087	Floating cranes	水上浮式起重机，浮吊
102070	Forklifts	铲车，叉车
102076	Gantry cranes	龙门起重机
102088	Goods hoists	货物提升机
102088	Goods lifts	货物升降机
102069	Hoists, lifts, elevators	提升机，升降机，电梯
102082	Jacks for lifting	千斤顶
102092	Lift cages	升降机吊笼，吊箱
102067	Lift trucks	升降运输机
102090	Lifting devices for animals	动物用升降装置
102091	Lifting devices for invalids	病人用升降装置
102061	Lifts	升降机
102069	Lifts, hoists, elevators	升降机，提升机，电梯
102066	Manure loaders	肥料装载机
102072	Moving staircases	自动扶梯
102089	Moving walkways	自动人行道，平行电梯
102075	Pulley blocks	滑轮组
102077	Pulleys	滑轮
104758	Transfer robots	转运机器人 【11】
102081	Trolleys for handling goods［self-propelled］	装卸货物用台车［自动式］
102080	Winches	绞车
102080	Windlasses	起锚机，卷扬机，绞盘

12-06
Ships and boats

12-06
船和艇

102125	Bathyscaphs	深海潜水器
102127	Boat hulls	船体
102098	Boats	艇
102101	Canoes	独木舟，小划子
102104	Catamarans	筏，双体船
102108	Centre-boards ［nautical］	帆船的活动船板［船舶的］
102131	Cleats for boats	艇用系缆墩
102131	Cleats for boats and ships	船艇用系缆墩
102131	Cleats for ships	船用系缆墩
102102	Dinghies	小游艇
102097	Ferry boats	渡轮
102109	Floating drydocks	浮式干船坞
102110	Floats for navigation	航海用浮舟
102126	Gangways for ships	船用舷梯
102112	Hydroplanes ［motor boats］	水面滑行快艇［摩托艇］
102100	Ice breakers	破冰船
102105	Launches	汽艇
102103	Life boats	救生艇
102118	Life rafts ［inflatable］	救生筏［充气式］
102096	Oars	桨
102128	Paddle wheels ［boat propulsion］	桨轮，明轮［船用推进器］
102114	Paddles for canoes	独木舟用桨
102115	Pontoons	趸船，浮舟
102111	Propellers for ships	船用推进器
102117	Rafts	筏子
102130	Rudders for ships	船舵
102123	Sailing boats	帆船
102122	Sails for ships	船帆
102111	Screws for ships	船的螺旋桨
102094	Ships	船
102116	Ships' keels	船的龙骨
102129	Ships' ladders	船的梯子
102113	Ships' masts	船的桅杆
102095	Ships' rigging	船的缆索
102107	Ships' superstructures	船的上部结构，船舶上层建筑

102121	Submarines	潜水艇	
102099	Tankers［ships］	油轮［船］	
102119	Trailer boats	拖船	
102106	Trawlers	拖网渔船	
102133	Trimarans	三体游艇	
102120	Tugboats	拖船	
102132	Turnbuckles for ships	船用螺旋扣	
104972	Underwater drones	水下机器人，水下无人机	【13】
104974	Underwater scooters	水下摩托车	【13】
104973	Water scooters［personal watercraft］	水上摩托车［摩托艇］	【13】
102124	Yachts	快艇，游艇	

12-07
Aircraft and space vehicles

12-07
航空器和太空运载工具

102134	Aeroplanes	飞机	
102135	Air balloons	热气球	
102134	Aircraft	航空器	
102136	Airships	飞船，飞艇	
104759	Drones［aircraft］	无人机［航空器］	【11】
104869	Flying boards	飞行板，悬浮滑板	【12】
102140	Gliders［aircraft］	滑翔机［航空器］	
102138	Gyroplanes	旋翼机	
102138	Helicopters	直升机	
102139	Hydroplanes［aircraft］	水上飞机［航空器］	
102137	Propellers for aircraft	航空器用推进器	
102143	Rudders for aircraft	航空器用方向舵	
102142	Space vehicles	太空运载工具	
102141	Stabilizers［aircraft］	水平尾翼［航空器］	

12-08
Motor cars，buses and lorries

Note：Including ambulances and refrigerator vans（road）.

12-08
汽车、公共汽车和货车

注：包括救护车和冷藏货车（公路）。

102144	Ambulances	救护车
102146	Automobiles	汽车
102145	Buses	公共汽车

102154	Cars driven electrically	电动汽车	
102152	Coaches	长途汽车	
102149	Garbage trucks	垃圾卡车	
102155	Go-karts ［motor-driven］	微型竞赛汽车，卡丁车［马达驱动式］	
102153	Hearses	灵车	
102151	Hoods for motor cars ［roof］	汽车车篷［车顶部］	
102148	Lorries	货车	
102159	Lorry loading platforms	货车装料台	
102147	Motor car bodies	汽车车身	
102146	Motor cars	汽车	
102148	Motor trucks	运货卡车	
102160	Racing cars	赛车	
102158	Refrigerator motor trucks	冷藏卡车	
102158	Refrigerator vans ［road］	冷藏货车［公路］	
102149	Refuse lorries	垃圾车	
102150	Tank trucks	油罐车	
102157	Trolleybuses	无轨电车	
102161	Vans ［lorries］	有篷货车［货车］	
102162	Vehicle bodywork	车辆车身	

12-09
Tractors

12-09
拖拉机

102163	Tractors	拖拉机	

12-10
Road vehicle trailers

Note：Including caravans.

12-10
公路车辆的挂车

注：包括篷车。

102164	Caravans	篷车	
102167	Itinerants' caravans	巡回篷车	
102165	Road vehicle trailers	公路车辆的挂车	
102166	Trailers ［camping］	挂车，挂车式活动房屋［野营］	

12-11
Cycles and motorcycles

12-11
自行车和摩托车

104572	Balance bikes	平衡训练车	【10】

102169	Bicycles	自行车	
102179	Brackets for cycle or motorcycle lamps	自行车或摩托车灯架	
102190	Brake levers for cycles or motorcycles	自行车或摩托车制动杆	
102199	Chain adjusters for cycles	自行车链调整器	
102196	Chain rings for cycles or motorcycles	自行车或摩托车链圈	
102196	Chain wheels for cycles or motorcycles	自行车或摩托车链盘	
104578	Chainguards for bicycles	自行车链罩	【10】
104589	Chainguards for motorcycles	摩托车链罩	【10】
102194	Chain-guides for cycle gear changes	自行车变速机构的导链器	
102173	Cycles	自行车	
104976	Delivery tricycles	送货三轮车	【13】
104975	Electric scooters	电动滑板车	【13】
102203	Fairings for motorcycles	摩托车的整流板、整流罩、导流罩	
102175	Forks for cycles or motorcycles	自行车或摩托车叉架	
102170	Frames for cycles or motorcycles	自行车或摩托车车架	
102197	Fuel tanks for motorcycles	摩托车油箱	
102172	Gear cases for cycles or motorcycles	自行车或摩托车齿转动装置外壳	
102189	Gear levers for cycles or motorcycles	自行车或摩托车用调速指拨、变速杆	
102202	Gear protectors for cycles	自行车齿轮防护罩、链罩	
102191	Handlebar grips	车把把套	
102177	Handlebars for cycles or motorcycles	自行车或摩托车车把	
102192	Luggage carriers for cycles or motorcycles	自行车或摩托车载物架	
102180	Monocycles	独轮车	
102174	Mopeds	机动脚踏两用车	
102184	Motor scooters	小型摩托车	
102188	Motor-assisted cycles	马达助力自行车	
102181	Motorcycles	摩托车	
102176	Mudguards for cycles or motorcycles	自行车或摩托车挡泥板	
102183	Pedal cranks for cycles or motorcycles	自行车或摩托车踏板曲柄	
102182	Pedals for cycles	自行车脚踏板	
102193	Pennant holders for cycles or motorcycles	自行车或摩托车旗架	
102178	Saddle covers for cycles or motorcycles	自行车或摩托车鞍座垫	
102185	Saddles for cycles or motorcycles	自行车或摩托车鞍座	
104656	Scooters	踏板车，滑板车	【10】
104870	Self-balancing boards	平衡滑板	【12】
104871	Self-balancing scooters	平衡车	【12】
102186	Sidecars	附于摩托车旁的单轮边车、跨斗	
102195	Sprocket wheels for cycles or motorcycles	自行车或摩托车链轮	

102168	Stands for cycles or motorcycles [retractable]	自行车或摩托车脚撑［可收放］	
102201	Tank covers for motorcycles	摩托车油箱盖	
102171	Toe clips for cycles	自行车踏脚套	
102204	Trailers for bicycles	自行车拖车	
102200	Tricycles [except toys]	三轮车［玩具除外］	
102187	Velocipedes	早期二轮三轮自行车	

12-12
Perambulators, invalid chairs, stretchers
Notes：(a) "Perambulators" means hand carriages for infants. (b) Not including toy perambulators (Cl. 21-01).

12-12
婴儿车、病人用轮椅、担架
注：(a)"婴儿车"指婴儿的手推车。(b) 不包括玩具婴儿车（21-01类）。

102212	Baby carriages	婴儿车	
102214	Baby walkers	婴儿学步助步车	
102207	Biers, wheeled	带轮棺材架、停尸架	
104977	Electric wheelchairs	电动轮椅	【13】
102213	Frames for pushchairs	折叠式婴儿车车架	
102213	Frames for strollers	手推童车的车架	【12】
102217	Handles for walking frames	助行架手柄	
102215	Invalid carriages	病人用滑动架	
102208	Invalid chairs	病人用轮椅	
104978	Mobility scooters	电动代步车，老年助力车	【13】
102209	Mudguards for baby carriages	婴儿车挡泥板	【12】
102209	Mudguards for perambulators	婴儿车挡泥板	
102212	Perambulators	婴儿车	
102210	Pushchairs	折叠式婴儿车	
102211	Quadricycles	手摇四轮车	
102206	Stretchers for the injured	伤员用担架	
102205	Stretchers, wheeled	带轮担架	
102210	Strollers	手推童车	
102216	Walking frames for disabled	残疾人用助行架	
102208	Wheelchairs	轮椅	
104651	Wheeled walkers	轮式扶车，助行车	【10】

12-13
Special-purpose vehicles

Notes: (a) Including only vehicles not specifically intended for transport, such as street cleaning vehicles, watering lorries, fire engines, snow ploughs and breakdown lorries. (b) Not including mixed-purpose agricultural machines (Cl. 15-03), or self-propelled machines for use in construction and civil engineering (Cl. 15-04).

12-13
专用车辆

注：(a) 仅包括不特定用于运输的车辆，如街道清洁车、洒水车、消防车、除雪犁车和救援车辆。(b) 不包括复合用途农业机械（15-03类）或用于建筑和土木工程的自驱动式机械（15-04类）。

102225	Armored vehicles	装甲车
102223	Breakdown vehicles	救援车
102226	Fire engines [vehicles]	消防车 [车辆]
102232	Golf buggies	高尔夫小车
102230	Ice machines [vehicles] for skating rinks	溜冰场整冰车 [车辆]
102222	Kitchens [mobile]	厨房 [移动式]
102231	Mobile shops	流动售货车
102227	Motor cars with platforms for watching races	带有观看比赛用平台的汽车
102228	Ski trail making devices	开辟滑雪道装置
102221	Snowplows [vehicles]	除雪犁车 [车辆]
102229	Snowblowers	吹雪机
102218	Sprinkling trucks	洒水车
102219	Street cleaning vehicles	街道清洁车
102219	Street-cleaning vehicles	街道清洁车
102224	Tanks [armored vehicles]	坦克 [装甲车辆]
102220	Trucks for liquid manure	液态肥料车
102218	Watering lorries	洒水车
102223	Wrecking cars	救援车

12-14
Other vehicles

Note: Including sleighs and air-cushion vehicles.

12-14
其他交通工具

注：包括雪橇、气垫车和气垫船。

102240	Air cushion vehicles	气垫车，气垫船
102233	Amphibian vehicles	水陆两用车
102236	Bob-sleighs	长橇
102235	Ice boats	冰上滑行船
102242	Kick-sleds	冰上或雪上用脚蹬滑行车

102241	Rescue sleds	营救雪橇	
102238	Ski bobs	雪橇车	
102237	Sleds	雪橇	
102234	Sleighs	马拉的雪橇	
102239	Sleighs [self propelled]	雪地车［自驱动式］	
102198	Snowmobiles	雪上摩托车	【13】[1]
104979	Snow scooters	雪地滑板车	【13】
102237	Toboggans	平底雪橇	

12-15
Tyres and anti-skid chains for vehicles

12-15
交通工具的轮胎和防滑链

102246	Anti-skid chains	防滑链
102250	Inner tube valve caps for pneumatic tyres	充气轮胎用内胎的阀盖
102244	Inner tubes for pneumatic tyres	充气轮胎用内胎
102245	Pneumatic tyres	充气轮胎
102247	Tyre spikes	轮胎毛刺
102247	Tyre studs	轮胎防滑钉
102248	Tyre treads	轮胎胎面
102243	Tyres for vehicle wheels, pneumatic	车轮的充气轮胎
102249	Valves for vehicle tyres	轮胎用气嘴

12-16
Parts, equipment and accessories for vehicles, not included in other classes or subclasses

Notes: (a) Not including safety belts for the seats of vehicles (Cl. 29-02), door handles for vehicles (Cl. 08-06). (b) Not including pantographs for electric locomotives or trams (Cl. 13-03).

12-16
其他大类或小类未包括的交通工具零部件、装置和附件

注：(a) 不包括交通工具座位安全带（29-02类）和交通工具门把手（08-06类）。(b) 不包括电力机车和有轨电车用集电弓（13-03类）。 【11】

102301	Accelerator pedals for vehicles	交通工具油门踏板
102273	Air-intake grilles for vehicles	交通工具进风口格栅
102254	Anchors	锚
102255	Anti-dazzle devices for vehicles	交通工具防眩装置
102279	Anti-glare windshields	防眩风挡玻璃
102258	Arms of windscreen wipers	风挡刮水器臂

1　由 12-11 类转移至 12-14 类。

102298	Balance weights for vehicle wheels	交通工具用轮平衡配重	
104980	Bicycle racks for vehicles	交通工具用自行车车架	【13】
102292	Boat fenders	护舷物，碰垫	
102300	Brake blocks for vehicles	交通工具制动闸瓦、刹车片	
102305	Brake shoes for vehicles	交通工具制动闸皮	
102271	Brakes for vehicles	交通工具制动器	
102303	Bumper guards	保险杠的护挡、防撞条	
102280	Bumpers for vehicles	交通工具保险杠	
102323	Cabins for vehicles	交通工具座舱	
102317	Central consoles for vehicles	交通工具用中控台	
102264	Chocks [to prevent vehicles from moving]	垫块［防止车辆移动］	
102316	Control and indicator panels for vehicles	交通工具用控制和指示面板	
102274	Covers for vehicles	交通工具盖外壳	
102290	Dashboards for vehicles	交通工具仪表板	
102257	Decorative beading for vehicles	交通工具装饰条	
102269	Decorative fittings for vehicles	交通工具装饰配件	
102267	Defrosters for vehicles	交通工具用除霜器	
102312	Door protectors for vehicles	交通工具门保护装置	
102293	Drag hooks for vehicles	交通工具拖钩	
102259	Earthing tapes against static electricity for vehicles	交通工具用防静电接地带	
102306	Exhaust pipes	排气管	
102270	Fittings for rearview mirrors	后视镜配件	
102295	Fittings for vehicle bonnets	交通工具引擎盖配件	
102315	Gear lever knobs	变速杆捏手	
102314	Gear levers	变速杆	
102297	Hand crank starters	手摇曲柄起动器	
102311	Handbrake levers	手刹车拉杆	
102319	Hatches for vehicles	交通工具舱口盖	
102268	Hub caps	轮毂盖	
102277	Hubs of vehicle wheels	轮毂	
102320	Interior linings for vehicles	交通工具内饰板	
102302	Luggage carriers for vehicles [except for cycles and motorcycles]	交通工具用行李架［自行车和摩托车除外］	
102261	Mud flaps for vehicles	交通工具挡泥板	
102272	Mudguards for motor cars	汽车挡泥板	
104982	Overhead consoles for vehicles	交通工具用顶置控制台	【13】
102252	Portholes	舷窗	

102299	Propeller hubs［for vehicles］	推进器毂［交通工具用］	
102304	Radiator cap ornaments	散热器罩装饰物	
102262	Radiator caps for vehicles	交通工具用散热器盖	
102283	Radiator covers for vehicles	交通工具用散热器罩	
102263	Radiator grilles for vehicles	交通工具用散热器格栅	
102284	Radiators for vehicles	交通工具用散热器、水箱	
102266	Rearview mirror cups	后视镜镜座	
102287	Rearview mirrors for vehicles［inside］	交通工具后视镜［内部］	
104760	Roof boxes for vehicles	车顶箱，车顶行李箱	【11】
102276	Running boards for road vehicles	公路车辆用脚踏板	
104981	Side view mirrors for vehicles［outside］	交通工具侧后视镜［外部］	【13】
102282	Ski racks for vehicles	车顶雪橇架	
102309	Spoilers for motor cars	汽车扰流板	
102285	Spokes for vehicle wheels	轮辐条	
102307	Steering wheels	方向盘	
102281	Sun visors for vehicles	交通工具用遮阳板	
102291	Suspension shock absorbers for road vehicles	公路车辆悬置减震器	
102286	Suspension springs for road vehicles	公路车辆悬挂弹簧	
102289	Suspensions for road vehicles	公路车辆悬挂装置	
102306	Tailpipes	排气管	
102260	Tow bars for vehicles	交通工具牵引杆	
102293	Tow hooks for vehicles	交通工具牵引钩	
102265	Tracks for track-laying vehicles	履带式车辆用履带	
102308	Tractor cabins	牵引车座舱	
102256	Trailer hitches for vehicles	交通工具用拖钩	
102298	Tyre balancers［weights］	轮胎平衡配重块［重物］	
102318	Vanity mirrors for vehicles	交通工具梳妆镜	
102253	Vehicle bonnets	交通工具引擎盖	
102251	Vehicle couplings	交通工具连接器	
102322	Vehicle doors	交通工具门	
102313	Vehicle passenger compartments	乘客车厢	
102310	Vehicle wheel covers［for transport］	交通工具轮罩［运输用］	
102275	Vehicle wheel rims	轮缘，轮辋	
102321	Vehicle wings	交通工具翼板	
104873	Washer jets for vehicles	交通工具的风挡清洗器喷嘴	【12】
104872	Washer reservoirs for vehicles	交通工具的风挡清洗器水箱	【12】
102288	Wheels for vehicles［except for rail vehi-	车轮，轮子［铁路车辆除外］	

cles]

102294	Wind deflectors [for vehicles]	挡风板[交通工具用]
102296	Windscreen wiper blades	风挡刮水器刮片
102278	Windscreens for vehicles	交通工具用挡风玻璃
102278	Windshields for vehicles	交通工具用挡风玻璃

12-17

Railway infrastructure components

Note: Not including railway rails and sleepers (Cl. 25-01), buffers for railway terminals (Cl. 25-99) and railway signals (Cl. 10-06).

12-17

铁路基础设施零件

注：不包括铁轨和铁路轨枕（25-01类）、铁轨终端缓冲垫（25-99类）和铁路信号设备（10-06类）。

【12】[1]

102325	Rail anchors	钢轨固定装置，钢轨地脚
102326	Rail joints	轨道接头
102324	Railway points	铁路道岔
102324	Railway switches	轨道转辙器
102327	Railway turntables	铁路转车台

12-99

Miscellaneous

12-99

其他杂项

| 102328 | Catapults for aeroplanes | 飞机弹射器 |
| 102329 | Wiping devices for oil dipsticks | 量油尺用擦油装置 |

---

[1] 新增 12-17 类，产品项由 12-99 类转移至 12-17 类。

Class 13
Equipment for production, distribution or transformation of electricity

Notes: (a) Including only apparatus which produces, distributes or transforms electric current. (b) Including electric motors, however. (c) Not including electrically-driven apparatus, such as electric watches (Cl. 10-02), or apparatus for the measurement of electric current (Cl. 10-04).

13-01
Generators and motors

Note: Including electric motors for vehicles.

102330	Dynamos
102331	Generators, electric
102332	Motors, electric
102333	Rotors of electric motors and generators
102334	Stators of electric motors and generators

13-02
Power transformers, rectifiers, batteries and accumulators

102349	Accumulator charging apparatus	
102344	Accumulator jars	
102346	Accumulator plates	
102336	Accumulators, electric	
102338	Apparatus for electrifying cattle fences	
102337	Batteries, electric	
102352	Battery boxes for portable telephones	
102354	Battery charger housings	
104874	Battery charging cases for mobile devices	【12】
102346	Battery plates	
104984	Charging stations for electric vehicles	【13】
104983	Charging stations for mobile devices	【13】

13 类
发电、配电或变电设备

注：(a)仅包括发电、配电或变电的设备。(b)也包括电动机。(c)不包括电动设备，例如电子表（10-02类）或电流测量仪（10-04类）。

13-01
发电机和电动机

注：包括交通工具的电动机。

直流发电机
发电机
电动机
电动机和发电机的转子
电动机和发电机的定子

13-02
电力变压器、整流器、电池和蓄电池

蓄电池充电设备
蓄电瓶
蓄电池极板
蓄电池
牲畜栅栏供电设备
电池
移动电话电池盒
电池充电器
移动设备用背夹电池
电池极板
电动交通工具充电站
移动设备充电站

104875	Current inverters	电流逆变器，变流器	【12】
102347	Current rectifiers	整流器	
102340	Dry batteries	干电池	
102351	Electrical chargers for telephones	电话用充电器	
102335	Grids for accumulators	蓄电池栅板	
102345	Ignition coils for motors	发动机点火线圈	
102343	Induction coils	感应线圈	
102350	Power supply units, universal	通用的电源装置	
102353	Rechargeable batteries	可充电电池	
102348	Self-induction coils	自感线圈	
102339	Step-down and step-up transformers	降压和升压变压器	
102339	Step-up and step-down transformers	升压和降压变压器	
102342	Transformers	变压器	
102341	Voltage regulators	电压调节器，稳压器	

13-03 Equipment for distribution or control of electric power

Note: Including conductors, switches and switchboards.

13-03 配电或电力控制设备

注：包括导线、导电体、开关、电闸和配电盘。

102355	Adapters for electrical connector sockets	电插座插头	
102356	Bows collectors for electric locomotives tramcars	电力机车或有轨电车用集电弓	
102388	Branch boxes [electricity]	分线盒[电力]	
102391	Cable clips [electricity]	电缆夹[电力]	
104762	Cable protectors	线缆保护物	【11】
102402	Cable terminal shoes	电缆端接头	
102359	Cables, electric	电缆	
102387	Capacitors	电容器	
102365	Circuit breakers	电路断路器	
102363	Conductors, electric	导电体，导线	
102390	Conduits [electricity]	导线管[电力]	
102371	Connecting plugs for coaxial cables	同轴电缆用连接插头	
102364	Connectors [electricity]	连接器[电力]	
102385	Contact breakers	接触式断路器，触断器	
102389	Contact plugs	接触插头	
102377	Contact poles for electric locomotives or tramcars	电力机车或有轨电车用集电杆	

102395	Control panels [electricity]	控制板，配电板[电力]	
102366	Covers for electric switches	电开关盖	
102367	Cut-outs	断路器	
102370	Decorative fittings for electric switches and sockets	电开关和插座用装饰配件	
102395	Distribution boards [electricity]	配电盘[电力]	
102401	Electrified rails for mounting spot lights	安装聚光灯用电轨	
102369	Electrodes	电极	
102361	Equipment for control of electric power	电力控制设备	
102368	Equipment for distribution of electric power	电力配电设备	
102378	Fuse holders	保险丝支架，熔丝座	
102374	Fuse terminals [electricity]	保险丝接柱，保险丝端钮[电力]	
102373	Fuses [electricity]	保险丝[电力]	
104761	Heat sinks	散热器，散热片	【11】
102396	Housings for electric conductors	导电体的外壳	
102399	Identification sheaths for electric conductors	导线识别包层	
102372	Insulated electric wires	绝缘电导线	
102375	Insulators [electricity]	绝缘体[电力]	
102388	Junction boxes [electricity]	接线盒，分线箱[电力]	
102400	Light dimmers	灯调光器	
102398	Marking caps [electricity]	标识端头[电力]	
102376	Pantographs for electric locomotives or tramcars	电力机车或有轨电车用集电弓	
102379	Potentiometers	电位器	
102380	Power points [electricity]	电源插座[电力]	
102381	Reducers [electricity]	节电器[电力]	
102382	Relays, electric	继电器	
102357	Resistance boxes [electricity]	电阻箱[电力]	
102383	Resistances [electricity]	电阻[电力]	
102384	Rheostats	变阻器	
102360	Safety covers for electric sockets	电插座安全罩	
102397	Sheathing for electric conductors	导电体表皮	
102380	Sockets [electricity]	插座[电力]	
102393	Stabilizers [electricity]	稳定器[电力]	
104665	Surge protection devices	过载保护设备，电涌保护设备	【10】
102394	Switchboards for electric connections	用于电连接的配电盘	
102362	Switches [electricity]	开关，电闸[电力]	

102358	Terminals [electricity]	接线柱，接线端子[电力]	
102386	Two-way switches	双向开关	
102392	Wire connectors [electricity]	接线器[电力]	

13-04
Solar equipment

Note: Not including solar heat collectors (Cl. 23-03).

13-04
太阳能设备

注：不包括太阳能集热器（23-03类）。

【12】[1]

104985	Portable solar power supplies	太阳能移动电源	【13】
102404	Solar cells	太阳能电池	
104662	Solar panels	太阳能电池板	【10】
104763	Supports for solar panels	太阳能电池板支架	【11】

13-99
Miscellaneous

13-99
其他杂项

102403	Electro-magnets	电磁铁	
104986	Electrostatic eliminators	除静电设备	【13】

---

[1] 新增13-04类，产品项由13-99类转移至13-04类。

Class 14
Recording, telecommunication or data processing equipment

14 类
记录、电信或数据处理设备 【12】[1]

14-01

Equipment for the recording or reproduction of sounds or pictures

Note: Not including photographic or cinematographic apparatus (Cl. 16).

14-01

声音或图像的记录或再现设备

注：不包括照相或电影摄影设备（16类）。

104764	Audio mixers	音频混频器，混音器，调音台	【11】
102428	Audio and video apparatus for reproducing sounds or images	再现声音或图像的音频和视频设备	
102422	Audiovisual teaching apparatus	视听教学设备	
102409	Baffles for loudspeakers	扬声器面板	
102426	Cassette players	磁带播放机，卡式录音机	
102408	Dictating apparatus	听写装置	
102430	Digital versatile disc players [DVD players]	数字多功能光盘播放器[DVD播放器]	
102431	Earphones for monitoring broadcasts or recordings	用于监听播音或录音的耳机	
102418	Electrophones	电唱机	
102419	Headphones	头戴式耳机	
102423	Horns for loudspeakers	扬声器用喇叭	
102411	Jukeboxes	自动唱片点唱机	
104987	Karaoke booths	自助K歌亭	【13】
102425	Laser disc players	激光光盘播放器	
102410	Loudspeakers	扬声器	
102414	Microphones [except for telephones]	麦克风[电话机用除外]	
102429	MP3 players	MP3播放器	
102415	Phonographs	电唱机，留声机	
102424	Portable audio cassette players	便携式磁带播放器，便携式录音机	
104643	Portable digital multimedia players	便携式数字多媒体播放器	【10】
102420	Radio headphones	带收音机的头戴式耳机	
102407	Record changers	自动换片器	
102405	Record player needles	电唱机唱针	
102416	Record player turntables	电唱机转盘	

---

1 由 "Recording, communication or information retrieval equipment 记录、通信、信息检索设备" 修改为 "Recording, telecommunication or data processing equipment 记录、电信或数据处理设备"。

102418	Record players	电唱机	
102427	Recorders for magnetic optical discs	磁光盘录音/录像机	
104988	Smart speakers	智能音箱	【13】
102412	Talking machines	留声机	
102406	Tape recorders	磁带录音机	
102417	Telephone answering apparatus	电话机自动应答设备	
102421	Tone arms for record players	电唱机的拾音臂	
102413	Video tape recorders	磁带录像机	

14-02

Data processing equipment as well as peripheral apparatus and devices

14-02

数据处理设备及其外围设备和装置

102449	Anti-noise casings for computer printers	用于计算机打印机的降噪声罩壳	
102448	Bar code readers	条形码阅读器	
102435	Card punches ［data processing］	卡片穿孔机［数据处理］	
102453	Cartridges for computer printers	计算机打印机的墨盒	
102456	Compact disc players ［data processing］	光盘驱动器［数据处理］	
102443	Computer casings	计算机机箱	
102460	Computer interfaces	计算机接口	
102452	Computer mouses	计算机鼠标	
102441	Computer plotters	计算机绘图仪，喷绘机	
102455	Computer printers	计算机打印机	
102444	Computer screens	计算机屏幕	
102454	Computer terminals	电脑终端机，计算机终端设备	
102434	Computers	计算机	
104989	Cryptocurrency wallets	加密货币钱包	【13】
102439	Data processing equipment	数据处理设备	
102468	Data transmission devices ［data processing］	数据传输设备［数据处理］	
104880	Devices for the projection of virtual keyboards	虚拟键盘的投影设备	【12】
102462	Digital picture frames	数码相框	
102447	Disk drives	磁盘驱动器	
102438	Document sorting machines ［data processing］	文件分类器［数据处理］	
104603	E-book readers	电子阅读器，电子书	【10】
102459	Electronic devices for reading magnetic cards	磁卡读取电子装置	

102442	Electronic pocket diaries	电子袖珍记事簿，电子袖珍词典	
102467	Handheld computers	掌上电脑	
102457	Hard disc players	硬盘驱动器	
102450	Joysticks for computers	计算机操纵杆	
102432	Keyboards for card perforators	卡片穿孔机键盘	
102440	Keyboards for data equipment	数据设备键盘	
104876	Keys for computer keyboards	电脑键盘的按键	【12】
102446	Micro-computers	微型计算机	
102451	Monitors［data processing］	显示器，监视显示器［数据处理］	
104877	Mouse scanners［data processing］	鼠标扫描器［数据处理］	【12】
104768	Multifunction printers	多功能打印机	【11】
102458	Multimedia communication terminals	多媒体通信终端	
102461	Network switches for computers	计算机网络交换机	
102463	Notebooks［laptop computers］	笔记本电脑［便携式电脑］	
104766	Point-of-sale［POS］terminals	销售点［POS］终端机	【11】
102433	Readers［data processing］	读出器，读卡器［数据处理］	
104649	Reading and talking pens	点读笔	【10】
102437	Scanners for punched cards	穿孔卡片用扫描器	
102445	Scanners［data processing］	扫描器，扫描仪［数据处理］	
104767	Security tokens［encryption devices］	安全令牌，密钥［密码装置］	【11】
104878	Slide scanners [data processing]	底片扫描仪、幻灯片扫描仪［数据处理］	【12】
104879	Somatosensory detectors [computer interfaces]	体感感应器［计算机接口］	【12】
104667	Tablet computers	平板电脑	【10】
102436	Tabulators for punched cards	穿孔卡片用制表机	
104990	Terminals for recharging electronic payment cards	电子支付卡充值终端	【13】
102466	Terminals with screens for Internet access	带显示器的联网终端	
102465	Touch screens	触摸式显示屏	
104882	Virtual reality glasses	虚拟现实眼镜	【12】
104881	Virtual reality headsets	头戴式虚拟现实设备	【12】
104765	Wrist tablet computers	腕戴式平板电脑	【11】

14-03

Telecommunications equipment, wireless remote controls and radio amplifiers

Note: Including telephone and television apparatus, as well as radio sets.

14-03

电信设备、无线遥控设备和无线电放大器 【12】[1]

注：包括电话和电视设备，以及无线电设备。

编号	英文名称	中文名称	备注
102473	Aerials for vehicles	交通工具用天线	
102523	Antenna sockets	天线插座	
102512	Basic apparatus for wireless telephones	无线电话机的基础设备	
104883	Beacons for wireless devices	无线设备用信标	【12】
102496	Communications equipment	通信设备	
102518	Cordless modems	无线调制解调器	
102517	Digital pagers	数字寻呼机	
102477	Emergency call boxes ［roadside］	应急呼救电话机箱［路边］	
102507	Facsimile machines	传真机	【11】
102507	Fax machines	传真机	【11】[2]
102476	Frame aerials ［radio and television］	框形天线［收音机和电视］	
102478	Frequency converters［radio and television］	频率转换器［收音机和电视］	
102524	Global positioning devices ［GPS］	全球定位装置［GPS］	
104772	Handheld wireless voting apparatus	手持无线投票装置	【11】
102528	Headsets for telephones ［earphones and microphones combined］	电话机的头戴式送受话器［耳机和话筒结合］	【10】
102474	Honeycomb coils for wireless apparatus	用于无线电设备的蜂窝线圈	
102503	Indicator boards ［call bells］	呼叫器板［呼叫铃］	
102521	Intercom phones	内部通话电话机	
102484	Intercommunication devices	内部通话装置	
104992	Live video broadcasting devices	视频直播机	【13】
102487	Megaphones	喊话筒，喇叭筒，传声筒	
102485	Microphones for telephones	电话机话筒	
102486	Microtelephones	小型话机	
102525	Mobile telephones	移动电话机	
102508	Modems	调制解调器	
102526	Navigational devices	导航装置	
104771	Phablets	平板手机	【11】
102519	Portable telephones	便携式电话机	
102471	Radio aerials	无线电设备用天线	

1　由"Communications equipment，wireless remote controls and radio amplifiers 通信设备、无线电遥控设备和无线电放大器"修改为"Telecommunications equipment ，wireless remote controls and radio amplifiers 电信设备、无线遥控设备和无线电放大器"。

2　由"Telecopiers 电传复印机"修改为"Fax machines 传真机"。

102475	Radio dials	无线电调谐度盘	
104991	Radio-frequency identification ［RFID］ bracelets	RFID 腕带，射频识别腕带	【13】
102490	Radio receivers	无线电接收机，收音机	
102488	Radiogoniometers	无线电测向器	
102489	Radios for vehicles	交通工具用无线电装置	
102513	Remote controls ［wireless］	遥控装置［无线电］	
102522	Satellite receivers	卫星接收机	
102516	Screens for telephony	电话机屏幕	
104770	Smartphones	智能手机	【11】
102470	Sound amplifiers	声音放大器	
102506	Speaking tubes	通话管	
102505	Street emergency telephone posts	路面应急电话柱	
102504	Switchboards for telecommunications	电信交换机	
102509	Telecommunication apparatus	电信设备	
102480	Telephone dials	电话机拨号盘	
102493	Telephone exchanges	电话交换机	
102520	Telephone handsets	电话机送话器	
102481	Telephone receivers	电话机受话器	
102469	Telephone relays	电话中继装置	【10】
102499	Telephones	电话机	
102472	Television aerials	电视天线	
102501	Television apparatus	电视设备	
102511	Television decoders	电视解码器	
102510	Video screens ［large screen television］	电视屏幕［大屏幕电视］	
102514	Videophones	电视电话	
102502	Videotelephony apparatus	电视电话设备	
102482	Walkie-talkie radios	无线对讲机	
104686	Wireless laser presentation remote controls	无线激光演示遥控装置，激光笔，翻页笔	【10】
102494	Wireless sets	无线电装置	
102515	Wireless tuners	无线电调谐器	
104769	Wrist smartphones	腕戴式智能手机	【11】

14-04
Screen displays and icons

Note: Including those for goods belonging to other classes.

14-04
显示界面和图标

注：包括属于其他大类的产品的显示界面和图标。

【8】

【10】

102529	Graphical user interfaces[computer screen layout]	图形用户界面[计算机屏幕版面设计]	
104993	Graphic symbols for screen display	屏幕显示的图形符号	【13】
102530	Icons [for computers]	图标[计算机用]	
104994	Web banners	网页横幅	【13】

14-05
Recording and data storage media

14-05
记录数据和存储数据的介质

【12】[1]

102535	Cartridges for magnetic tapes	磁带盒	
102535	Cassettes for magnetic tapes	磁带盒	
102538	Compact discs	光盘	
102539	Computer cassettes for discs	计算机磁盘盒	
102537	Floppy discs	软盘	
102533	Magnetic tapes	磁带	
102550	Memory cards [electronic]	记忆卡，存储卡[电子]	
102534	Phonograph records	留声机唱片	
102464	USB memory devices	USB 存储设备	

14-06
Holders, stands and supports for electronic equipment, not included in other classes

14-06
其他类未列入的电子设备用支架、立架和支撑装置

【12】[2]

101404	Brackets for radio sets for vehicles	交通工具用收音机托架	
102548	Computer keyboard stands	计算机键盘支架	
102544	Fixing devices [brackets] for loudspeakers	扬声器用固定装置[支架]	
102551	Holders for remote controls	遥控装置支架	
104775	Selfie sticks	自拍杆	【11】
102541	Stands for loudspeakers	扬声器立架	
104774	Stands for mobile telephones	移动电话立架	【11】
102540	Supports for computer terminals	计算机终端用支撑装置	

---

1 新增加 14-05 类，产品项由 14-99 类转移至 14-05 类。
2 新增加 14-06 类，产品项由 08-08 类和 14-99 类转移至 14-06 类。

102543	Supports for telephones	电话机用支撑装置	
102542	Supports for television apparatus	电视设备用支撑装置	

14-99　　　　　　　　　　　　　　　　　　　　　　14-99
Miscellaneous　　　　　　　　　　　　　　　　　　其他杂项

102547	Boxes for compact discs［packaging］	光盘盒［包装］	
102546	Computer mouse pads	计算机鼠标垫	
102549	Data transmission cables	数据传输线缆	
102531	Demagnetization apparatus	去磁装置	
102536	Electronic tubes	电子管	
104884	Optical fiber connectors	光纤连接器	【12】
102532	Photo-transmission diodes	图像传输二极管	
102545	Protective filters for visual display units	显示器用视力保护滤光器	
104664	Styluses for touch screens	触屏笔，电子笔	【10】
104773	USB hubs	USB 集线器	【11】

Class 15
Machines, not elsewhere specified

15 类
其他类未列入的机械

15-01
Engines

Notes: (a) Including non-electric engines for vehicles. (b) Not including electric motors (Cl. 13).

15-01
发动机

注：(a) 包括交通工具的非电力发动机。(b) 不包括电动机（13类）。

104778	Actuators [machines]	作动器，促动器 [机械]	【11】
102553	Carburettors for motors	发动机汽化器、化油器	
102555	Cylinders for motors	发动机气缸	
102570	Electronic boxes for engines	发动机电子盒	
102567	Engine heaters	发动机加热器	
102557	Engine pistons	发动机活塞	
102569	Engine units	发动机组	
104776	Exhaust manifolds for combustion engines	内燃机排气歧管	【11】
102556	Exhaust silencers	排气消声器	
104777	Filters for engines	发动机过滤器	【11】
102554	Gear and gearing casings	齿轮箱，变速箱	
102552	Hot air engines	热空气发动机，热气机	
102565	Ignition regulators for motors	发动机点火调节器	
102558	Jet engines	喷气式发动机	
102559	Motors	发动机	
102561	Mufflers for motors	发动机消声器	
102561	Silencers for motors	发动机消声器	
102564	Sparking plugs for motors	发动机火花塞	
102566	Steam engines	蒸汽机	
102560	Turbine rotors	涡轮机转子	
102562	Turbine stators	涡轮机定子	
102563	Turbines	涡轮机	
102568	Valves for engines	发动机气缸气门	
104678	Ventilators for engines	发动机通风装置	【10】

15-02
Pumps and compressors

Note: Not including hand or foot pumps (Cl. 08-05), or fire extinguishing pumps (Cl. 29-01).

15-02
泵和压缩机

注：不包括手动、脚动的泵（08-05类），或消防泵（29-01类）。

102572	Air dispensers for inflating tyres	轮胎充气桩

102578	Air pumps for condensers	冷凝器气泵
102577	Air pumps for laboratories	实验室气泵
102581	Boiler feed pumps	锅炉给水泵
102583	Central heating pumps	集中供暖泵
102580	Centrifugal pumps	离心泵
102571	Compressors	压缩机
102579	Direct-action pumps	直动泵
102576	Fuel injection pumps	燃料喷射泵
102584	Grease guns［machines］	注油泵［机械］
102577	Laboratory air pumps	实验室气泵
102575	Pumps for inflating tyres［machines］	轮胎充气泵［机械］
102573	Pumps for liquids	液体泵
102582	Suction and injection pumps for brine	盐水抽吸及压注泵
102574	Vacuum pumps	真空泵，真空抽气机

15-03

Agricultural and forestry machinery

Notes:（a）Including ploughs and combined machinery, i.e., both machines and vehicles, for example, reaping and binding machines.（b）Not including hand tools（Cl. 08）.

15-03

农业和林业机械 【12】[1]

注:（a）包括犁和既是机器又是交通工具的联合机械，例如收割捆扎机。(b) 不包括手动工具（08类）。

102585	Agricultural machines	农业机械
102620	Beet lifters［machines］	甜菜挖掘机［机械］
102622	Binding and reaping machines	收割捆扎机
102603	Chaffcutter blades	切草机刀片
102604	Chaffcutters	切草机
102594	Fertilizer spreaders	施肥机
102623	Fodder presses	饲料压扎机
102600	Fumigators for the treatment of plants	用于作物处理的熏蒸消毒器
102601	Grain driers［machines］	谷物干燥机［机械］
102602	Grain separators	谷物清选机
102605	Harrows［agricultural machines］	耙［农业机械］
102814	Harvesters [forest]	收割机［林木］
102592	Hay cutters［machines］	干草切割机［机械］
102598	Hay tedders［machines］	干草翻晒机［机械］
102588	Hoeing machines	锄地机

---

[1] 由"Agricultural machinery 农业机械"修改为"Agricultural and forestry machinery 农业和林业机械"。产品项"Harvesters [forest] 收割机［林木］"和"Machines for felling trees 伐木机"由15-99类转移至15-03类。

102611	Land rollers [machines]	田间滚轧机[机械]
102626	Lawn aerators	草坪打孔通气机
102624	Lawn mowers	草坪修剪机
104631	Lawn trimmers	草坪修剪机，割草机
102591	Lime spreaders [agriculture]	石灰撒播机[农业]
102781	Machines for felling trees	伐木机
102610	Machines for pricking out	移植机
102619	Machines for the chemical treatment of plants	作物的药物处理机
102595	Manure spreaders	肥料撒播机
102617	Milking machines	挤奶机
102599	Mowing machines [agriculture]	割草机[农业]
102608	Planting machines	播种机
102590	Ploughs	犁
102606	Ploughshare blades	犁头刀片
102590	Plows	犁
102606	Plowshare blades	犁头刀片
102615	Plowshares	犁头
102586	Potato diggers [machines]	土豆挖掘机[机械]
102607	Power driven cultivators	动力驱动耕耘机
102609	Rakes [machines]	耙[机械]
102622	Reaping and binding machines	收割捆扎机
102627	Robotic lawn mowers	自动草坪修剪机
102618	Root slicers [machines]	块茎切割机[机械]
102613	Scarifiers [agriculture]	松土机[农业]
102614	Seeders	播种机
102614	Sowing machines	播种机
102597	Steam driers [agriculture]	蒸汽干燥机[农业]
102596	Stone removing machines for grain	谷物去石机
102616	Sulfurators [agriculture]	硫化处理机械[农业]
102587	Threshing machines	脱粒机
102593	Top-cutting machines for root crops	块根作物切顶机
102625	Tree-dozers	推树机，除根机
102589	Trussing machines	捆束机
102621	Vineyard plows	葡萄园用犁
102612	Weeding machines	除草机

【10】

15-04
Construction and mining machinery

Notes: (a) Including machines used in civil engineering and self-propelled machines such as excavators, concrete mixers and dredgers. (b) Not including hoists and cranes (Cl. 12-05).

15-04
建筑机械、采矿机械、选矿机械 【12】[1]

注: (a) 包括土木工程用的机械、自驱动式机械, 例如挖掘机、混凝土搅拌机和挖泥机。
(b) 不包括提升机和起重机 (12-05类)。

102803	Apparatus for boring the ground	钻地设备
102630	Bulldozers	推土机
102633	Civil engineering machines	土木工程机械
102629	Concrete mixers	混凝土搅拌机
102628	Construction machines	建筑机械
102789	Crushers	轧碎机
102642	Dredger buckets	挖泥机铲斗
102631	Dredgers	挖泥机
102638	Drilling machines [construction]	钻孔机[建筑]
102641	Excavator buckets	挖掘机铲斗
102632	Excavators	挖掘机
102635	Mixing machines [construction]	搅拌机, 混合机[建筑]
102784	Ore crushers	矿石破碎机
102811	Ore separators	选矿机
102636	Pile driver rams	打桩机夯锤
102640	Road making machines	筑路机
102643	Road rollers [motor driven]	压路机[动力驱动]
102812	Rock drills	凿石机
102797	Rock drills [machines]	钻岩机[机械]
102637	Shovels, mechanical	单斗挖掘机
102634	Tar spraying machines	柏油喷洒机, 沥青喷洒机
102639	Vibrators [construction]	振捣机[建筑]
102796	Winding machines [mining]	矿井提升机械[采矿]

15-05
Washing, cleaning and drying machines

Notes: (a) Including appliances and machines for treating linen and clothes, such as ironing machines and wringers. (b) Including dishwashing machines and industrial drying equipment.

15-05
洗涤、清洁和干燥机械

注: (a) 包括亚麻制品、服装的处理设备和机械, 例如熨平机、绞干机。(b) 包括碗盘清洗机和工业干燥设备。

102673	Automatic cleaners for swimming pools	游泳池自动清洁器

---

1 由 "Construction machinery 建筑机械" 修改为 "Construction and mining machinery 建筑机械、采矿机械、选矿机械"。"采矿机械、选矿机械" 由 15-99 类转移至 15-04 类。

102673	Automatic swimming pool cleaners	游泳池自动清洁器	
102665	Boot and shoe polishing machines	靴及鞋的擦光机	
102661	Bottle washing machines	刷瓶机	
102649	Brushing machines for shoes	刷鞋机	
104996	Cabinets for cleaning and freshening clothing	衣物清洁清新柜	【13】
102646	Carpet beating vacuum cleaners	地毯拍打真空吸尘器	
102671	Carpet shampooers	地毯清洗机	
102666	Centrifugal drying machines	离心干燥机	
102674	Cleaner heads [including brushes]	清洁器头[包括刷子]	
102669	Clothes driers [machines]	衣物干燥机[机械]	
102652	Dish racks for dishwashers [machines]	洗碗机的碗碟架[机械]	
102655	Dishwashers [machines]	洗碗机[机械]	
102644	Drying cabinets	干燥箱	
102663	Drying machines	干燥机	
102654	Drying machines for laundry purposes	洗衣房用干燥机	
104998	Dust mite vacuum cleaners	除螨仪	【13】
102667	Filling indicators for vacuum cleaners	真空吸尘器用填塞指示器	
102659	Floor cleaning machines	地板清洁机	
102651	Floor polishers, electric	地板电动抛光机，地板电动打蜡机	
102670	High-pressure cleaners	高压清洗机，高压清洁器	
102660	Ironing machines	熨平机，熨烫机	
102648	Laundry apparatus	洗衣房设备	
102659	Machines for cleaning floors	地板清洁机	
102668	Machines for washing drinking glasses	玻璃杯清洗机	【12】[1]
102650	Mangles	衣物轧干机，衣物脱水机	
102662	Rinsing machines for barrels	刷桶机	
104885	Robotic vacuum cleaners	机器人吸尘器，扫地机器人	【12】
102653	Sewer cleaning machines	下水道清洁机	
102658	Shoe cleaning machines	鞋类清洁机	
104779	Steam mops	蒸汽拖把	【11】
104995	Sterilizing cabinets [except for medical purposes]	消毒柜[非医用]	【13】
104780	Sweeping machines for chimneys	烟囱清扫机	【11】
102664	Transparent doors for washing machines	洗衣机用透明门	
104997	Ultrasonic washing devices [portable]	超声波洗衣设备[便携式]	【13】
102645	Vacuum cleaners [industry or household]	真空吸尘器[工业或家用]	

1　由"Washing machines for glasses 眼镜清洗机"修改为"Machines for washing drinking glasses 玻璃杯清洗机"。

102647	Washing installations for motor cars	汽车用清洗设备	
102656	Washing machines	洗衣机	
102657	Washing machines for laundry purposes	洗衣房用洗衣机	
102672	Water suction apparatus	吸水设备	

15-06

Textile, sewing, knitting and embroidering machines, including their integral parts

15-06

纺织、缝纫、针织和绣花机械及其零部件

102696	Balling machines	线球机，纱球机	
102709	Bobbins for sewing machines	缝纫机线轴	
102676	Bobbins ［spinning］	线轴［纺纱］	
102700	Braiding machines ［textile］	编织机［纺织］	
102677	Buttonholing machines	锁眼机	
104587	Carding machines	梳棉机，梳理机	【10】
102695	Combs ［weaving］	精梳机［纺织］	
102686	Cotton gins	轧棉机	
102685	Cutting machines for textiles	纺织品裁剪机	
102697	Darning machines	织补机	
102703	Embroidery frames	绣花机绣框	
102680	Embroidery machines	绣花机，刺绣机	
102675	Fabric stretching frames	纺织品拉幅机	
102708	Heddles	综片	
102694	Hemming machines	缝边机	
102702	Hosiery looms	织袜机	
102691	Knitting looms	针织机	
102701	Knitting machines	编织机	
102692	Looms for tulle and lace	薄纱和花边织机	
102710	Pedals for sewing machines ［treadles］	缝纫机用踏板［踏板］	
104640	Pedals ［treadles］ for looms	织机踏板［踏板］	【10】
102710	Pedals ［treadles］ for sewing machines	缝纫机用踏板［踏板］	
102684	Reels for textile machines	纺织机用卷轴	
102681	Roll calenders ［textile］	滚筒轧光机［纺织］	
102705	Sewing machine tables	缝纫机台面	
102682	Sewing machines	缝纫机	
102679	Shuttle pins	摆梭销	
102707	Shuttles for looms ［battens］	织机用梭子［板条］	
102706	Shuttles for sewing machines	缝纫机摆梭	

102707	Shuttles [battens] for looms	织机用梭子[板条]	
102678	Spindles	锭子	
102704	Spinning frames	精纺机	
102687	Spinning machines	纺纱机	
102698	Spinning wheels	手纺车	
102688	Thread humidifiers [spinning]	纺线增湿器[纺纱]	
104670	Thread separators for looms	织机用线分离器	【10】
102689	Twisting mills	捻纱机	
102683	Unwinding machines	退卷机	
102693	Warping machines	整经机	
102690	Weaving looms	纺织机	
102699	Weaving machinery	纺织机械	

15-07
Refrigeration machinery and apparatus

Notes: (a) Including household refrigeration apparatus. (b) Not including refrigerator wagons (rail) (Cl. 12-03) or refrigerator vans (road) (Cl. 12-08).

15-07
制冷机械和冷藏设备

注：(a)包括家用冷藏设备。(b)不包括冷藏车（铁路用）（12-03类）或冷藏车（公路用）（12-08类）。

102716	Freezers	制冷器，冷藏机	
102714	Ice machines and apparatus	制冰机和制冰设备	
102712	Refrigerated sales counters	冷藏销售柜	
104999	Refrigerated showcases	冷藏陈列柜	【13】
102713	Refrigerating apparatus	冷冻设备	
102715	Refrigerator doors	冰箱门	
102711	Refrigerators	冰箱	

15-08
[Vacant]

15-08
[空缺] 【3】[1]

15-09
Machine tools, abrading and founding machinery

Note: Including 3D printers.

15-09
机床、研磨和铸造机械

注：包括3D打印机。 【13】[2]

104781	3D printers	3D打印机	【11】

---

1 原类别标题和所有产品项转移至新建的31类，15-08类成为空缺。
2 第11版增加注释内容："(a)Including 3D printers.(a)包括3D打印机。"第13版删除注释内容："(b)Not including earth working machinery and material separators(Cl.15-99).(b)不包括土方工程机械和原料分离机（15-99类）。"

102717	Abrading machines	研磨机	
102734	Apparatus for loading blast furnaces	鼓风炉进料装置，高炉进料装置	
102755	Band saws	带锯机	
102750	Bending brakes	压弯机，弯板机	
102725	Bending machines	弯曲机，折弯机	
102733	Boring machines [except for rock]	镗床，钻孔机 [钻岩机除外]	
102774	Brick and tile molding machines	砖瓦成型机	
102721	Calenders for paper manufacture	造纸用压光机	
102773	Cask planing machines	龙门刨床	
102724	Casting carriages	铸桶车	
102741	Casting machines	铸造机	
102723	Chamfering machines	倒棱机，切角机	
102778	Circular saws [machines]	圆锯机 [机械]	
102731	Cold working machines for metals	金属冷加工机	
105000	Computer numerical control [CNC] machine tools	数控雕刻机	【13】
102772	Control desks for machine tools	机床控制台	
102719	Coolers for foundries	铸造用冷却装置	
102768	Cork stopper making machines	软木塞制造机	
102767	Draw plates for metal	金属拉模板	
102728	Edging machines for leather	皮革边加工机械	
102738	Electroplating equipment	电镀设备	
102729	Embossing machines	压花机，压纹机	
102742	Eyelet fixing machines	冲孔固定机	
102735	Filing machines	锉床	
102770	Forging presses	锻压机	
102720	Grinding and crushing machines for industry	工业用碾碎和压碎机	
102769	Grinding machines for sharpening, trueing, adjusting	用于磨利、精修、调整的磨床	
102760	Lathes [machine tools]	车床 [机床]	
102736	Machine tools for woodworking and metalworking	木材加工和金属加工用机床	
102722	Machines for boring, drilling, grooving rifle barrels	用于镗孔、钻孔、开来复槽的机械	
102727	Machines for cutting out	用于切断的机械	
102730	Machines for stamping metals	金属冲压机，金属压印机	

102780	Metalworking machines	金属加工机械
102732	Milling machines, fixed	固定式铣床
102776	Mills for making cement	生产水泥用碾磨机
102739	Millstones	粉碎机，研磨机
102777	Moulds for concrete [construction]	混凝土铸模［建筑］
102761	Opticians' lathes	光学仪器制造师用车床
102726	Pipe benders	弯管机
102751	Planing machines	龙门刨床
102744	Planishing machines [machine tools]	精轧机［机床］
102746	Polishing machines for metal	金属抛光机
102762	Potters' wheels	陶工旋盘
102737	Power hammers	动力锤
102749	Presses for fuel briquettes	煤球压制机
102775	Presses for molding soap	肥皂成型压力机
102771	Presses, hydraulic	液压机
102745	Punching machines [industry]	冲孔机［工业］
102752	Riveting machines	铆接机
102766	Rolling mills for metal	金属滚轧机
102765	Rolling presses for paper making	造纸滚压机
102757	Sandblast machines	喷砂机
102747	Sanding machines	砂轮机
102754	Sawing machines, fixed	固定式锯床
102764	Screw-making machines	制螺钉机
102718	Sharpening machines	修磨机，磨锐机
102740	Slotting machines	插床，立式刨床
102759	Spindle molding machines	心轴成型机
102743	Stone sawing or cutting machines	石料锯切机
102748	Tailstocks for lathes	车床尾架
102758	Tapping machines	攻丝机
102774	Tile and brick molding machines	砖瓦成型机
102753	Welding apparatus for thermoplastic materials	热塑性材料焊接设备
102756	Welding machines	焊接机，电焊机
102763	Wire drawing machines	拉丝机
102779	Wood choppers [machines]	劈木机［机械］

15-10
Machinery for filling, packing or packaging

15-10
填装、打包和包装机械 【12】[1]

102805	Bottle capping machines	瓶子压盖机
102785	Corking machines	封塞机
102794	Machines for filling bags or sacks	包袋填装机
102804	Machines for filling bottles	灌瓶机
102802	Machines for weighing and filling bags	称重并装包的机械
102793	Packing machines	包装机械

15-99
Miscellaneous

15-99
其他杂项

102795	Balancing machines for vehicle wheels	车轮平衡机	
102808	Ball bearings	球轴承,滚珠轴承	
102790	Belting machines	包带机	
104787	Crankshafts for machines	机械用曲轴	【11】
102791	Driving belts [for machines]	传动皮带 [机械用]	
105002	Fog machines	造雾机	【13】
102807	Frames for making mattresses	制造气垫的构架	
102786	Gear levers for machinery	机械变速操纵杆	
102809	Grease separators for waste water [machines]	废水的油脂分离器 [机械]	
104782	Indoor cultivation apparatus	室内栽培设备	【11】
104783	Industrial robots	工业机器人	【11】
102783	Jigs for repairing vehicle bodies	修理机动车身夹具	
104785	Lacquering machines	喷漆机,喷涂机	【11】
102806	Lasts for shoemaking [machine parts]	制鞋用鞋楦头 [机械部件]	
105001	Linear actuators [machines]	独立线性驱动器,线性致动器	【13】
102810	Liquid and steam separators	汽液分离器	
102787	Machines for making cigarettes	制香烟机	
102799	Machines for mechanical handling of radioactive material	处理放射性物质的机械	
102813	Machines for skinning animals [except for use in the food industry]	动物剥皮机 [食品工业用除外]	
102798	Mixers, industrial	工业用搅拌机	

1　新增加 15-10 类,产品项由 15-99 类转移至 15-10 类。

102788	Nailing machines	钉接机	
104786	Oil dampers for machines	机械用油阻尼器	【11】
104784	Robots for guiding people	向导机器人	【11】
102817	Snow guns	人工造雪机，雪炮	
102782	Stapling machines	压钉机	
102800	Tobacco mixing and sifting machines	烟草搅拌和筛选机	
102801	Tyre fitting machines	轮胎组装机	
102792	Vulcanizing boilers	硫化罐	
102815	Wastepaper presses	废纸压床	
102816	Winders	绕线机	

Class 16
Photographic, cinematographic and optical apparatus

Note: Not including lamps for photography or filming (Cl. 26-05).

16类
照相设备、电影摄影设备和光学设备

注：不包括照相和摄影用灯（26-05类）。

16-01
Photographic cameras and film cameras

16-01
照相机和电影摄影机

102824	Camcorders	便携式摄像机	
102818	Cinematographic cameras	电影摄影机	
104788	Dashboard cameras	行车记录仪	【11】
102819	Diaphragms [photography]	光圈[摄影]	
102820	Filming apparatus	电影摄制设备	
104887	Photo booths	自助照相亭	【12】
102821	Photographic cameras	照相机	
102823	Shutters [photography]	快门[摄影]	
102826	Surveillance cameras	监控摄像机	
102822	Television cameras	电视摄像机	
104886	Thermal imaging cameras	热成像摄像机，热感应摄像机	【12】
102827	Webcams	摄像头，网络摄像机	

16-02
Projectors and viewers

16-02
放映机、投影仪和看片器

102828	Diapositive projection apparatus	幻灯片投影仪	
102829	Film projectors	电影放映机	
102832	Overhead projectors	高射投影仪	
102828	Slide projectors	滑动式投影仪，幻灯片放映机	
105003	Smart projectors	智能投影机	【13】
102830	Viewers for films	胶片看片器	
102831	Viewers for slides	幻灯片看片器	

16-03
Photocopying apparatus and enlargers

Note: Including microfilming equipment and apparatus for viewing microfilms, as well as office machines known as "photocopying" apparatus which use other than photographic processes (in particular, thermal or magnetic processes).

16-03
影印设备和放大机

注：包括缩微设备、观看缩微胶片的设备和被通称为"影印机"的办公设备，该设备不采用照相工艺（特别是热工艺或磁工艺）。

102835	Blueprint apparatus	晒图设备	
102834	Easels for photographic enlarging	放相用定位板	
102833	Enlargers [photography]	放大机[摄影]	
102836	Microfilm reading apparatus	缩微胶片阅读设备	
102838	Microfilming apparatus	缩微仪器	
102839	Photocopying apparatus	影印设备，复印设备	
102840	Printers [photography]	晒片机，印相机[摄影]	
102841	Toner cartridges for office copying apparatus	办公复印设备的墨盒	

16-04
Developing apparatus and equipment

16-04
显影器械和设备

102845	Developing baths [containers] for photography	摄影用显影槽[容器]	
102843	Developing equipment for photographic prints	照片冲印的显影设备	
102842	Film developing apparatus and implements	胶片显影器械和器具	
102844	Tanks for developing films	胶片显影容器	

16-05
Accessories

Note: Including filters for photographic cameras, exposure meters, tripods and photographic flash apparatus.

16-05
附件

注：包括照相机用滤镜、曝光计、三脚架和照相闪光设备。

104573	Ball heads for tripods [photography]	云台[摄影]	【10】
104789	Battery pack grips for photographic cameras	照相机电池手柄	【11】
102851	Cardboard frames for photographs	摄影用卡纸架	
102867	Cassettes for microfilms	缩微胶片暗盒	

102854	Diapositive loaders	幻灯片装片机
102846	Exposure meters	曝光计
102868	Exposure tables [photography]	曝光台［摄影］
102852	Film cassettes	胶片暗盒
102853	Film loaders [photography]	胶片装片机［摄影］
102857	Film splicers	胶片接片机
102870	Films	胶片
102860	Filters [photography]	滤镜［摄影］
102861	Flash apparatus [photography]	闪光设备［摄影］
102861	Flashlamps for photography	摄影闪光灯
102850	Frames for transparencies [slides]	幻灯片框架［幻灯片］
102855	Holders for diapositives	幻灯片托架
102856	Mounting corners for photographs	相角，相片角贴
102847	Photo reels	胶片卷盘
102862	Photometers [photography]	曝光计，曝光表［摄影］
102849	Printing masks [photography]	印相遮光板［摄影］
102866	Projection screens	投影屏，银幕
102858	Remote controls [except wireless] for diapositive projectors	幻灯片投影仪用远程控制器［无线的除外］
102859	Shutter releases [photography]	快门释放装置，快门线［摄影］
102850	Slide frames [photography]	幻灯片框架［摄影］
102848	Spools for film projectors	胶片放映机卷轴
102863	Stands for photographic or cinematographic cameras	照相机或电影摄影机支架
102864	Titlers for films	电影字幕机
102865	Tripods for cameras [photography]	照相机三脚架［摄影］
102869	Viewfinders [photography]	取景器［摄影］

16-06
Optical articles

Notes: (a) Including spectacles and microscopes. (b) Not including measuring instruments embodying optical devices (Cl. 10-04).

16-06
光学制品

注：(a) 包括眼镜和显微镜。(b) 不包括含有光学器件的测量仪器（10-04类）。

102871	Anti-dazzle spectacles	防眩眼镜	
102873	Arms of spectacle frames	镜架腿	
102875	Binoculars	双筒望远镜	
102872	Bridges for spectacle frames	眼镜框架的鼻梁架	
104793	Camera lens caps	照相机镜头盖	【11】

104794	Camera lens hoods	照相机镜头遮光罩	【11】
104792	Camera lenses	照相机镜头	【11】
102887	Combination of lenses	组合透镜	
104791	Contact lenses	隐形眼镜	【11】
102899	Fastenings for glasses	眼镜扣紧物	
102875	Field glasses	野外双筒望远镜	
102882	Goggles	护目镜	
102897	Gun sights	枪炮瞄准器	
102874	Hinges for spectacles	眼镜的铰链	
104618	Holders for telescopic sights	望远镜瞄准器支架	【10】
102885	Judas-holes	监视孔	
104795	Lenses for smartphone cameras	智能手机摄像头用镜头	【11】
102877	Lenses，simple	单透镜	
102879	Magnifying glasses	放大镜	
102884	Microscopes	显微镜	
102894	Mirrors〔optics〕	镜〔光学〕	
102886	Monocles	单片眼镜	
102876	Opera glasses	看戏用小望远镜	
102885	Peepholes for doors	门窥视镜	
102889	Periscopes	潜望镜	
102890	Pince-nez	夹鼻眼镜	
102893	Prisms〔optics〕	棱镜〔光学〕	
102891	Refractors	折射透镜，折射望远镜	
104796	Ski goggles	滑雪护目镜	【11】
104790	Smartglasses	智能眼镜	【11】
102896	Spectacle frames	眼镜架	
102898	Spectacle lenses	眼镜片	
102880	Spectacles	眼镜	
102881	Spyglasses	小型望远镜	
102885	Spy-holes for doors	门的窥视镜，猫眼	
102892	Stereoscopes	立体镜，体视镜，实体镜	
102895	Sunglasses	太阳镜	
104797	Swimming goggles	泳镜	【11】
102878	Telescopes	望远镜	
102883	Telescopic sights for firearms	武器望远瞄准器	

16-99
Miscellaneous

16-99
其他杂项

102900	Microscope slides	显微镜载物片	

Class 17
Musical instruments

Note: Not including cases for musical instruments (Cl. 03-01), or equipment for the recording or reproduction of sounds (Cl. 14-01).

17-01
Keyboard instruments

Note: Including electronic and other organs, accordions, and mechanical and other pianos.

102901	Accordions	手风琴
102904	Concertinas	六角形手风琴
102905	Harmoniums	簧风琴，小风琴，脚踏式风琴
102902	Keyboard instruments	键盘乐器
102903	Keyboards for musical instruments	乐器键盘
102912	Keys for musical instruments	乐器键
102909	Mechanical pianos	机械钢琴
102913	Organ pipes	风琴管
102910	Organ stops	风琴音栓
102906	Organs	风琴
102908	Pianos	钢琴
102911	Sound boards for pianos	钢琴音板，钢琴共鸣板

17-02
Wind instruments

Note: Not including organs, harmoniums and accordions (Cl. 17-01).

102925	Bagpipes	风笛
102915	Bassoons	巴松管，低音管
102916	Bugles	军号，喇叭
102917	Clarinets	单簧管，竖笛
102919	Cornets [musical instruments]	短号 [乐器]
102929	Euphoniums	次中音号
102921	Flutes	笛，长笛
102922	Harmonicas	口琴
102918	Horns [musical instruments]	号角，喇叭 [乐器]
104624	Hulusies [musical instruments]	葫芦丝 [乐器] 【10】

102920	Hunting horns	猎号，猎笛	
102924	Kazoos	卡祖笛，小笛	
102922	Mouth organs	口琴	
102923	Oboes	双簧管	
102927	Ocarinas	奥卡利那笛，洋埙	
102928	Piccolos	短笛	
102914	Reeds for musical instruments	管乐器簧片	
102930	Saxophones	萨克斯管	
102931	Trombones	拉管，长号	
102932	Trumpets［musical instruments］	小号［乐器］	
104675	Tsuns［musical instruments］	埙［乐器］	【10】
102926	Wind instruments	管乐器	
102926	Wind musical instruments	管乐器	
104675	Xuns［musical instruments］	埙［乐器］	【10】

17-03
Stringed instruments

17-03
弦乐器

102946	Balalaikas	巴拉莱卡琴，俄式三弦琴	
102934	Banjos	班卓琴，五弦琴	
102933	Bows for musical instruments	乐器的琴弓	
102937	Double bass	低音提琴	
102942	Dulcimers	扬琴	
104605	Erhues［musical instruments］	二胡［乐器］	【10】
102939	Guitars	吉他，六弦琴	
102940	Harps	竖琴	
102941	Mandolins	曼陀林琴	
102936	Pegs for stringed instruments	弦乐器的弦轴、弦钮、琴栓	
104641	Pipaes［musical instruments］	琵琶［乐器］	【10】
102938	Stringed instruments	弦乐器	
102936	Tuning pegs for stringed instruments	弦乐器的调音弦轴	
102947	Ukuleles	尤克里里琴，夏威夷四弦琴	
102945	Violin chin rests	小提琴腮托	
102944	Violins	小提琴	
102943	Violoncellos	大提琴	
102935	Zithers	筝，扁琴，齐特拉琴	

17-04
Percussion instruments

102954	Bass drum sticks	低音鼓槌
102950	Bells	钟，铃
102963	Big drums [musical instruments]	大鼓 [乐器]
102948	Carillons	钟乐器，钟琴，编钟
102949	Castanets	响板
102948	Chimes	套钟，排钟
102951	Cymbals	铙钹
102958	Drums [musical instruments]	鼓 [乐器]
102952	Gongs	锣
102959	Kettledrums	定音鼓，铜鼓
102964	Maracas	沙球
102955	Marimbas	马林巴琴
102956	Percussion instruments	打击乐器
104648	Ratchets	棘轮
102962	Small bells	小铃
102953	Small globular bells	小型球状铃
102957	Tambourines	小手鼓
102960	Triangles [musical instruments]	三角铁 [乐器]
102961	Xylophones	木琴

【10】

17-05
Mechanical instruments

Notes: (a) Including music boxes. (b) Not including mechanical keyboard instruments (Cl. 17-01).

注：(a) 包括音乐盒、八音盒。(b) 不包括机械式键盘乐器（17-01类）。

102969	Barrel organs	手摇风琴
102966	Calliopes [musical instruments]	汽笛风琴 [乐器]
102967	Mechanical musical instruments	机械乐器
102968	Mechanical singing birds	机械鸣禽
102965	Music boxes	音乐盒，八音盒

17-99
Miscellaneous

102970	Conductors' batons [music]	指挥棒 [音乐]

102972	Dampers for musical instruments	乐器制音器，乐器减音器	
104798	Jews' harps	犹太竖琴	【11】
102972	Mutes for musical instruments	乐器弱音器	
104690	Pedals for musical instruments	乐器踏板	【11】[1]
105004	Stands for musical instruments	乐器支架	【13】
102971	Tuning forks	音叉	
102973	Tuning whistles	调音笛	

---

1 由 17-01 类转移至 17-99 类。

Class 18
Printing and office machinery

18 类
印刷和办公机械

18-01
Typewriters and calculating machines

Note: Not including computers and other apparatus to be placed in Cl. 14-02.

18-01
打字机和运算机器

注：不包括属于14-02类的计算机及其他设备。

102984	Abacus	算盘
102981	Accounting machines	记账机，会计机
102974	Adding machines	加法器
102985	Ballot counting or voting machines	选票计算或投票记录机
102976	Calculating machines [except computers]	运算机器［计算机除外］
102988	Calculators [except computers]	计算器［计算机除外］
102975	Cash registers	现金出纳机，收银机
102980	Checkwriters	支票机
102979	Paper guides for typewriters	打字机纸张导轨
102982	Stenographic machines	速记机，速录机
102983	Stenotypes [office machines]	速记打字机［办公机械］
102987	Typewriter keys	打字机键
102986	Typewriter platens	打字机压纸卷轴
102978	Typewriter ribbons	打字机色带
102977	Typewriters	打字机
102989	Validation and payment consoles with screens [except computers]	带屏幕的确认支付机［计算机除外］

18-02
Printing machines

Notes: (a) Including typesetting machines, stereotype machines and apparatus, typographic machines and other reproducing machines such as duplicators and offset equipment, as well as addressing machines, franking and cancelling machines. (b) Not including computer printers (Cl. 14-02) and photocopying machinery (Cl. 16-03).

18-02
印刷机械

注：(a) 包括排版机、铅版印刷机、活版印刷机和其他复制机，例如复制机、胶印机、印地址机、邮资盖戳机和盖销机。(b) 不包括计算机打印机（14-02类）和影印设备（16-03类）。 【11】[1]

102994	Address plates	地址印刷板
102991	Address plates for addressing machines	印地址机用地址印刷板

---

[1] 注释（b）由 "Not including photocopying machinery (Cl. 16-03).不包括影印设备（16-03类）."修改为 "Not including computer printers (Cl. 14-02) and photocopying machinery (Cl. 16-03).不包括计算机打印机（14-02类）和影印设备（16-03类）."

102990	Addressing machines	印地址机
103008	Anti-noise casings for printing machines	印刷机抗噪声罩
103001	Cancelling machines	盖销机
102996	Duplicators	复制机，拷贝机
102992	Franking machines	邮资盖戳机
102998	Inking apparatus for printing machinery	印刷机械用油墨设备
103007	Inking rollers for printing machines	印刷机用油墨辊
102997	Mimeograph apparatus and machines	油印设备和机械
102999	Offset printing machines	胶版印刷机
103000	Printing machines	印刷机械
103006	Printing presses	印刷机
103003	Stamping machines	压印机，打戳机，烫金机
102993	Stereotype machines and apparatus	铅版印刷机和设备
103009	Toner cartridges for printing machines	印刷机械的墨盒、硒鼓
103005	Typecasting machines	铸铅字机
102995	Typesetting apparatus	排版设备，排字设备
103004	Typographic machines	活版印刷机

18-03
Type and type faces

18-03
活字和字体

103010	Alphabets ［printing characters］	字母［印刷字符］
103013	Figures for vehicle number plates	交通工具号牌用数字
103013	Figures for vehicle registration plates	交通工具号牌用数字
103016	Letters for signs	符号字母
103018	Letters for vehicle number plates	交通工具号牌用字母
103018	Letters for vehicle registration plates	交通工具号牌用字母
103014	Luminous letters	发光字母
103015	Monograms	拼合字
103017	Printing matrices	印刷字模
103010	Printing type	印刷活字
103012	Type for subtitles ［films］	字幕用活字［电影］
104677	Typefaces	字体，字样　【10】
103011	Typewriter type	打字机铅字

LIST OF GOODS IN CLASS ORDER CLASS 18

18-04

Bookbinding machines, printers' stapling machines, guillotines and trimmers (for bookbinding)

Note: Including machines and similar devices for cutting paper, analogous to guillotines and trimmers.

103022	Bookbinding machines
103026	Envelope opening apparatus and machines
103023	Envelope sealing apparatus and machines
103019	Folding machines [bookbinding]
103024	Guillotines [bookbinding]
103021	Machines or devices for cutting paper
103024	Paper cutters [machines]
103020	Printers' stapling machines
103025	Stitchers [bookbinding]
103024	Trimmers [bookbinding]

18-99

Miscellaneous

103027	Cases [typography]
103028	Composing frames [typography]
103031	Composing tables for printing
103029	Document destroyers
103030	Labellers [machines]
103033	Paper sorters
103034	Table supports for pocket calculating machines

18-04

装订机、印刷工用订书机、切纸机和修边机（装订用）

注：包括类似切纸机、修边机的切纸机械和类似装置。

装订机
封套拆封设备和机械
封套封口设备和机械
折页机［装订］
切纸机［装订］
切纸机械或装置
切纸机，裁切机［机械］
印刷工用订书机
订书机［装订］
修边机［装订］

18-99

其他杂项

字盘［活版印刷］
排字架［活版印刷］
印刷排字表盘
文件销毁机，文件粉碎机，碎纸机
标签机，贴标机，打标机［机械］
纸张分选机，纸张分类机
袖珍计算器的工作盘支座

Class 19

Stationery and office equipment, artists' and teaching materials

19 类

文具、办公用品、美术用品和教学用品

19-01

Writing paper, cards for correspondence and announcements

Note: Including all paper, in the widest sense of the term, which is used for writing, drawing, painting or printing, such as tracing paper, carbon paper, newsprint, envelopes, greetings cards and illustrated postcards, even if they embody a sound recording.

19-01 【3】[1]

书写用纸、通信用卡片和通知用卡片

注：包括广义而言的纸张，即用于书写、绘图、绘画或印刷的所有纸张，即使其中记录有声音，例如描图纸、复写纸、新闻用纸、信封、贺卡和插图明信片。

103049	Aerograms	航空邮简	
103048	Announcement cards	通知卡片	
103054	Carbon paper	复写纸	
103037	Drawing paper	绘图纸	
103038	Envelopes [stationery]	信封 [文具]	
103045	Greetings cards	贺卡	
103047	Illustrated postcards	插图明信片	
103036	Letter cards	信函卡片	
103035	Mailing wrappers for printed matter	印刷品邮寄包装纸	
103044	Mourning cards	哀悼卡，致哀卡	
103041	Newsprint	新闻纸	
104799	Origami paper	手工折纸	【11】
103043	Paper for architectural plans	建筑设计图用纸	
103042	Photographic paper	相纸	
103046	Picture postcards	美术明信片	
103050	Postcards	明信片	
103052	Printing paper	印刷纸，晒图纸，打印纸	
103040	Security paper	证券纸，保险纸，防伪纸	
104888	Sticky notes	便签，便条	【12】
103053	Tracing paper	描图纸	
103051	Writing paper	书写用纸	

---

[1] 原 19-05 类的类别标题和所有产品项合并入此类。

LIST OF GOODS IN CLASS ORDER CLASS 19

19-02
Office equipment

Notes: (a) Including equipment used at cash desks, such as change sorters. (b) Some office equipment is to be placed in other subclasses or classes; for example, office furniture in Cl. 06, office machines and equipment in Cl. 14-02, Cl. 16-03, Cl. 18-01, Cl. 18-02 or Cl. 18-04, and writing materials in Cl. 19-01 or Cl. 19-06 (see Alphabetical List).

19-02
办公用品

注：(a) 包括收款台上用的设备，如零钱拣选机。(b) 不包括办公家具（06类）、办公机械和设备（14-02、16-03、18-01、18-02 或者 18-04 类）和书写用具（19-01 或者19-06类）。

103082	Adhesive tape dispensers	胶带分割器	
103097	Apparatus for counting bank notes	纸币计数设备，点钞机	
103088	Apparatus for making rolls of coins	硬币卷的成型设备	
103096	Apparatus for smoothing bank notes	纸币平整设备	
103086	Banknote clips	纸币夹子	
104891	Binder clips	长尾夹	【12】
103098	Boxes for paper clips	曲别针盒，纸夹盒	
104890	Brass fasteners for paper [foldback pins]	纸用黄铜紧固件［弯折夹］	【12】
103091	Cancelling stamps [tools] for postmarks	邮戳盖销图章［工具］	
103070	Card index cabinets [mobile]	卡片索引柜［可移动］	
103064	Card index guide tabs	卡片索引突舌	
103078	Card index plates	卡片索引板	
103059	Cashboxes	钱箱	
103063	Change boxes [money]	零钱盒［货币］	
103065	Change sorters [money]	零钱拣选器［货币］	
103073	Coin plates	硬币盘	
103067	Correspondence trays	信件格，信件盘	
103071	Dampers [office equipment]	湿手盒，蘸水盒［办公用品］	
103066	Dating and numbering devices for office use	办公用号码机、日期机	
103095	Dispensers for correction fluid	修正液分配器	
103105	Dispensers for correction ribbons	修正带分配器	
104800	Dispensers for correction tapes	修正带分配器	【11】
103094	Draft holders	绘图用夹持器、固定器	
103087	Drawing clips	绘图夹子	
104689	Drawing pins	图钉	【11】[1]
103084	Elastic bands for office use	办公用弹性皮筋	

---

[1] 由 08-08 类转移至 19-02 类。

103069	Electric apparatus for erasing[office equipment]	电动擦除装置［办公用品］	
103060	Filing boxes［office equipment］	文件盒，卷宗盒［办公用品］	
103101	Filing trays［office equipment］	文件格盘，卷宗格盘［办公用品］	
103083	Folders for hanging files	悬挂文件夹，悬挂卷宗夹	
103099	Holders for paper clips	曲别针托座，纸夹托座	
103102	Holders for stamps［seals］	图章托座［图章］	
103106	Holders for visiting cards［office equipment］	名片托座［办公用品］	
103056	Letter fasteners	信件扣钉	
104801	Letter openers	开信刀	【11】
103103	Lettering apparatus, hand-operated［office equipment］	手动操作印字装置［办公用品］	
103090	Memo pad holders	记事簿托座	
103081	Money boxes for counting change	可计数的钱盒	
103086	Money clips	钱夹子	
103089	Money shovels	搓钱铲	
103072	Numbering stamps	编号印字器	
103075	Office punches	办公用打孔器	
103062	Office seals	办公印章	
103061	Office staplers	办公用订书机	
103085	Paper clips	曲别针，纸夹	
103057	Paper fasteners	纸张扣钉，装订夹	
103068	Paper knives	裁纸刀	
103074	Paper punches［for office use］	纸张打孔器［办公用］	
103079	Paperweights	镇尺，纸镇，书镇	
103093	Perforating stamps	穿孔印戳	
103104	Pin trays［office equipment］	大头针盘［办公用品］	
103092	Rubber stamps	橡皮图章	
103077	Spindle files	票插、纸插	
103076	Spring clamps for holding papers	固定纸用弹簧夹	
103055	Staple removers	起钉器	
104889	Staples for paper	订书钉	【12】
103080	Stencils［stationery］	蜡板［文具］	
103058	Supports for shorthand pads	速记簿托架	
103058	Supports for stenography tablets	速记簿托架	
103100	Telephone number finders	电话号码查找器	
104689	Thumbtacks	图钉	【11】[1]

1　由 08-08 类转移至 19-02 类。

19-03
Calendars

Note：Not including diaries（Cl. 19-04）.

19-03
日历

注：不包括日记簿（19-04类）。

103111	Advent calendars	降临节倒计时日历
103110	Bases for loose-leaf desk diaries	活页台式日历座
103107	Calendars ［also as advertising material］	日历［兼作广告用品］
103109	Pages for loose-leaf desk diaries	活页台式日历的活页
103110	Tear-off calendar holders	撕页式日历的座、托架
103108	Tear-off calendars	撕页式日历
103252	Wall charts for vacation planning	休假日程的墙上挂历　【12】[1]

19-04
Books and other objects of similar outward appearance

Note：Including covers of books，bindings，albums，diaries and similar objects.

19-04
书本及与其外观相似的其他物品

注：包括封面、书籍装帧、剪贴簿、日记簿和其他类似物品。

103134	Accounting books	会计账簿
103137	Address books	地址簿
103265	Album leaves fitted with pockets	插袋式相册内页　【12】[2]
103116	Albums of all sorts ［stamps, photographs, postcards］	各种剪贴簿［邮票、照片、明信片］
103117	Almanacs	年鉴
103118	Binding rings	装订环
103128	Bindings ［book］	装帧［书本］
103123	Book covers	书的封面封底，图书封面
103133	Book jackets	书籍护封
103126	Booklets	小册子
103125	Books	书本
103130	Catalogs	目录册
103130	Catalogues	目录册
103114	Diaries	日记簿
103136	Document folders	文件夹
103139	Filing containers for compact discs	插光盘档案簿

1　由"Cards for checking holidays 假日检查卡片"修改为"Wall charts for vacation planning 休假日程的墙上挂历"，并由19-08类转移至19-03类。
2　由19-99类转移至19-04类。

103140	Filing containers for diskettes	插磁盘档案簿	
103141	Filing containers for visiting cards	插名片档案簿	
103267	Filing pages for coins for collectors	硬币收藏页	【12】[1]
103112	Jackets for papers	纸张护封	
103129	Magazines	杂志	
103135	Music books	乐谱册	
103120	Note pads	便条本，记事本	
103121	Notebooks［books］	笔记簿［书本］	
103113	Office files	办公卷宗夹	
103127	Office ledgers	办公账册	
103124	Photograph albums	相册	
103112	Portfolios［stationery］	公文夹，文件夹［文具］	
103122	Postage stamp classifiers	邮票分类册	
103132	Postcard albums	明信片册	
103244	Printed leaves of albums	相册印刷页	【12】[2]
103119	Scoring pads for bridge	桥牌记分簿	
103115	Scrap books	剪贴册	
103138	Shorthand pads	速记簿，速记记事贴	
103124	Snapshot albums	快照相册	
103131	Stamp albums	集邮册	

19-05
［Vacant］

19-05
［空缺］ 【3】[3]

19-06
Materials and instruments for writing by hand, for drawing, for painting, for sculpture, for engraving and for other artistic techniques

Note: Not including paintbrushes (Cl. 04-04), drawing tables and attached equipment (Cl. 06-03), or writing paper (Cl. 19-01).

19-06
用于书写、绘图、绘画、雕塑、雕刻和其他艺术技法的用品和工具

注：不包括油漆刷（04-04类）、绘图桌及其附属设备（06-03类）或者书写用纸（19-01类）。

104802	3D printing pens	3D 打印笔	【11】
103192	Ball-point pens	圆珠笔	
103164	Bevel protractors	斜角量角器	

1　由 19-99 类转移至 19-04 类。
2　由 19-08 类转移至 19-04 类。
3　原类别标题和所有产品项目并入 19-01 类，19-05 类成为空缺。

103181	Bevel squares	斜角规，分度规	
103161	Blackboard erasers	黑板擦	
103150	Burins	雕刻刀	
103152	Canvas stretchers for painters	绘画用画布张紧器	
103151	Cartridges for drawing ink	描图墨水筒	
103186	Chalk holders	粉笔托，粉笔持笔器	
103159	Crayons	彩色笔，蜡笔，炭笔，色粉笔	
103156	Curve tracers	曲线描绘器	
103180	Cutting squares	切割直角尺	
103142	Desk blotting mats	桌面吸墨垫	
103146	Desk mats	桌面垫板	
103155	Dividers	分规，圆规	
103160	Drawing apparatus	绘图设备	
103185	Drawing boards［except tables］	绘图板［桌子除外］	
103154	Drawing compasses	绘图圆规	
103166	Drawing implements	绘图工具	
103197	Drawing machine heads	绘图仪机头	
103199	Drawing pens	绘图笔	
103190	Drawing rules	绘图尺	
103179	Drawing squares	绘图直角尺	
103191	Electric engraving stylus	电雕刻铁笔	
103162	Ellipsographs	椭圆规	
103182	Eraser shields	擦图片	
103183	Erasing rubbers	橡皮擦	
103148	Fountain pen nibs	自来水笔笔尖，钢笔笔尖	
103173	Fountain pens	自来水笔，钢笔	
103184	French curves	曲线板，曲线规	
103195	Hand blotters	手动吸墨器	
104617	Highlighters	荧光笔	【10】
103144	Inkstands	墨水台，墨水瓶托座	
103145	Inkwells	墨水池	
103196	Lead sharpeners［pencils］	笔芯研磨器［铅笔］	
103157	Line chalks	画线粉笔	
104617	Markers	马克笔	【10】
103175	Office rulers	办公用尺	

103149	Paint boxes for painters	绘画用颜料盒	
103153	Painters' easels	绘画用画架	
103167	Painters' palettes	绘画用调色板	
103200	Painting kits for water colorists	水彩画绘画用具	
103168	Pantographs for drawing	绘图用缩放仪	
103172	Pen holders	笔杆	
103170	Pen trays	置笔座	
103170	Pencil boxes	铅笔盒	
103187	Pencil holders	笔插，笔筒，铅笔持笔器	
103194	Pencil sharpeners	卷笔刀，铅笔刀	
103158	Pencils	铅笔	
103169	Pens	钢笔	
103188	Propelling pencils	自动铅笔	
103189	Protractors [also nautical]	量角器[也用于航海]	
103174	Refills for ball-point pens	圆珠笔笔芯	
103199	Ruling pens	鸭嘴笔，直线笔	
103178	School blackboards	学校用黑板	
103143	Sharpeners for chalks	粉笔刀，粉笔磨刀	
104803	Signing machines	签名机	【11】
103193	Stands for pens	钢笔架	
103171	Stencils [patterns]	镂空模板，描绘板[图案]	
103176	Styles	铁笔	
103177	Stylographs	尖头自来水笔，针管笔	
103198	Thermocauteries for pyrography	烙画用热烙器	
103163	Toolmakers' squares	精密直角尺	
103165	Water color saucers for artists	画家用水彩调色盘	
103147	Writing slates	书写用石板	

19-07
Teaching materials and apparatus 　教学用具和教学设备　【12】[1]

Notes: (a) Including maps of all kinds, globes and planetariums. (b) Not including audio-visual teaching aids (Cl. 14-01).

注：(a) 包括各种地图、地球仪和天象仪。(b) 不包括音视频教学辅助设备（14-01类）。

103209	Astronomical globes	天球仪，天体仪
103208	Astronomical maps	天文图，天象图
103214	Atlases	地图集

1　由"Teaching materials 教学用品"修改为"Teaching materials and apparatus 教学用具和教学设备"。

103211	City plans	城市平面图，城市规划图	
104804	Flight simulators for training	训练用飞行模拟装置	【11】
103202	Geographical maps	地图，地理图	
105005	Laser pointers	激光指示器	【13】
103273	Map holders［teaching material］	地图支架［教学用具］	【12】[1]
103206	Maps of the world in two hemispheres	世界两半球地图	
104805	Medical simulators for training	训练用医学模拟装置	【11】
103212	Panoramic tables［sightseeing］	全景图，全景地图［观光游览］	
103207	Planetariums	天象仪，星象仪	
103210	Planispheres for navigation	航海航空用平面天球图	
103213	Pointers	教鞭	
103203	Road maps	道路交通图	
103201	Teaching apparatus［except audiovisual aids］	教学设备［音视频教学辅助设备除外］	
103204	Teaching materials	教学用具	
103205	Terrestrial globes	地球仪	

19-08
Other printed matter

Note：Including printed advertising materials.

19-08
其他印刷品

注：包括印刷的广告品。

103224	Accounting sheets	财务票据	
103216	Admission tickets	入场券	
103229	Advertisement inserts	广告插页	【11】
103229	Advertisement insets	广告插页	
103241	Advertisement posters	广告画，海报	
103242	Advertising placards	广告招贴	
103250	Architects' plans	建筑设计图	
103243	Bank checks	银行票据	
103219	Calculating tables	计算表格	
103223	Cards for card indexes	卡片索引卡	
103215	Cards for registering absences	考勤登记卡片	
103257	Chip cards	芯片卡，IC卡	
103221	Credit cards	信用卡	
103217	Embroidery designs［patterns］	刺绣设计图样［图案］	
103234	Engravings	雕版印刷品	
103253	Forms［printed］	表格［印刷品］	

---

[1] 由19-99类转移至19-07类。

103233	Graphs	标绘图，曲线图
103220	Identification cards	身份证
103231	Labels	标签
103259	Lottery forms ［printed］	彩票表格［印刷品］
103258	Magnetic cards	磁卡
103248	Medical prescription pads	处方签
103247	Menstrual cycle indicators	月经周期指示图表
103239	Music paper	乐谱纸
103238	Newspapers	报纸
103227	Parking discs	停车时间计录卡
103249	Patterns for dressmaking	服装制作样板，裁缝图样
103232	Printed leaves of ledgers	账簿印刷页
103237	Printed matter, including advertising materials	印刷品，包括广告印刷品
103254	Prospectus	计划书，说明书，样张
103246	Railway timetables	铁路时刻表
103218	Seals for letters	信件封签
103256	Smart cards	智能卡
103251	Stamp album leaves	邮票贴片页
103255	Stickers	标贴，邮票
103228	Tables for indicating distances	距离指示图表
103228	Tables indicating distances	距离指示图表
103231	Tags	标签
103245	Templates for cutting	裁切模板
103236	Test pictures for oculists' instruments	眼科检查用图
103235	Timetables	时刻表
103240	Topographical plans	地形测量图表
103226	Transfers	转印贴花纸，转移印花纸
103225	Transfers for registration plates	车辆牌照用转移印花纸
103222	Visiting cards	名片

19-99
Miscellaneous

19-99
其他杂项

103262	Binding strips ［bookbinding］	装订黏合条［装订用］
103266	Book markers	书签
103264	Calculating discs	计算盘
103261	Folders for film negatives ［loose leaves］	电影胶片夹［活页］
103270	Folders for photographic negatives and prints	相片底片和画片用夹

103260	Label fasteners	标签紧固件	【12】[1]
103274	Magnetic boards	磁力板	
103271	Memo boards	备忘板，留言板	
103268	Newspaper holders [for reading]	报刊托架[阅读用]	
103263	Page turners	翻页器	
103269	Slide rules	滑尺，计算尺	

---

[1] 由"Strings for securing labels 安检卡挂带、挂绳"修改为"Label fasteners 标签紧固件"。

Class 20
Sales and advertising equipment, signs

20 类
销售设备、广告设备和标志物

20-01
Automatic vending machines

20-01
自动售货机

103285	Automatic teller machines [on-line banking terminals]	自动取款机[在线银行终端]	
103278	Automatic vending machines for cigarettes	自动售烟机	
103281	Automatic vending machines for drinks	饮料自动售货机	
103282	Automatic vending machines for ice cream cornets	蛋卷冰激凌自动售货机	
103276	Automatic vending machines for sweets	糖果自动售货机	
103279	Coin-operated automatic vending machines	投币式自动售货机	
103284	Control panels for vending apparatus	售货设备的控制面板	
104633	Machines for collecting bottles or cans	瓶子回收机，罐子回收机	【10】
103277	Money changing machines	货币兑换机	
104647	Queue management devices	排队取号机	【10】
105006	Self-service leasing machines for portable power banks	自助移动电源租赁机	【13】
104806	Self-service payment terminals	自助支付终端	【11】
103280	Transport ticket vending machines	交通售票机	
103283	Water dispensers	售水机	

20-02
Display and sales equipment

Note: Not including articles of furniture (Cl. 06).

20-02
陈列设备和销售设备

注：不包括家具和家居用品（06类）。

103306	Dispensers for bags [packaging]	袋分配器[包装]
103304	Dispensers for wrapping paper	包装纸分配器
103288	Display racks	陈列架
103291	Display stalls [open-air]	陈列货摊[露天]
103288	Display stands	陈列立架
103309	Display stands for ties	领带陈列架
103308	Display stands for watches	手表陈列架
103297	Display units	陈列装置
103286	Display units for bobbins of thread	棉线轴的陈列装置

103310	Display units for the sale of flowers or plants	花草销售陈列装置	
103292	Display units for writing implements	书写用具陈列装置	
103287	Dressmakers' busts for displaying or fitting	裁缝用于展示或试穿的半身模特	
103311	Exhibition stands	展示架，展览架	
103302	Fuel pumps [service stations]	泵式加燃料机[加油站]	
103296	Magazine display stands	杂志陈列架	
103301	Makeup shade charts	化妆品色调图表	
103293	Mannequins	展示服装用假人模特	
103290	Petrol pumps [service stations]	泵式加汽油机[加油站]	
105007	Product pusher devices	货架自动推进设备	【13】
103305	Racks for postcards	明信片陈列架	
103289	Rollers for dispensing cloth [in shops]	售布卷筒[商店用]	
104652	Rollup poster stands	卷曲式海报立架	【10】
103299	Sales stands	售货台，售货架	
103294	Shade cards or charts for hair dyes	染发剂色调卡或者色调图表	
103307	Showcases for watches [display units]	表陈列柜[陈列装置]	
104658	Showcases [display units]	陈列柜[陈列装置]	【10】
103298	Stands for displaying bottles	瓶子陈列架	
103312	Stands for displaying samples	样品陈列架	
103295	Stands for millinery	女帽及妇女头饰的陈列架	
103300	Stands for ready-made clothes	成衣陈列架	
103303	String dispensers	绳子分配器	
103293	Tailors' dummies	裁缝用假人模特	

20-03

Signs, signboards and advertising devices

Notes: (a) Including luminous advertising devices and mobile advertising devices. (b) Not including packaging (Cl. 09), or signalling devices (Cl. 10-06).

20-03

标志物，招牌、布告牌和广告设备

注：(a) 包括发光和可动的广告设备。(b) 不包括包装物（09类）或者信号装置（10-06类）。

103316	Advertisement boards	广告张贴板
103314	Advertisement screens	广告屏幕
103317	Advertising devices [luminous or not, mobile or static]	广告设备，广告装置[发光或不发光的，可动或静止的]
103330	Advertising pillars	广告柱子

103318	Apparatus for animated advertising	动画广告设备	
103313	Barber poles	理发馆标志彩柱	
103324	Billboards	广告牌，布告板	
103319	Boundary markers for hunting and fishing reservations	渔猎保留地的边界标志物	
105008	Checkout dividers	收银台分隔器	【13】
103323	Commemorative plaques	纪念牌匾	
103328	Game scoreboards	比赛记分牌	
103333	Holders for advertising labels	广告标牌支架	
103335	Holographic signs, indicators and devices	全息标志物、指示物和装置	
103325	Identity plaques	身份标志牌，胸牌	
103320	License plates for vehicles	交通工具牌照	
103326	License tags	许可牌照	
103323	Memorial tablets	纪念牌，纪念匾	
103322	Nameplates	名牌，铭牌，标示牌	
103327	Nationality plates for vehicles	交通工具国籍牌照	
103329	Pictographs	象形符号标志物	
104642	Plant labels	植物标识牌	【10】
103320	Registration plates for vehicles	交通工具牌照	
104892	Shop signs	店铺标志物，店铺招牌	【12】
103334	Signboards for taxis	出租车标识牌	
103331	Signboards for vehicles	交通工具标识牌	
103332	Video screens [electronic notice boards]	显示屏幕[电子布告牌]	

20-99
Miscellaneous

20-99
其他杂项

104635	Mascots	吉祥物	【10】

Class 21
Games, toys, tents and sports goods

21 类
游戏器具、玩具、帐篷和体育用品

21-01
Games and toys

Notes: (a) Including scale models. (b) Not including toys for animals (Cl. 30-12). [1]

21-01
游戏器具和玩具

注：(a) 包括比例模型。(b) 不包括动物用玩具（30-12类）。

编号	英文	中文	备注
103386	Articles of clothing for dolls	玩偶用服装	
105010	Baby gyms	婴儿游戏架	【13】
103400	Backgammon sets	西洋双陆棋	
103336	Balloons for children	儿童用气球	
104895	Billiard balls	台球	【12】
103379	Billiard cue rests	台球杆的架杆	
103384	Billiard cues	台球杆	
100573	Billiard tables	台球桌，弹子台	【12】[2]
103401	Board games	棋盘类游戏器具	
103374	Buckets [toys]	桶 [玩具]	
103380	Chalk for billiard cues	台球杆滑粉块	
103377	Checkerboards	西洋跳棋盘	
103346	Checkers [games]	西洋跳棋 [游戏器具]	
103351	Chess [games]	国际象棋 [游戏器具]	
103352	Chessboards	国际象棋盘	
103353	Chessmen	国际象棋子	
103343	Construction sets for children	儿童用积木	
104894	Construction toys with interlocking bricks	互锁块积木玩具	【12】
103358	Counters for games	游戏用筹码	
103356	Courses and obstacles for miniature golf	小型高尔夫的球场和障碍物	
103382	Cribbage boards	克里比奇牌戏积分板	
103399	Cuddly toys	怀抱玩具，毛绒玩具	
103345	Cups for dice	骰子筒	
104599	Dance pads [electronic games]	跳舞毯 [电子游戏]	【10】
103354	Darts [games]	飞镖 [游戏器具]	
103348	Diabolos [toys]	响铃，空竹 [玩具]	
103347	Dice for games	游戏用骰子	

---

1 原英文注释为（Cl. 30-99），由于第12版中产品项"动物用玩具"由30-99类转移至新增加的30-12类，编译时进行了修改。
2 由 06-03 类转移至 21-01 类。

103370	Dolls	玩偶	
103371	Dolls' heads	玩偶头	
103349	Dominos [games]	多米诺骨牌［游戏器具］	
103377	Draughtboards	国际跳棋盘	
103346	Draughts [games]	国际跳棋［游戏器具］	
104808	Drones [toys]	无人机［玩具］	【11】
103395	Electronic billiards	电子台球，电子弹子戏	
103396	Electronic games	电子游戏	
103392	Electronic games consoles	电子游戏操控台、控制器，掌上游戏机	
103391	Electronic games stations	电子游戏设备	
103387	Electronic toys	电动玩具	
103398	Figurines [toys]	小塑像［玩具］	
104809	Foosball tables	桌上足球	【11】
104809	Football tables	桌上足球	【11】
103394	Game cartridges for electronic games or electronic games stations	电子游戏器具或电子游戏设备的游戏卡	
103359	Gameboard pieces	游戏盘棋子	
103369	Gameboards	游戏棋盘	
103360	Games, including educational games	游戏器具，包括有教育意义的游戏器具	
104614	Glove puppets	布袋式手偶，手套式手偶	【10】
105009	Go-karts [toys]	微型竞赛汽车，卡丁车［玩具］	【13】
103371	Heads for dolls	玩偶头	
103338	Hoops [toys]	环［玩具］	
103385	Jack-in-the-boxes	（揭开盖子即有小人儿跳出的）玩偶匣	
103383	Jigsaw puzzles	拼板玩具，七巧板	
103388	Joysticks for toys	玩具操纵杆	
103363	Kaleidoscopes [toys]	万花筒［玩具］	
103339	Kites [toys]	风筝［玩具］	
103364	Lotto [games]	洛托卡牌戏［游戏器具］	
103402	Marbles	弹珠	【12】[1]
103378	Marionettes	牵线木偶	
103362	Mechanical toys	机械玩具	
103390	Paper dolls	纸偶	
103368	Pawns [chess]	棋子［国际象棋］	
103337	Playing cards	扑克牌	
103372	Prams for dolls	玩偶用小车	
103378	Puppets	木偶	
103357	Rattles [toys]	拨浪鼓，摇铃［玩具］	
103393	Remote-controlled toys	遥控玩具	

1　由"Balls for games [e.g. billiards, marbles]游戏用球［例如：台球、弹子球］"修改为"Marbles 弹珠"。

104807	Robots [toys]	机器人［玩具］	【11】
103340	Rocking horses	摇摆木马	
103373	Roulette [games]	轮盘赌［游戏器具］	
103366	Scale models	比例模型	
104893	Scale models to build	拼装模型	【12】
103367	Scooters [toys]	滑板车，踏板车［玩具］	
103365	Scorers for games	游戏用记分器	
103344	Skipping ropes	跳绳	
103381	Soap-bubble pipes [toys]	肥皂泡吹管［玩具］	
103375	Spinning tops [toys]	旋转陀螺［玩具］	
103350	Stilts	高跷	
100566	Tables for bridge	桥牌桌	【12】[1]
100567	Tables for games	游戏桌	【12】[2]
103355	Table golf	台式高尔夫	
103361	Toys	玩具	
103342	Tracks for racing cars [toys]	赛车轨道［玩具］	
103389	Tricycles [toys]	三轮车［玩具］	
103397	Vehicles [toys]	车辆［玩具］	
103341	Wooden horses [toys]	木马［玩具］	
103376	Zanzibars [dice games]	桑给巴尔骰子［骰子游戏］	

21-02

Gymnastics and sports apparatus and equipment

Notes: (a) Including sports apparatus and equipment that are necessary for the practice of various sports and which normally have no other specific purpose, such as footballs, skis and tennis rackets, excluding all other sporting objects classified in other classes and subclasses according to other functions (for example, canoes, boats (Cl. 12-06), air guns (Cl. 22-01), mats for sports (Cl. 06-11)). (b) Including, subject to the reservation mentioned under (a), training equipment, and apparatus and equipment necessary for outdoor games. (c) Not including sports clothing (Cl. 02), toboggans or sleighs (Cl. 12-14).

21-02

体育和运动的器械及设备

注：（a）包括用于各种运动锻炼所必需且通常无其他特定用途的运动器械和设备，例如足球、滑雪板、网球拍。不包括根据其他功能可以分入其他大类或小类的运动用品，例如独木舟、小艇（12-06类）、气枪（22-01类）、运动用地垫（06-11类）。（b）在（a）所限定的条件下，包括训练设备和器械，以及户外运动所必需的设备。（c）不包括运动服装（02类），雪橇或雪地车（12-14类）。

【12】[3]

103425	Apparatus for developing muscles	肌肉锻炼器械

---

1 由06-03类转移至21-01类。
2 由06-03类转移至21-01类。
3 修改了21-02类注释中的（a），修改前是"（a）Including, as sports equipment: apparatus and equipment necessary for the various sports which have no other specific purpose, such as footballs, skis and tennis rackets, to the exclusion of all other objects which may also be used in practicing a given sport."（a）包括运动器材，即各种运动中所必需的且没有其他特殊用途的设备和器材，如足球、滑雪板、网球拍，不包括某一特定运动训练中也可以使用的其他物品。"

103420	Athletics equipment	运动设备，运动器材	
103413	Balls for sports	运动用球	
103412	Balls [toys]	球[玩具]	
104896	Bandy sticks	曲棍球棒	【12】
103440	Baseball bats	棒球球棒	
105011	Belay devices [climbing equipment]	系索保护装置，自锁保护器[攀爬设备]	【13】
103421	Bindings for skis and their parts	滑雪板用固定器及其零部件	
103445	Bowling alleys	保龄球球道	
107896	Bowling pins	保龄球球瓶	
103444	Chest expanders	拉力器，扩胸器	
103459	Climbing ropes	登山绳	
105012	Climbing walls	攀岩墙	【13】
103441	Crampons for climbing	攀登用冰爪	
103465	Cricket balls	板球	
103466	Cricket bats	板球棒	
103446	Croquet sets	槌球用品	
103467	Croquet balls	槌球用球，门球用球	
103468	Croquet mallets	槌球棒，门球杆	
103419	Discuses [sports]	铁饼[运动]	
103424	Dumbbells	哑铃	
103422	Exercising apparatus	锻炼器械	
103447	Fencing masks	击剑面罩	
103448	Flippers for swimming	游泳用的脚蹼	
103462	Flying discs [toys]	飞盘，飞碟[玩具]	
103437	Flying trapezes	空中飞人吊架	
103451	Frames for gymnastic exercises	体操训练用架	
104897	Goals for sports	运动用球门	【12】
103417	Golf clubs	高尔夫球杆	
103455	Golf pegs	高尔夫球座	
103455	Golf tees	高尔夫球球座	
103408	Gymnasium apparatus	健身器械	
103423	Gymnastics apparatus and equipment	体操器械和设备	
103442	Hand straps for ski poles	滑雪杖缚手带	
103442	Hand straps for ski sticks	滑雪杖缚手带	【12】
103454	Heel grips for ski bindings	滑雪板用脚跟夹紧装置	
103414	Horizontal bars [sports]	单杠，双杠[运动]	

103426	Hurdles	跨栏	
103404	Ice hockey pucks	冰球	
103464	Ice hockey sticks	冰球棒	
103427	Ice skates	溜冰鞋	
103472	Inline skates	直排溜冰鞋	
103443	Machines for physical exercise	体能训练机	【12】[1]
103449	Nose clips for swimmers	游泳鼻夹	
103471	Paragliders	滑翔伞	
103403	Playing bowls	保龄球	
103430	Protective tips for skis	滑雪板的防护端	
103432	Racquets for games	运动、游戏用球拍	
103409	Rings for beach games	海滩游戏环	
103428	Roller skates	旱冰鞋	
103439	Roller skis	滚轮滑雪板	
103411	Rowing exercising machines	划船练习器	
103407	Shuttlecocks	羽毛球，毽子	
103469	Skateboards	滑板	
103410	Ski edges	滑雪板边刃	
103452	Ski pole discs	滑雪杖挡雪轮	【12】
103450	Ski pole handles	滑雪杖手柄	
103415	Ski poles	滑雪杖	
103452	Ski stick discs	滑雪杖挡雪轮	
103450	Ski stick handles	滑雪杖手柄	【12】
103415	Ski sticks	滑雪杖	
103470	Ski tips [spare parts]	滑雪板顶部件［备用零件］	
103457	Skin-divers' masks	赤身潜水者的面罩	
103435	Skis	滑雪板	
103405	Skittles [games]	撞柱游戏用小柱［游戏器具］	
103473	Snowboards	滑雪板	
103474	Snowshoes	雪鞋具	
103433	Soles of skis	滑雪板底板	
103461	Sticks for playing sports	体育运动用棒	【12】[2]
103434	Surface coverings of soles of skis	滑雪板底板的表面覆盖物	
103453	Surfboards	冲浪板	
103448	Swim fins	游泳用鸭脚蹼	

1　由"Physical appliances 体育器械"修改为"Machines for physical exercise 体能训练机"。
2　由"Bandy sticks 曲棍球棒"修改为"Sticks for playing sports 体育运动用棒"。

100569	Table tennis tables	乒乓球台	【12】[1]
103416	Training bicycles, stationary	训练用固定脚踏车	
103436	Trampolines	蹦床	
103418	Treadmills [exercising devices]	跑步机[锻炼器械]	
103438	Valves for inflatable balls	充气球用气门	
103460	Water skis	滑水板	
103431	Weights for athletics	运动用重物	
103458	Wind-surfing boards	帆板	

21-03
Other amusement and entertainment articles

Notes: (a) Including fairground roundabouts and automatic machines for games of chance. (b) Not including games and toys (Cl. 21-01), or other articles to be placed in Cl. 21-01 or Cl. 21-02.

21-03
其他娱乐和游艺用品

注：（a）包括露天旋转木马和碰运气游戏的自动机器。（b）不包括游戏器具和玩具（21-01类），或者其他列入21-01或21-02类中的物品。

103481	Amusement apparatus	娱乐设备	
103486	Amusement railways	游艺铁路	
103476	Automatic machines for games of chance	碰运气游戏的自动机器	
103478	Carrousels	旋转木马	
103491	Climbing frames [play equipment]	攀登梯架[游戏设备]	
103480	Confetti	五彩纸屑	
103485	Fairground shooting galleries	露天游艺射击靶场	
103482	Ferris wheels	摩天轮，大观缆车	
103477	Firecrackers for parties	聚会用礼花筒	
103494	Frames for outdoor games	户外游戏架	
105013	Inflatable tubes for aquatic activities	水上活动用充气管道	【13】
103488	Jokes and tricks	捉弄和恶作剧用具	
103489	Masks for disguise	乔装面具	
103478	Merry-go-rounds	旋转木马	
103490	Mirrors for fairgrounds	游乐场用镜，哈哈镜	
103483	One arm bandits	老虎机	
103484	Paper streamers [entertainment articles]	彩纸带[娱乐用品]	
104810	Pinatas	皮纳塔	【11】
104810	Piñatas	皮纳塔	【11】
104645	Puppet theaters	木偶戏表演台	【10】
103479	Roundabouts for children's playgrounds	儿童游乐场中的旋转木马	

1　由06-03类转移至21-01类。

103478	Roundabouts [fairground]	旋转木马［游乐场］	
103493	Sand pits	沙坑，玩沙池	
103486	Scenic railways	过山车	
103475	Seesaws	跷跷板	
103487	Slides [chutes]	滑梯［滑道］	
104692	Swimming pools [transportable]	游泳池［可移动式］	【11】[1]
103475	Swings	秋千	
103486	Switchback railways [for amusement]	曲线形轨道［娱乐用］	
103487	Toboggan slides	乘橇滑梯，乘橇滑道	
103488	Tricks and jokes	恶作剧和捉弄用具	
103492	Water slides	水滑道	

21-04
Tents and accessories thereof

Notes: (a) Including poles, pegs and other similar articles. (b) Not including other camping articles to be placed in other classes according to their nature, such as chairs (Cl. 06-01), tables (Cl 06-03), plates (Cl. 07-01), and caravans (Cl. 12-10).

21-04
帐篷及其附件

注：(a)包括撑杆、栓柱和其他类似物品。(b)不包括根据其用途分在其他类中的露营物品，如椅子（06-01类）、桌子（06-03类）、盘子（07-01类）、旅行用大篷车（12-10类）。

103499	Circus tents [big tops]	马戏团帐篷［大顶］	
104634	Marquees [tents]	大营帐［帐篷］	【10】
103497	Pegs for tents	帐篷拴柱	
104898	Rooftop tents for vehicles	交通工具用车顶帐篷	【12】
103495	Tent groundsheets	帐篷防潮布	
103496	Tent poles	帐篷支撑杆	
103498	Tents	帐篷	

21-99
Miscellaneous

21-99
其他杂项

---

[1] 由 21-02 类转移至 21-03 类。

Class 22

Arms, pyrotechnic articles, articles for hunting, fishing and pest killing

22 类

武器，烟火用品，用于狩猎、捕鱼及捕杀有害动物的用具

22-01
Projectile weapons

22-01
射击武器

103524	Air guns	气枪
103509	Anti-hail guns	防雹炮
103504	Bows [archery]	弓[射箭]
103512	Breeches of firearms	枪支后膛
103511	Butts of firearms	枪托
103523	Cannons	大炮
103510	Carbines	卡宾枪，轻型自动或半自动步枪
103530	Cartridge clips for firearms	枪支子弹夹
103502	Crossbows	弩
103506	Cylinders of firearms	枪支旋转弹膛
103505	Firearms	枪支
103507	Gun barrels	枪管，炮筒
103501	Gun carriages	炮架
103522	Gun rests	枪架
103527	Gun silencers	枪炮消声器
103523	Guns	炮，枪
103514	Guns for underwater fishing	水下捕鱼枪
103525	Handshields for shotguns	猎枪护手
103508	Harpoon guns	鱼叉枪，捕鲸炮
103518	Howitzers	榴弹炮
103517	Machine guns	机关枪
103519	Pistols	手枪
103520	Revolvers	左轮手枪
103526	Rifle magazines	步枪弹仓
103513	Rifles	步枪
103521	Slings for firearms	枪支背带
103500	Slingshots	弹弓
103516	Spear guns	鱼叉枪
103503	Spear guns for underwater fishing	水下捕鱼用鱼叉枪

103529	Sub-machine-guns	轻型机关枪	
103515	Triggers for guns	枪扳机	
103528	Warning guns for protection against trespassers	防侵犯警告用枪	

22-02
Other weapons

22-02
其他武器

105014	Anti-drone guns	无人机干扰枪，无人机反制器	【13】
103532	Bayonets	刺刀	
103531	Bladed weapons	带刃武器	【12】[1]
103533	Boomerangs	回力镖，回旋镖	
103535	Brass knuckles	指节铜套	
105015	Daggers	匕首，短剑	【13】
104899	Electroshock weapons	电击武器	【12】
103537	Fencing foils	击剑用钝头剑	
103534	Fencing-foil tips	击剑用钝头剑尖头	
103540	Flame throwers	火焰喷射器	
103539	Sabres	军刀	
103536	Swords	剑	
103538	Truncheons	警棍	

22-03
Ammunition, rockets and pyrotechnic articles

22-03
弹药、火箭和烟火用品

103557	Ammunition	弹药
103542	Ammunition caps	弹药火帽
103550	Arrows	箭
103547	Blank cartridges	空弹，空包弹
103545	Blasting caps	雷管
103548	Blasting cartridges	爆破筒
103546	Cartridges [ammunition]	弹药筒 [弹药]
103544	Detonating capsules	起爆雷管
103549	Detonators	雷管
103563	Distress signal rockets	求救信号弹
103554	Floating and underwater mines	水雷

---

[1] 由"Side arms 随身武器"修改为"Bladed weapons 带刃武器"。

103553	Grenades [missiles]	手榴弹[投射弹]
103556	Guided missiles	导弹
103561	Ignition fuses	引信，引爆装置
103555	Magnetic mines	磁性水雷
103541	Missile boosters	导弹助推器
103558	Projectiles	射弹
103559	Pyrotechnic articles	烟火用品
103543	Rifle bullets	步枪子弹
103551	Rockets [fireworks or missiles]	火箭[花炮或投射弹]
103552	Signalling flares	信号照明弹
103562	Torches [pyrotechnic]	烟花喷筒[烟火]
103560	Torpedoes	鱼雷

22-04
Targets and accessories

Note: Including the special device for actuating mobile targets.

22-04
靶及附件

注：包括驱动活动靶子的专用装置。

103566	Clay pigeons	飞碟靶
103565	Clay-pigeon launchers	飞碟靶发射器
103564	Targets	靶

22-05
Hunting and fishing equipment

Note: Not including articles of clothing (Cl. 02), or weapons (Cl. 22-01 or Cl. 22-02).

22-05
狩猎和捕鱼器械

注：不包括服装（02类）或武器（22-01或22-02类）。

103594	Artificial fish with hooks [bait]	带钩的人造鱼[鱼饵]
103584	Artificial flies for fishing	钓鱼用人造蝇饵
103585	Artificial worms for fishing	人造鱼虫
103591	Bait buckets	鱼饵桶
103567	Bait for fishing	捕鱼鱼饵
103568	Decoy-birds	擒鸟诱饵
103593	Decoys for hunting	狩猎用诱饵
103575	Disgorgers [fishing]	鱼钩脱除器[捕鱼]
103582	Fish hooks	鱼钩
103595	Fishing bait holders	鱼饵用固定物
103583	Fishing harpoons	捕鱼鱼叉
103587	Fishing lines	鱼线

103586	Fishing lures	鱼饵	
105016	Fishing net clearers	渔网整理机	【13】
103579	Fishing nets	渔网	
103596	Fishing rod holders	鱼竿架	
103597	Fishing rod props	鱼竿支架	
103571	Fishing rods	鱼竿	
103577	Fishing tackle	钓鱼具	
103589	Fishing traps	诱捕渔具，渔栅	【12】[1]
103580	Floats for fishing	鱼漂	
103578	Landing nets［fishing］	袋网，抄网［捕鱼］	
103592	Lobster creels	捕虾篓	
103570	Nets［for ferrets and rabbits］	网［捕雪貂和兔用］	
103572	Pots and nets for shrimping	捕虾用笼和网	
103581	Reel type brakes［fishing rods］	卷轴型制动器［鱼杆］	
103569	Reels for fishing lines	鱼线卷轴	
103588	Reels for fishing rods	鱼竿绕线轮	
103590	Sinkers for fishing	钓鱼用铅坠	
103583	Spears for fishing	捕鱼鱼叉	
103574	Spoon bait	匙形假饵	
103576	Swivels for fishing	钓鱼用连接转环	【12】[2]
103573	Trawls	拖网	

22-06
Traps, articles for pest killing

22-06
捕捉器、捕杀有害动物的用具

103605	Animal traps	动物捕捉器	
103610	Atomizers for insecticides［except aerosol dispensers and agricultural atomizers］	杀虫剂喷雾器［气雾分配器和农用喷雾器除外］	
104571	Baits for mouse traps	捕鼠器用饵	【10】
103606	Caterpillar lanterns［traps］	诱虫灯［捕捉器］	
103609	Fly swatters	蝇拍	
103608	Flypaper holders	粘蝇纸固定座	
103600	Insect or bird catching nets	昆虫或鸟捕捉网	
103598	Insect traps	昆虫捕捉器	
103607	Lark mirrors	诱鸟反光镜	
104811	Mosquito repellent bracelets	驱蚊手环	【11】

---

1 由"Pots for lobsters，eels，etc. 捕龙虾、鳗鲡等的笼"修改为"Fishing traps 诱捕渔具，渔栅"。
2 由"Spinners for fishing lines 鱼线旋绕器"修改为"Swivels for fishing 钓鱼用连接转环"。

103611	Moth traps	飞蛾捕捉器	
103604	Mousetraps	捕鼠器	
103603	Rat traps	捕鼠器	
104812	Refills for mosquito repellent bracelets	驱蚊手环添补物	【11】
103599	Traps and articles for destruction of pests	消灭有害动物的捕捉器和用具	
103601	Traps for animals	动物捕捉器	
103602	Traps for insects [also electric]	昆虫捕捉器[包括电动的]	

22-99
Miscellaneous

22-99
其他杂项

103612	Armor	盔甲
103615	Camouflage nets	伪装网
103614	Paravanes	水雷排除器
103613	Shields [arms]	盾[武器]

Class 23
Fluid distribution equipment, sanitary, heating, ventilation and air-conditioning equipment, solid fuel

23 类
流体分配设备、卫生设备、加热设备、通风和空气调节设备、固体燃料

23-01
Fluid distribution equipment
Note: Including pipes and pipe fittings.

23-01
流体分配设备
注：包括管和管配件。

编号	英文	中文	标记
103616	Adapters for pipe joints	管接头用配接器	
103621	Anti-splash nozzles for taps	龙头防溅喷嘴	
103629	Apparatus for supply of gas	煤气供应设备	
103634	Cocks and taps	旋塞和龙头	
103635	Coiled pipes [parts of appliances]	蛇形管[设备部件]	
103650	Connecting devices for gas bottles	煤气罐连接装置	
103665	Control handles for taps	龙头的控制把手	
103649	Douche bags	冲洗袋，灌洗袋	
103661	Drainpipes	排水管	【11】[1]
103628	Drinking fountains	喷嘴式饮水器	
103633	Extensible connections for flexible piping	可延伸的软管接头	
103622	Faucet handles	龙头柄	
103645	Faucets	龙头	
103648	Fire hose nozzles	消防水带喷嘴	
103653	Fire hoses	消防水带	
103647	Fire hydrants	消防栓	
104900	Fire sprinklers	消防喷淋头	【12】
103639	Flexible pipes	软管	
104813	Floor drains [indoor and outdoor]	地漏[户内外的]	【11】
103625	Fluid distribution equipment	流体分配设备	
103666	Garden hoses	花园浇花用软管	
104814	Grates for floor drains [indoor and outdoor]	地漏格栅[户内外的]	【11】
104694	Gratings for storm drains	下水道格栅	【11】[2]
103643	Gutters	檐沟，排水槽	

1　由"Drainpipes, not for walls 非墙用排水管"修改为"Drainpipes 排水管"。
2　由 25-02 类转移至 23-01 类，并由"Gratings for gullies 沟渠格栅"修改为"Gratings for storm drains 下水道格栅"。

103620	Hydrants	给水栓	
103651	Hydraulic output regulators	液压输出调节器	
104630	Irrigation installations	灌溉设备	【10】
103659	Joint or packing rings for tubes and pipes	管子连接环，管子密封环	
103659	Joint rings for tubes and pipes	管子连接环	
103631	Joints for pipes	管接头	
103637	Lawn sprinklers	草地洒水器，草地喷灌器	
103658	Leaf gratings for down pipes	落水管树叶格栅	
103652	Mixing taps	混合龙头	
103659	Packing rings for tubes and pipes	管子密封环	
103657	Pipe and plate packed joints	盘管密封接头	
103638	Pipes of concrete or cement	混凝土或水泥制管	
103624	Pressure reducers for gas	煤气减压器	
103632	Pressure reducers ［pipe fittings］	减压器，节流器［管配件］	
103640	Rigid piping	硬管	
104695	Safety devices for drain gratings	排水沟格栅安全装置	【11】[1]
103655	Safety valves for cisterns	贮水器安全阀	
103636	Siphons for decanting fluids	流体移注虹吸管	
103656	Sluice gates	水闸门	
103662	Slurry tanks	泥浆槽	
103667	Sprinklers for sinks	水槽的喷洒装置	
103642	Standpipes	消防竖管、室外消防栓	【12】[2]
104693	Storm drains	下水道	【11】[3]
103654	Stove pipes	炉烟管	
103623	Suction roses	吸水管喷嘴	
103644	Tanks for gaseous or liquid substances	气体或液体储槽	
103626	Tap bases	龙头座	
103619	Tap casings	龙头套接短管	
103645	Taps	龙头	
103634	Taps and cocks	龙头和旋塞	
103663	Thermostatic mixers	恒温龙头，恒温混水器	
103641	Valves ［taps］	阀［龙头］	
103664	Washing nozzles	洗涤喷嘴	
103627	Water filters	水过滤器	
103646	Water hose nozzles	水管喷嘴	
103660	Water purifiers	水净化器	
103712	Water purifying installations	净水装置	【13】[4]
103617	Water softening apparatus	水软化设备	

1 由25-02类转移至23-01类。
2 由"Street fountains 街道喷泉装置"修改为"Standpipes 消防竖管、室外消防栓"。
3 由25-02类转移至23-01类，并由"Gully-holes 集水孔"修改为"Storm drains 下水道"。
4 由23-08类转移至23-01类，并由"水处理装置"修改为"净水装置"。

| 103618 | Water sprinklers | 洒水器 |
| 103630 | Waterspouts | 排水口 |

23-02
[Vacant]

23-02
[空缺]

【12】[1]

23-03
Heating equipment

23-03
加热设备

103755	Air humidifiers for heating radiators	暖气片用空气增湿器
103725	Animal or plant husbandry heaters	畜牧业或种植业供热器
103752	Ashpan sifters	炉灰盘筛
103750	Atomic piles	原子反应堆
103745	Bakers' ovens	面包师用烤炉
103743	Bath heaters	浴室供热器
103756	Bleeding taps for heating radiators	暖气片用排气龙头
103721	Braziers	火钵，火盆
103744	Brick and tile kilns	砖瓦窑
103757	Bunsen burners	喷灯，本生灯
103722	Burners [heating]	燃炉[加热用]
103754	Control panels for bath heaters	浴室供热器控制面板
103758	Convectors	对流散热器
103739	Draught regulators for fireplaces	壁炉通风调节器
103741	Draught regulators [heating]	通风调节器[供热用]
103748	Fire grates	炉栅
103731	Flame deflectors for oil-fired heating devices	燃油加热装置的火焰挡板
103762	Flued stoves	暖气炉
103728	Footwarmers	脚炉，暖足器
103759	Furnaces	炉，熔炉
104612	Garden fireplaces	花园壁炉	【10】
103729	Gas fireplaces	燃气壁炉
103733	Glassmaking furnaces	制造玻璃用熔炉
103759	Hearths	炉床，炉膛
103760	Heat recuperators	同流换热器
103761	Heating boilers	供热锅炉
103724	Heating equipment	加热设备

1　23-02类整体拆分成23-06类、23-07类以及23-08类，由"Sanitary appliances 卫生设备"修改为"[Vacant][空缺]"，并转移所有产品项。

103747	Hot air generators	热气发生器	
103720	Igniters for gaseous fuel burners	气体燃料炉的点火器	
103730	Indoor fireplaces	室内壁炉	
103749	Infrared lamps for heating	加热用红外线灯	
103751	Intake pipes for central heating	集中供热的输入管	
103742	Jets for gas burners	煤气炉的喷嘴	
103723	Mantelpieces for fireplaces	壁炉架	【13】[1]
103736	Nuclear reactors	核反应堆	
103763	Outdoor heaters	户外取暖器	
103734	Ovens［industrial］	烤箱，炉［工业用］	
103732	Pottery kilns	陶器窑	
103738	Radiators for heating	暖气片	
103740	Sauna heaters	桑拿浴室供热器	
103746	Smelting furnaces［electric］	熔炉［电的］	
103753	Solar heat collectors	太阳能集热器	
103735	Steam boilers for heating	加热用蒸汽锅炉	
103737	Stoves［heating］	炉［加热用］	
104901	Waste heat recovery units	热能回收装置	【12】
103727	Water heaters［electric］	热水器［电的］	
103726	Water heaters［gas］	热水器［煤气］	

23-04
Ventilation and air-conditioning equipment

23-04
通风和空气调节设备

103777	Air conditioners	空调机	
103770	Air conditioning apparatus	空调设备	
105017	Air dehumidifiers	空气除湿器	【13】
103765	Air deodorizing apparatus	空气除臭设备	
103771	Air humidifiers	空气加湿器	
103767	Air purifiers	空气净化器	
103772	Air sterilizing apparatus	空气消毒设备	
103773	Air vents	通风排气孔	
103772	Apparatus for air sterilization	空气消毒设备	
103768	Hoods for ventilation	通风罩	
103766	Smoke extractors	抽油烟机	
103764	Ventilating fans	通风扇	

---

[1] 由"Chambranles for heating arrangements 加热装置装饰框"修改为"Mantelpieces for fireplaces 壁炉架"。

103775	Ventilation ducts	通风管	
103774	Ventilation grids	通风栅格	
103769	Ventilation valves	通风阀	
103776	Ventilator blades	通风机叶片	

23-05
Solid fuel

23-05
固体燃料

103781	Briquettes [fuel]	煤球［燃料］	
103782	Charcoal	木炭	
103783	Coal	煤	
103778	Coal briquettes	煤球	
103779	Fire starters	引燃物	
103780	Nuts [fuel]	小煤块［燃料］	
103784	Solid fuels	固体燃料	

23-06
Sanitary appliances for personal hygiene

23-06
个人卫生用卫生设备 【12】[1]

103673	Baby baths	婴儿浴盆	
103671	Bath tubs	浴盆，浴缸	
103672	Bath tubs for sitz-baths	坐浴用浴缸	
103675	Bidets	坐浴盆，妇洗器	
104315	Hair washing basins	洗头盆	【13】[2]
103670	Hot air bath appliances	热气浴设备	
103711	Isolation tanks [for relaxation]	隔离舱［放松用］	
103718	Lavabos	洗手盆	
103702	Lavatory basins	盥洗盆	
103717	Overflows	溢流口	
103715	Plugs for sinks	水槽塞子	
103694	Saunas	桑拿浴室，蒸汽浴室	
103669	Shower cabinets	淋浴房	
103716	Shower trays	淋浴房底盘	
103686	Showers	淋浴器	
103678	Sink drains	洗涤槽排水口	
103707	Sink strainers	洗涤槽滤器	

1　新增加 23-06 类，产品项由 23-02 类转移至 23-06 类。
2　由 28-03 类转移至 23-06 类。

103677	Sink units	洗涤槽组	
103688	Sinks	洗涤槽	
103687	Spray heads for showers	淋浴器喷头	
103674	Steam baths equipment	蒸汽浴设备	
103697	Sudation apparatus, non medical	非医疗用发汗设备	
103704	Turkish bath cabinets, portable	移动式土耳其蒸汽浴室	
103702	Washbasins	洗脸盆	
103668	Wash-hand basins	洗手盆	

23-07
Equipment for urination and defecation　　便溺设备　　【12】[1]

101652	Babies' potties	婴儿便盆	【13】[2]
101641	Bucket latrines	卫生便池	【13】[3]
103689	Cesspools, fixed or movable	固定或移动式污水池	
101640	Chamber pots	便壶	【13】[4]
104816	Commode chairs	座厕椅	【11】
103679	Flushing cisterns	抽水马桶水箱	
103680	Flushing devices for water closets	抽水马桶冲洗装置	
103692	Latrines	便池	
103690	Septic tanks	化粪池	
103719	Toilet seat adapters for babies	婴幼儿用马桶座圈适配器	
103681	Toilet seat covers	马桶座盖	
103701	Toilet seats	马桶座	
103699	Urinals [public]	小便池［公共用］	
103700	Water closets	抽水马桶	
103706	Water-closet outlet floats	抽水马桶出水口浮子	
103682	Water-closet pans	抽水蹲便器	

23-08
Other sanitary equipment and accessories, not included in other classes or subclasses　　其他大类或小类未包括的卫生设备及附件　　【12】[5]

104838	Applicators for toilet bowl cleaning gel	马桶洁厕凝胶用打胶装置	【12】

---

[1] 新增加 23-07 类，产品项由 23-02 类转移至 23-07 类。
[2] 由 09-09 类转移至 23-07 类。
[3] 由 09-09 类转移至 23-07 类，并由 "Sanitary buckets 卫生桶" 修改为 "Bucket latrines 卫生便池"。
[4] 由 09-09 类转移至 23-07 类。
[5] 新增加 23-08 类，除两个新增产品项外，其余产品项由 23-02 类转移至 23-08 类。

103709	Bathroom shelves [except furniture]	浴室搁架[家具除外]	
103713	Decanting apparatus for waste water	废水滗析设备	
103714	Deodorant holders [for sanitary equipment]	除臭剂用架[卫生设备用]	
103708	Glass holders [for bathroom]	玻璃托架[浴室用]	
104328	Hand driers	手烘干机,干手机	【12】[1]
104837	Holders for toilet rim blocks	马桶清洁块用挂托	【12】
103703	Lavatory-brush holders	盥洗刷架	
103695	Liquid soap dispensers	皂液分配器	
103676	Sanitary units [including for hospitals]	卫生装置[包括医院用]	
103705	Sewer traps	除臭用下水道弯管	
103693	Soap dishes	肥皂托	【13】
103684	Soap dispensers	肥皂分配器	
103693	Soap holders	肥皂托	
103683	Toilet paper dispensers	卫生纸分配器	
103698	Toilet paper holders	卫生纸托架	
105018	Toothpaste dispensers	牙膏分配器	【13】
103685	Towel dispensers	擦手纸巾分配器	
103710	Towel holders [sanitary equipment]	毛巾架[卫生设备]	
104815	Towel rails	毛巾架,毛巾杆	【11】
103696	Traps for sanitary apparatus	卫生设备存水用弯管	

23-99
Miscellaneous

23-99
其他杂项

103787	Refuse incinerators	垃圾焚化炉,尸体焚化炉
103786	Trash burners	垃圾焚烧器
103785	Water distillation apparatus	水蒸馏设备

---

[1] 由 28-03 类转移至 23-08 类。

Class 24
Medical and laboratory equipment

Note: The term "medical equipment" covers also surgical, dental and veterinary equipment.

24-01
Apparatus and equipment for doctors, hospitals and laboratories

24类
医疗设备和实验室设备

注：术语"医疗设备"还包括外科、牙科和兽医用设备。

24-01
医生、医院和实验室用的仪器和设备

编号	英文	中文	备注
103790	Anaesthetic apparatus	麻醉机	
103819	Anaesthetic masks	麻醉面罩	
103827	Apparatus and installations for medical or laboratory diagnosis	医疗或实验室用诊断设备和装置	
103824	Apparatus for thermotherapy	温热疗法设备	
104903	Artificial lung ventilation apparatus	肺通气装置，呼吸机	【12】
103792	Audiometers	听力计	
103793	Autoclaves [medicine]	高压消毒器[药用]	
104906	Blood glucose meters	血糖仪	【12】
103789	Blood testing apparatus	血液化验设备	
103825	Blood transfusion and sampling apparatus	输血和采血设备	
103826	Chromatographs	色谱仪	
103798	Compression diaphragms [Roentgen apparatus]	压缩遮光板[X射线装置]	
104904	Defibrillators	除颤仪，除颤器	【12】
103797	Dental appliances [fixed]	牙科设备[固定式]	
103799	Diathermy apparatus	透热疗法设备	
103818	Disinfecting and sterilizing chambers	消毒和杀菌箱	
103791	Disinfection equipment for premises	房间用消毒设备	
103800	Drills [dental]	牙钻[牙科用]	
104905	Electrocardiographs	心电图仪	【12】
104907	Electrosurgical apparatus	电外科手术器械，手术电刀	【12】
103829	Exercise devices for disabled persons	残疾人用康复装置	
103794	Eye testing apparatus and equipment	眼睛检查仪器和设备	
103805	Fixed apparatus and equipment for doctors	医生用固定仪器和设备	
103801	Fixed apparatus and equipment for hospitals	医院用固定仪器和设备	
103803	Fixed apparatus and equipment for laboratories	实验室用固定仪器和设备	

104625	Hydrotherapy apparatus [medical apparatus]	水疗设备［医疗设备］	【10】
103795	Incubators for newborn infants	新生儿保育箱	
103831	Incubators [medical apparatus]	（用于放置早产婴儿的）恒温箱［医疗设备］	
103821	Insufflation apparatus for pneumothorax	气胸注入设备	
103802	Irradiation apparatus	辐照设备，放射设备	
104908	Laser scalpels	激光手术刀	【12】
103832	Light therapy apparatus	光疗设备	
103822	Mass spectrographs	质谱仪	
103804	Medical apparatus and equipment [fixed]	医疗仪器和设备［固定式］	
104637	Medical rehabilitation apparatus	医疗康复设备	【10】
103806	Microtomes	超薄切片机	
103823	Operating tables	手术台	
103807	Oxygen tents	氧气帐，氧幕	
103808	Ozonizers for medical use	医用臭氧发生器	
103788	Particle accelerators	粒子加速器	
103830	Physiotherapy apparatus	物理治疗设备	
103820	Portable microlathes for dental and bone surgery	牙科和骨科手术用便携式微型车床	
103796	Relaxing apparatus [for medical use]	放松设备［医用］	
103813	Resuscitators	复苏器，人工呼吸器	
103810	Saliva aspirators [dental]	唾液汲出器［牙科用］	
103828	Spirometers for medical purposes	医用肺活量计	
103809	Spray guns for dentists	牙医用喷枪	
103814	Sterilizers for medical use	医用消毒器	
103818	Sterilizing and disinfecting chambers	杀菌和消毒箱	
103815	Sudation apparatus for medical use	医用发汗设备	
104902	Surgical microscopes	手术显微镜	【12】
103816	Ureteromy apparatus	输尿管切开术设备	
103817	Vibrators for dentists	牙医用振动器	
103811	X-ray production apparatus	X射线机	
103812	X-ray tubes	X射线管	

24-02

Medical instruments, instruments and tools for laboratory use

Note: Including only hand-operated instruments.

24-02

医疗器械、实验室用器械和实验室用工具

注：仅包括手动操作的器械。

103895	Acupuncture instruments	针刺器械

104909	Anti-snoring devices	防打鼾装置，止鼾器	【12】
103838	Apparatus for keeping the mouth open [dentistry]	保持口腔打开用器具［牙科］	
103863	Apparatus for taking blood samples	取血样用器械	
103888	Blood pressure measuring apparatus	血压测量仪	
103889	Breast pumps for nursing mothers	哺乳母亲用的吸奶器	
103854	Castrating instruments	阉割器械	
103878	Chains for calving cattle	家畜接生用链条	
103892	Clips for surgical purposes	外科手术用剪	
103887	Cooling coils [for laboratories]	蛇形冷却管［实验室用］	
103843	Crucibles [for laboratories]	坩埚［实验室用］	
103844	Curettes [medicine]	刮匙［药用］	
103845	Cystoscopes	膀胱镜	
103846	Dental forceps	牙科镊子	
103847	Dental instruments	牙科器械	
103869	Dentists' spatulas	牙医用压舌板	
103885	Devices for calculating blood sedimentation rate	用于计算血沉率的装置	
103834	Dilators [medical instruments]	扩张器［医疗器械］	
103833	Douches for injections	注射冲洗器	
103841	Droppers for medical or laboratory purposes	医疗或实验室用滴管	
103873	Dropping tubes	输液滴管	
103881	Ear cleaners [medical]	耳朵清洁器［医用］	
103886	Ear syringes	洗耳球	
103851	Forceps	手术钳，医用镊子	
103852	Gastroscopes	胃镜	
103891	Graduated glassware	带刻度的玻璃器皿	
103880	Grinding wheels for dentists	牙医用砂轮	
104615	Gua sha scrapers	刮痧板	【10】
103883	Haemostatic clamps	止血钳	
103855	Hand-operated instruments and tools for laboratories	实验室用手动操作器械和工具	
103858	Hand-operated medical instruments	手动操作医疗器械	
103835	Hypodermic needles	皮下注射针	
103839	Injection tubes	注射管	
103893	Instruments and utensils for medical or laboratory diagnosis	医疗或实验室诊断用器械和器具	
103842	Knives for surgical purposes	外科手术刀	

103890	Laboratory glassware	实验室用玻璃器皿	
103867	Laboratory siphons	实验室用虹吸管	
103856	Lancets	柳叶刀，采血针	
103857	Laryngoscopes	喉镜	
103859	Medical instruments	医疗器械	
103868	Medical probes	医用探针	
103866	Medical syringes	医用注射器	
103874	Medical thermocauteries	医用热灼器	
103853	Medicine injectors	药品注射器	
103860	Mirrors for doctors and dentists	医生和牙医用反射镜	
103896	Mortars [for laboratories]	研钵[实验室用]	
104638	Moxibustion instruments	艾灸器械	【10】
104639	Needles for acupuncture	针灸用针	【10】
103836	Needles for medical purposes	医用针	
103882	Oxygen masks	氧气面罩	
103861	Pipettes	移液管，滴管	
103837	Retorts	蒸馏器	
103864	Retractors	牵开器	
103884	Saws for surgical purposes	外科手术用锯	
103865	Scalpels	手术刀	
104818	Specimen cups with lids	带盖标本杯	【11】
103870	Specula	窥器，子宫镜	
103871	Sphygmometers	脉搏计，血压计	
103872	Stethoscopes	听诊器	
103840	Surgical instruments	外科用器械	
103894	Surgical staplers	外科缝合器	【12】[1]
103848	Swabs for taking mucus smears	用于涂抹黏液的棉签、拭子	
103849	Syringe nozzles	注射针头，灌洗器喷头	
103897	Test strips for medical or laboratory purposes	医疗或实验室用试片，试纸	
103850	Test tubes	试管	
103879	Tooth extractors	牙齿拔出器	
103875	Trepans [surgery]	环锯[外科]	
103876	Trocars	套管针	
103877	Urinometers	尿比重计	
103862	Washing bottles [for laboratories]	冲洗瓶[实验室用]	

---

1 由"Clippers for surgical use 外科手术用剪"修改为"Surgical staplers 外科缝合器"。

24-03
Prosthetic articles

103904	Artificial eyes	假眼	
104910	Artificial heart valves	人造心脏瓣膜	【12】
103901	Artificial limbs	假肢	
103900	Artificial teeth	假牙	
103898	Bridges［dental］	假牙牙床［牙科用］	
103899	Dental plates	齿板	
103905	Denture fixing devices	假牙固定器	
104913	Implantable pacemakers	可植入的起搏器，体内起搏器	【12】
103902	Pins for artificial teeth	用于假牙上的牙冠钉	
103903	Prosthetics	修补物，假体	
104912	Stent grafts	体内枝状支架	【12】
104911	Stents	体内管状支架	【12】
103906	Surgical nails	外科用钉	

24-04
Materials for dressing wounds, nursing and medical care

Note: Including absorbent dressings.

注：包括吸水性敷料剂。

103909	Absorbent bandages	吸水绷带
103940	Ankle pads［medical］	踝垫［医用］
103910	Apparatus for cutting plaster-of-paris bandages	切割熟石膏绷带用器械
103928	Atomizers for medicine［except aerosol dispensers］	医用雾化器［气雾分配器除外］
103933	Bedpans	床上便盆
103913	Belts［bandages］	带［绷带］
103931	Catamenial absorbents	月经吸收物
103908	Comforters	安抚奶嘴
103945	Condoms	避孕套
103921	Cradle-splints for injured limbs	伤肢用支夹板
103934	Cupping glasses［medical］	拔火罐［医用］
103944	Cushions for pelvis support	骨盆支架衬垫
103942	Cutting devices for adhesive plaster	橡皮膏用切割装置
103916	Drainage tubes for medical purposes	医用引流管

103926	Dressings	敷料	
103925	Ear plugs	耳塞	
103925	Ear stoppers	耳塞	
103937	Feeding devices for invalids	病人用喂食工具	
103920	Fumigators	烟熏器	
103936	Hernia bandages	疝气带	
103938	Ice bags for medical purposes	医用冰袋	
104628	Incontinence pads	失禁垫	【10】
103922	Inhalers	吸入器，哮喘用吸入器	
104629	Intrauterine devices [IUD]	子宫内避孕器[IUD]	【10】
103923	Irrigators [medical]	冲洗器[医用]	
103930	Jock straps	护裆三角带	
103914	Medical compresses	医用敷布	
103924	Medical equipment for enemas	灌肠用医疗器械	
104914	Medical infusion bags	医用输液袋	【12】
105020	Menstrual cups	月事杯，月经杯	【13】
103940	Orthopedic ankle supports and braces	整形外科用踝支撑和固定架	
103943	Orthopedic arch supports	整形外科用弓形支架	
105019	Pacifier clips	奶嘴夹	【13】
105019	Pacifier holders	奶嘴固定防掉链	【13】
103908	Pacifiers for babies	婴儿用安慰奶嘴	
103927	Pessaries	子宫托，子宫帽	
103935	Plasters for callosities	胼胝用膏药	
103919	Plasters for rheumatism, sciatica	用于风湿病和坐骨神经痛的膏药	
103939	Rectal syringes for injection of enemas	用于注射和灌肠的直肠注射器	
103939	Rectal syringes for injections and enemas	用于注射和灌肠的直肠注射器	
103941	Sanitary towels	月经带，卫生巾	
103917	Slings [surgical]	悬带[外科用]	
103918	Splints [surgical]	夹板[外科用]	
103929	Sticking plasters for medical purposes	医用胶布，橡皮膏	
103934	Suction cups [medical]	吸杯[医用]	
103911	Surgical bandages	外科绷带	
103930	Suspensory bandages	悬吊绷带	
103907	Teething rings	婴儿咬环	
103912	Umbilical tapes	脐带状带	
103932	Urinals [receptacles]	小便壶[容器]	
103915	Weaning devices	断奶器	

24-99
Miscellaneous

24-99
其他杂项

104568	Acupressure mats	针压按摩垫	【10】
103948	Dental braces	牙齿矫正器	
103947	Dental floss holders	牙线托	
105021	Devices for magnetic therapy	磁疗设备	【13】
103946	Hearing aids for the deaf	聋人助听器	
105022	Orthokeratology lenses	OK镜，角膜塑形镜	【13】
104819	Posture correction devices	姿势校正装置	【11】

Class 25
Building units and construction elements

25 类
建筑构件和施工元件

25-01
Building materials

Note: Including bricks, beams, pre-shaped strips, tiles, slates and panels.

25-01
建筑材料

注：包括砖、梁、未成形板、瓦、瓷砖、石板和镶板。

103985	Acoustic building elements	声学建筑元件	
103995	Anchoring components [building]	锚式构件[建筑]	
103957	Angle irons	角铁，角钢	
103986	Angle irons [L-shaped sections]	角铁，角钢[L形截面]	
103992	Anti-noise screens [building materials]	降噪屏[建筑材料]	
103981	Architectural moldings	建筑线脚	
103958	Battens [carpentry]	板条[木工]	
103974	Beams [construction]	梁[建筑]	
104820	Blocks for breakwaters	防波堤用块材	【11】
103978	Blocks for construction	建筑块材	
103953	Boundary stones	界石	
103965	Brackets [woodwork]	托架[木制品]	
103954	Bricks	砖	
103956	Building materials	建筑材料	
103987	Building stones	建筑石料	
103984	Ceramic tiles for building	建筑瓷砖，饰面砖	
103976	Cladding for building	建筑外壁覆面物	
103951	Clapboards	护墙楔形板，护墙板	
103983	Conduits for cables	线缆管道	
103975	Construction elements [angles]	施工元件[角形物]	
103964	Cork sheets [construction]	软木薄板[建筑]	
103952	Curbs for sidewalks	人行道的路缘石	
103994	Decorative panels for building	建筑装饰板	
103991	Edge lists for lawns and beds of flowers	草坪和花坛的边沿	
103988	Fence pickets	栅栏尖桩	
103949	Fish plates [rail]	接合板，鱼尾板[钢轨]	
103974	Girders	梁	
103961	Joists	托梁	

103952	Kerbs for pavements	人行道的路缘石	
103963	Laths	板条	
103976	Linings for building	建筑衬砌	
103966	Longitudinal girders	纵向大梁	
103962	Panelling	镶板	
103968	Panelling [building]	镶板 [建筑]	
103993	Panels for electric conductors	电导体板	
103969	Paving stones	铺路石	
103970	Piles [stakes]	桩 [栅栏]	
103971	Plates [building]	板 [建筑]	
103973	Plinths	柱基，墙基石，勒脚	
103988	Posts for fences	栅栏柱	
103980	Railroad ties	铁路轨枕	
103982	Railway rails	铁轨	
103980	Railway sleepers	铁路轨枕	
103955	Refractory materials	耐火材料	
103990	Reinforced glass	强化玻璃	
103979	Rods for reinforcing concrete	加强混凝土钢筋	
103972	Roofing plates	屋顶盖板	
103996	Scantlings [carpentry]	细木条，小木块 [木工]	
104657	Sections [building materials]	型材 [建筑材料]	【10】
103967	Sheeting piles	板桩	
103951	Shingle boards	屋顶板，墙板	
103971	Slabs [building]	厚板 [建筑]	
103950	Slates for building	建筑石板	
103960	Supports [props]	支撑物 [支柱]	
103977	Tiles	瓦，瓷砖	
103989	Tufa stones	凝灰岩石	

25-02

Prefabricated or pre-assembled building parts

Notes: (a) Including windows, doors, outdoor shutters, partition walls and gratings. (b) Not including staircases (Cl. 25-04).

25-02

预制或预装建筑构件

注：(a) 包括窗户、门、户外百叶窗、隔断墙和栅栏。(b) 不包括楼梯（25-04 类）。

104021	Abutments for bridges	桥墩	
104570	Artificial grass tiles	人造草砖	【10】
104000	Awnings	遮篷，屋檐	

104915	Balconies	阳台	【12】
104001	Balustrades	栏杆	
104002	Balustrading	栏杆	
104001	Banisters	栏杆立柱	
104003	Barriers	栅栏	
104059	Bases for posts	柱基	
104043	Blinds［outdoor］	百叶窗［户外］	
104824	Bollards	系船柱，缆桩	【11】
104068	Bowls［masonry］	碗状物［砖石建筑］	
104034	Canopies for doors	门用遮篷	
104020	Casement windows	竖铰链窗	
104038	Ceilings	天花板	
104008	Chimney caps	烟囱帽	
103998	Chimney cowls	烟囱风帽	
104053	Chimney pots	烟囱顶管	
104012	Chimneys for buildings	建筑物烟囱	
104016	Columns［building］	柱［建筑］	
104597	Corbels	枕梁	【10】
104019	Cornices［building］	飞檐［建筑］	
104004	Crash barriers for roads	道路防撞护栏，防撞隔离墩	
104029	Devices for adjusting slats for blinds	用于调节百叶板的装置	
104030	Dome lanterns	圆顶灯笼式天窗	
104023	Domes	圆屋顶	
104055	Door casings	门框，门套	
104055	Door frames	门框	
104056	Door panels	门板	
104041	Doors	门	
104032	Dormer windows	天窗	
104057	Elevator doors	电梯门	
104054	False ceilings	假天花板，装饰性吊顶	
104051	Fanlights	楣窗，扇形窗	
104015	Fences	栅栏	
104039	Floors	地板	
104061	Flower boxes［outdoor］	花槽，花盒，花箱［户外］	
104067	Flower stands［masonry］	花坛，花架［砖石建筑］	
104607	Folding doors	折叠门	【10】
104010	Forcing frames［horticulture］	栽培温床［园艺］	

104009	Framework [building]	骨架[建筑]	
104069	French windows	落地窗	
104071	Gabions	石筐,石笼	
104611	Garage doors	车库门	【10】
104040	Gates	大门	
104005	Grade-crossing gates	平面交叉道口栏栅	
104026	Gratings [parts of buildings]	格栅[建筑构件]	
104033	Handrails	扶手栏杆	
104004	Highway line guards	高速公路防护装置	
104823	Insulated building panels	绝缘建筑板	【11】
104046	Latticework	网格结构	
104072	Lawn grid plates	草坪格板	
104005	Level-crossing gates	水平交叉道口栏栅	
104057	Lift doors	电梯门	
104031	Lintels	楣,过梁	
104052	Lock gates	闸门	
103997	Manhole covers	检修孔盖	
104049	Mine props	矿井支柱	
104064	Openwork partition	网眼式分隔物	
104035	Palisades	栅栏	
104025	Parapets	胸墙,女儿墙	
104037	Parquets	镶木地板	
104036	Partition walls	隔断墙	
104014	Partitions [building]	分隔物[建筑]	
104022	Pavings	铺筑过的路面	
104049	Pitprops [mining]	坑木,坑道支柱[采矿]	
104017	Prefabricated or pre-assembled building parts	预制或预装建筑构件	
104821	Removable floor tiles for outdoor use	户外用可拆卸地砖	【11】
104073	Rest barriers [outdoor]	固定栅栏[户外]	
104044	Roofs	屋顶	
104013	Screens for hothouses	温室遮盖物	
104822	Sewer manholes	下水道检修孔	【11】
104058	Shop shutters	商店百叶窗	
104048	Shutters [venetian]	百叶窗[威尼斯式]	
103999	Sills [windowsills]	槛[窗台]	
104030	Skylights	天窗	
104028	Slats for blinds	百叶板	

104063	Snow fences [for roofs]	防雪栅栏[屋顶用]	
104059	Sockets for posts	柱座	
105023	Speed bumps	减速带	【13】
104047	Stained-glass windows	有色玻璃窗	
104064	Stone windows	石窗	
104018	Storm windows	遮挡风雪的护窗，防风窗，外层窗	
104042	Thresholds	门槛	
104065	Tiling	瓦屋顶	
104051	Transoms	门顶窗，气窗，楣窗	
104066	Tree protectors	树木保护装置	
104045	Turnstiles	十字转门	
104007	Vault safes	拱顶保险库	
104027	Venetian shutters [outdoor]	威尼斯百叶窗[户外]	
104060	Ventilation shutters	通风百叶窗	
104050	Waste disposal chutes	废物处理滑道	
104685	Windbreaks [building]	防风墙[建筑]	【10】
104011	Window frames	窗框	
104024	Windows	窗	
103999	Windowsills	窗台	

25-03
Houses, garages and other buildings

25-03
房屋、车库和其他建筑

104827	Artificial reefs	人工鱼礁	【11】
104094	Barns	谷仓	
104083	Beach huts	海滩棚屋	
104115	Boathouses	船库，艇库	
104074	Bomb shelters	防空洞	
104104	Bridge piers	栈桥	
104106	Bridges [civil engineering]	桥[土木工程]	
104080	Buildings	建筑物	
104089	Buildings [transportable]	建筑物[活动式]	
104081	Bungalows	平房	
104087	Burial vaults	拱顶墓穴	
104078	Carports	停车棚	
104084	Changing cubicles	更衣室	
104131	Children's play-houses	儿童娱乐室	
104128	Columbaria	骨灰安置所	

243

104090	Crypts	地窖，地下室	
104601	Dolphins ［structures］	系缆桩［建筑］	【10】
104125	Dustbin shelters	垃圾箱遮棚	
104118	Filling stations	加油站	
104121	Floating bridges	浮桥	
104123	Footbridges	人行桥	
104092	Garages	车库	
104093	Gasometers	贮气罐	
104109	Greenhouses	温室	
104095	Hangars	飞机库	
104107	Hen houses	鸡舍	
104137	Horticultural cloches	园艺用钟形玻璃罩	
104096	Houses	房屋	
104116	Inflatable marquees	充气篷，充气房	
104124	Kiosks	亭子	
104136	Letter boxes	信箱，邮筒	
104091	Locks ［canal］	水闸［运河］	
104077	Market shelters	市场摊棚	
104098	Mausoleums	陵墓	
104130	Miniature buildings ［except toys］	微缩建筑物［玩具除外］	
104134	Modular shelters	组合式遮蔽所	
104099	Monuments	纪念碑	
104120	Mooring booms	系泊臂	
104138	Newspaper boxes	报箱	
105024	Outdoor fountains	室外喷泉	【13】
104082	Paint spray booths	喷漆房	
104126	Passenger shelters	旅客遮雨棚	
104103	Pavilions ［building］	亭［建筑］	
104133	Pergolas	（用藤架等做顶的）凉亭，蔓棚	
104117	Posts for electricity mains cables	电力电缆杆	
104135	Power stations ［civil engineering］	发电站［土木工程］	
104129	Protective shelters for building materials	建筑材料的保护掩体	
104108	Pylons	高压电缆塔	
104101	Recesses for telephones	放电话机的壁龛	
104825	Rooftop wind turbines	屋顶风轮机	【11】
104114	Sarcophagi	石棺	

104122	Sentry boxes [cabins]	岗亭[小屋]	
104118	Service stations	服务站，维修站	
104095	Sheds	棚屋	
104075	Sheds for animals	动物棚	
104076	Sheds for bicycles	自行车棚	
104079	Sheds [building]	棚屋[建筑]	
104132	Shelters for service stations	服务站或维修站的遮挡棚	
104110	Silos	筒仓，地窖，竖井	
104102	Skating rinks [structure]	溜冰场[建筑]	
104111	Solariums [construction]	日光浴室[建筑]	
104086	Supports for carrying cables	牵引缆索支架	
104826	Supports for rooftop wind turbines	屋顶风轮机支架	【11】
104105	Swimming pools [non-transportable]	游泳池[非移动式]	
104085	Telephone booths	电话间	
104085	Telephone boxes	电话亭	
104112	Terraces	露台	
104119	Theatre stages	剧场舞台	
104127	Toll houses	收费站	
104113	Tombstones	墓碑	
104097	Transmitter masts	发射塔	
104088	Water towers	水塔	
104684	Wind turbines [construction]	风轮机[建筑]	【10】
104100	Windmills	风车，风车磨坊	
104687	Yurts	蒙古包	【10】

25-04

Steps, ladders and scaffolds

25-04

台阶、梯子和脚手架

104144	Feet of ladders	梯脚
104140	Ladders	梯子
104147	Portable observation ladders	可移动式观测梯
104143	Scaffoldings and their components	脚手架及其组件
104142	Stair banisters	楼梯护栏
104145	Staircase steps	楼梯台阶
104141	Staircases	楼梯
104139	Step stools	凳梯
104146	Tubes for scaffolding	脚手架用管

25-99
Miscellaneous

25-99
其他杂项

104155	Airtight and watertight padding [construction]	气密及水密的填料[建筑]
104152	Buffers for railway terminals	铁轨终端缓冲垫
104153	Canopies for thrones, chairs of state or altars	御座、元首宝座或祭坛用华盖
104148	Draft excluder strips	嵌缝条，填缝条
104148	Draught excluder strips	嵌缝条，填缝条
104149	Garden pools	庭院水池
104156	Packing for doors and windows to prevent draft	门窗缝隙填料
104157	Painters' stands	画家或油漆工用台架
104154	Slipways for ships	轮船滑道，船台
104150	Weather strips	防风、防雨密封条
104151	Windbreaks [for protecting plants]	防风篱[保护植物用]

Class 26
Lighting apparatus

26-01
Candlesticks and candelabra

104158	Candle drip rings	蜡烛滴油环	
104161	Candle holders	蜡烛托架	
104586	Candle jars	烛罐，烛瓶，烛杯	【10】
104162	Candle lights for graves	墓地用蜡烛台	
104159	Candlesticks	烛台	
104160	Holders for garden candles	花园蜡烛用托架	

26-02
Torches and hand lamps and lanterns

104164	Battery lamps	电池灯	
104171	Chinese lanterns	中国灯笼	
104168	Electric torches	手电筒	
104828	Flaming torches	火炬	【11】
104163	Grill-protected portable lamps	有保护格的手提灯	
104166	Hand lamps	手提灯	
104170	Head torches	头灯	【12】[1]
104165	Miners' lamps	矿灯	
104169	Pocket torches	袖珍手电筒	
104167	Portable lanterns	手提灯笼	

26-03
Public lighting fixtures

Note：Including outside lamps, stage lighting and searchlight projectors.

注：包括户外灯、舞台照明设备和探照灯。

105026	Emergency lights［except portable lamps］	应急灯［手提灯除外］	【13】
104175	Floodlight projectors	泛光灯	
104177	Garden lamps	庭院灯	

1　由"Forehead lamps［e.g. for miners and speleologists］头灯［例如：矿工和洞穴学者用］"修改为"Head torches 头灯"。

105025	Ground lights	地埋灯	【13】
104175	Light projectors	投光灯	
104173	Public lighting fixtures	公共场所照明装置	
104175	Searchlight projectors	探照灯	
104178	Solar powered garden lamps	太阳能庭院灯	
104175	Spotlights	聚光灯	
104174	Stage lighting	舞台照明设备	
104172	Street lamp posts	路灯柱	
104176	Street lamps	路灯	

26-04

Luminous sources, electrical or not

Note: Including bulbs for electric lamps, luminous plaques and tubes, and candles.

26-04

电或非电的光源

注：包括电灯泡、发光板、发光管和蜡烛。

104189	Arc lamps	弧光灯	
104181	Bulbs for electric lamps	电灯灯泡	
104180	Bulbs for lighting fixtures	照明装置用灯泡	
104182	Bulbs for signalling lamps	信号灯灯泡	
104185	Burners [lighting]	发光体[照明]	
104183	Candles	蜡烛	
104184	Candles for Christmas trees	圣诞树用蜡烛	
104829	Curtain lights	灯帘	【11】
104191	Dark room lamps [photography]	暗室灯[摄影]	
104187	Electric candles	电烛	
104179	Electric lights for Christmas trees	圣诞树用挂灯、圣诞树用串灯	【12】[1]
104188	Filaments for light bulbs	灯泡的灯丝	
104190	Fluorescent lamps	荧光灯管	
104201	Garden candles	花园蜡烛	
104199	Halogen bulbs	卤素灯泡	
104198	Illuminated Advent stars	可发光的耶稣降临星	【11】[2]
104192	Lamp mantles	汽灯纱罩，汽灯燃罩	
104193	Lamp wicks	灯芯	
104585	Light cables [lighting]	光纤[照明]	【10】
104203	Light emitting diodes	发光二极管	

---

1 由"Christmas bulbs 圣诞灯泡"修改为"Electric lights for Christmas trees 圣诞树用挂灯、圣诞树用串灯"。
2 由"Illuminated stars for windows [Christmas decoration] 窗户用星灯[圣诞装饰物]"修改为"Illuminated Advent stars 可发光的耶稣降临星"。

104200	Light festoons	花彩灯	
104194	Luminous plaques [lighting]	发光板[照明]	
104196	Luminous tubes [lighting]	发光管[照明]	
104197	Oil lamps	油灯	
104195	Sodium vapor lamps	钠蒸气灯	
104668	Tealights	茶蜡	【10】
104186	Wax candles	蜡烛	

26-05
Lamps, standard lamps, chandeliers, wall and ceiling fixtures, lampshades, reflectors, photographic and cinematographic projector lamps

26-05
灯，落地灯，枝形吊灯，墙壁和天花板装置，灯罩，反光罩，摄影和电影投光灯

104210	Bracket lamps	墙灯，壁灯
104211	Ceiling lights	顶篷灯，吸顶灯
104215	Chandeliers	枝形吊灯
104221	Floor lamps [torchères]	落地灯[炬形灯柱座]
104207	Globes [lamps]	球形灯罩[灯]
104226	Halogen lamps	卤素灯
104213	Hangings for lamps	灯吊架
104205	Lamp brackets	灯架
104222	Lamp glasses	灯玻璃制品
104218	Lamp stands	灯座，灯台
104225	Lamps	灯
104216	Lamps for medical purposes [lighting]	医用灯[照明]
104209	Lamps for photography or cinematography [except flashlamps]	摄影或电影用灯[闪光灯除外]
104208	Lamps [non portable]	灯[非手提式]
104204	Lampshades	灯罩
104206	Light diffusers	散光器
104217	Light diffusing grilles	散光格栅
104223	Light organs	灯元件
104224	Night-lights [lamps]	夜灯[灯]
104219	Reflectors for photography or cinematography	摄影或电影用反光罩
104212	Reflectors of lamps	灯反光罩
104214	Standard lamps	落地灯
104220	Supports for studio lighting apparatus	演播室照明设备支架

104666	Table lamps	桌灯，台灯	【10】
104221	Torchères [floor lamps]	炬形灯柱座 [落地灯]	

26-06
Luminous devices for vehicles

26-06
交通工具发光装置

104580	Boat lanterns	船灯	【10】
104234	Cycle lamps	自行车灯	
104232	Direction indicators for vehicles	交通工具方向指示灯	
104231	Dome lights for vehicles	交通工具穹顶灯	
104227	Flashing direction indicators for vehicles	交通工具闪光转向指示灯	
104230	Headlights for vehicles	交通工具前灯	
104228	Lighting equipment for vehicles	交通工具照明设备	
104233	Lights for vehicles	交通工具灯	
104235	Navigation lights for vehicles	交通工具导航灯、航行灯	
104236	Rear lamp clusters for vehicles	交通工具组合后灯	
104231	Roof lights for vehicles	交通工具顶篷灯	
104229	Signalling lights for vehicles	交通工具用信号灯	

26-99
Miscellaneous

26-99
其他杂项

104241	Arc lamp regulators	弧光灯调节器
104237	Extinguishers for candles	灭烛器
104239	Lamp sockets	灯口
104238	Simulated logs [for fireplaces]	模拟原木燃烧的装置 [壁炉用]
104240	Snuffers	熄烛器，烛花剪

Class 27
Tobacco and smokers' supplies

27-01
Tobacco, cigars and cigarettes

104242	Cigar filter tips
104248	Cigar tips
104249	Cigarette filter tips
104247	Cigarette filters
104244	Cigarettes
104245	Cigarillos
104243	Cigars
104250	Quids
104246	Tobacco

27-02
Pipes, cigar and cigarette holders

104253	Cigar holders
104254	Cigarette holders
104252	Hookahs
104251	Mouthpieces for tobacco pipes
104255	Tobacco pipes

27-03
Ashtrays

104256	Ashtrays

27-04
Matches

104257	Matches

27-05
Lighters

104259	Cigarette lighters

27 类
烟草和吸烟用具

27-01
烟草、雪茄和香烟

雪茄过滤嘴
雪茄过滤嘴
香烟过滤嘴
香烟过滤嘴
香烟
小雪茄
雪茄
烟草咀嚼块，口嚼烟
烟草

27-02
烟斗、雪茄和香烟烟嘴

雪茄烟嘴
香烟烟嘴
水烟袋
烟斗烟嘴
烟斗

27-03
烟灰缸

烟灰缸

27-04
火柴

火柴

27-05
打火机

香烟打火机

104830	Cigarette lighters for cars	汽车点烟器	【11】
104258	Electric cigar lighters	电子雪茄打火机	

27-06
Cigar cases, cigarette cases, tobacco jars and pouches

27-06
雪茄盒、香烟盒、烟草罐和烟草袋

Notes: (a) Not including packaging (Cl. 09). (b) Including cases for electronic smoking supplies.

注：(a) 不包括包装（09类）。(b) 包括电子烟用品盒。 【13】[1]

104267	Cases for cigarette paper	卷烟纸用盒	
105027	Cases for electronic cigarettes	电子烟盒	【13】
105028	Cases for electronic hookahs	电子水烟袋盒	【13】
104266	Cigar boxes	雪茄匣	
104262	Cigar cases	雪茄盒	
104263	Cigarette cases	香烟盒	
104268	Humidors	烟草保湿盒	
104265	Snuffboxes	鼻烟盒	
104261	Tobacco boxes	烟草匣	
104264	Tobacco jars	烟草罐	
104260	Tobacco pouches	烟草袋	

27-07
Electronic cigarettes and other electronic smoking supplies

27-07
电子烟和其他电子吸烟用具 【13】[2]

104604	Electronic cigarettes	电子烟	【10】
105029	Electronic hookahs	电子水烟袋	【13】
105030	Electronic tobacco pipes	电子烟管	【13】

27-99
Miscellaneous

27-99
其他杂项

104277	Cigar trimmers	雪茄修切器	
104274	Cigarette extinguishers	灭烟器	
104273	Cigarette paper	卷烟纸	
104276	Cigarette-lighter holders	香烟打火机座	

---

1 增加注释内容："(b) Including cases for electronic smoking supplies. (b) 包括电子烟用品盒"。
2 第12版新增加27-07类，产品项由27-99类转移至27-07类。第13版小类名称由"Electronic cigarettes 电子香烟"修改为"Electronic cigarettes and other electronic smoking supplies 电子烟和其他电子吸烟用具"。

104271	Cleaners for tobacco pipes	烟斗清洁器
104269	Match holders	火柴托
104275	Pipe stands	烟斗架
104278	Portable rolling apparatus for cigarettes	便携式卷烟装置
104272	Tobacco pipe scrapers	烟斗刮刀
104270	Tobacco tampers	烟草填实用具

Class 28
Pharmaceutical and cosmetic products, toilet articles and apparatus

28 类
药品，化妆品，梳妆用品和设备

Note: Not including packaging (Cl. 09).

注：不包括包装（09类）。 【13】[1]

28-01
Pharmaceutical products

28-01
药品

Notes: (a) Including for animals. (b) Including chemicals in cachet, capsule, lozenge, pill and tablet forms, also for plants. (c) Not including materials for dressing wounds and nursing (Cl. 24-04).

注：(a) 包括动物用药品。(b) 包括扁囊剂、胶囊剂、锭剂、丸剂、片剂形状的化学药品，也可用于植物。(c) 不包括包扎伤口和护理用品（24-04类）。 【10】[2]

104280	Cachets, pharmaceutical	扁囊剂药品	
104281	Capsules, pharmaceutical	胶囊药品	
104279	Contraceptives	避孕药	
104831	Dietary supplement tablets	膳食补充片	【11】
104283	Lozenges	锭剂	
104282	Pharmaceutical tablets	药片	
104284	Pills	药丸	
104285	Suppositories	栓剂	

28-02
Cosmetic products

28-02
化妆品

Note: Including for animals.

注：包括动物用化妆品。

104291	Cosmetic pencils	化妆笔
104287	Deodorant sticks	体香棒
104293	Eye liners	眼线笔
104288	Hemostatic pencils	止血笔
104290	Lipstick tubes	唇膏管，口红管
104292	Lipsticks	唇膏，口红
104289	Soap	肥皂，香皂
104286	Styptic pencils	止血笔

---

1 增加注释内容："Note:Not including packaging (Cl. 09)．注：不包括包装（09类）。"

2 注释（b）由"(b) Including chemicals in cachet, capsule, lozenge, pill and tablet forms. (b) 包括扁囊剂、胶囊、锭剂、丸剂，药片形状的化学药品。"修改为"(b) Including chemicals in cachet, capsule, lozenge, pill and tablet forms, also for plants. (b) 包括扁囊剂、胶囊剂、锭剂、丸剂、片剂形状的化学药品，也可用于植物。"

28-03
Toilet articles and beauty parlor equipment

Notes: (a) Including razors, apparatus and appliances for massaging, hair removing or hair dressing. (b) Not including toilet and make-up brushes (Cl. 04-02), or grooming articles for animals (Cl. 30-10).

28-03
梳妆用品和美容院设备

注：(a) 包括剃须刀，按摩、剪发、美发用器械和设备。(b) 不包括梳妆刷和化妆刷（04-02类）或者动物用梳洗用品（30-10类）。

104356	Anti-cellulite appliances	减脂肪器具	
104325	Anti-wrinkle appliances	抗皱纹器具	
104320	Anti-wrinkle dressings [cosmetic products]	抗皱纹敷料［化妆品］	
104310	Apparatus for curling and waving the hair	卷发和烫发用设备	
104298	Atomizers, vaporizers and sprayers for perfumes [except packaging]	香水喷雾器［包装除外］	
104332	Bobby pins	发夹	【12】
104353	Chiropodists' scrapers	手足病医生用刮刀	
104322	Combs	梳	
104331	Corn cutters	鸡眼刀	
104922	Cosmetic sheet masks	片状面膜	【12】
104305	Cotton sticks [toilet]	棉花棒［梳妆］	
104339	Curlers for permanent waves	烫发卷发器	
104321	Curlpapers [hairdressing]	卷发纸［美发］	
104351	Cushions for vibromassage	振动按摩垫	
105032	Diffusers for perfumes or essential oils	香水或精油扩散器，香薰机	【13】
104352	Dispensers for cosmetics	化妆品分配器	
104335	Dispensers for razor blades	剃须刀刀片分配器	
104306	Dressing combs	理发梳	
104358	Ear-piercing apparatus	穿耳洞设备	
104312	Electric razor heads	电动剃须刀刀头	
104348	Electric razors	电动剃须刀	
104349	Electric toothbrushes [appliances]	电动牙刷［器具］	
105036	Electronic muscle stimulators [except for medical purposes]	电子肌肉刺激器［医用除外］	【13】
105034	Eye masks [for cosmetic purposes]	眼罩［美容用］	【13】
104918	Facial hair trimmers	面部毛发修剪器，鼻毛剪	【12】
104916	Facial mask making appliances	面膜制作机	【12】

104919	Facial massagers	面部按摩器	【12】
104311	Gloves for massage	按摩用手套	
104294	Hair barrettes	发卡	【12】
104917	Hair claw clips	头发爪夹	【12】
104345	Hair clippers	理发推子	
104329	Hair curler heaters	卷发加热器	
104299	Hair curlers	卷发器	
104308	Hair curling pins	卷发针，卷发发夹	
104330	Hair cutters	剪发器	
104301	Hair drier hoods	头发干燥罩	
104354	Hair driers	头发烘干机，吹风机	
104295	Hair fasteners [except jewellery]	头发固定物 [首饰除外]	
104332	Hair grips	发夹	【12】
104333	Hair nets	发网	
104332	Hair pins	发针	
104299	Hair rollers	发辊	
104294	Hair slides	发夹，发插	
104923	Hair straightening irons	头发拉直器，直发器	【12】
104340	Hair tweezers	拔毛镊，除毛器	
104319	Hair waving clips	头发波浪夹	
104307	Hair-removing appliances	脱毛器具	
104317	Hand mirrors	手持镜	
104344	Hand rests for manicuring	修指甲用手托	
104297	Holders for electric razors [including recharging holders]	电动剃须刀架 [包括充电座]	
104346	Holders for electric toothbrushes [including recharging holders]	电动牙刷架 [包括充电座]	
104297	Holders [including recharging holders] for electric razors	电动剃须刀架 [包括充电座]	
104346	Holders [including recharging holders] for electric toothbrushes	电动牙刷架 [包括充电座]	
104301	Hoods for hair driers	头发干燥罩	
104334	Horsehair gloves	马毛手套	
104303	Hygienic collars [hairdressing]	卫生脖围 [美发]	
105037	LED masks [for cosmetic purposes]	LED 光疗面罩 [美容用]	【13】
104302	Manicure hand rests	修指甲用手托	
104355	Massage appliances	按摩器具	

104318	Mirrors for ladies' handbags	女士手袋用镜子	
104304	Nail clippers	指甲剪	
104316	Nail files	指甲锉	
104338	Nail nippers	指甲钳	
104921	Nail polish dryers	指甲油干燥机，美甲灯	【12】
104343	Nail polishers	指甲磨光器	
104347	Oral waterjets	口腔冲牙器	
104300	Perfume burners	精油炉，香熏炉	
104339	Perm rods	烫发、卷发用发卷	【12】
104337	Pins for hair curlers	卷发器用插针	【12】[1]
104337	Pins for hair rollers	发辊用插针	【12】
104323	Powder compacts	粉饼盒	
104313	Powder puffs	粉扑	
104314	Razor blades	剃须刀刀片	
104324	Razors	剃须刀	
104832	Sex toys	性玩具，成人用品，情趣用品	【11】
104342	Shaving dishes	剃须盘	
104663	Solarium apparatus	日光浴装置，美黑设备	【10】
104341	Spraying apparatus for hairdressers	理发师用喷雾设备	
105035	Steam eye masks	蒸汽眼罩	【13】
104350	Sunlamps	美黑晒灯	
105033	Toe separators	脚趾分隔器	【13】
104920	Tongue cleaners	舌苔清洁器	【12】
105031	Toothbrush holders	牙刷架，牙刷座	【13】
104296	Toothpicks	牙签	
104327	Vibrators for massage	振动按摩器	
104357	Washing sponges	洗澡海绵	

28-04
Wigs and false beauty articles

28-04
假发和人造美妆用品 【12】[2]

104359	False beards	假胡须	
104367	False eyelashes	假睫毛	
104360	False hair	假发	
104364	False hairpieces	人造毛发	

---

1 由"Pincers for heated hair curlers 加热卷发器用钳子"修改为"Pins for hair curlers 卷发器用的插针"。
2 由"Wigs, false hairpieces 假发、人造毛发"修改为"Wigs and false beauty articles 假发和人造美妆用品"。产品项"False eyelashes 假睫毛""False nails 假指甲"由 28-99 类转移至 28-04 类。

104362	False moustaches	假髭
104368	False nails	假指甲
104365	Hair plaits	发辫
104361	Toupees	男用假发
104363	Wigs	假发

28-05
Air fresheners

28-05
空气清新剂 【12】[1]

| 104370 | Air fresheners [except apparatus] | 空气清新剂[器具除外] |

28-99
Miscellaneous

28-99
其他杂项

104366	Back scratchers	搔背器
104369	Blocks of washing products	块状洗涤剂
104371	Deodorants [tablets] for dishwashing machines	洗碗机用除臭剂[药片]

---

[1] 新增加 28-05 类，产品项由 28-99 类转移至 28-05 类。

Class 29
Devices and equipment against fire hazards, for accident prevention and for rescue

29 类
防火灾、防事故、救援用的装置及设备

29-01
Devices and equipment against fire hazards

Notes: (a) Including fire extinguishers. (b) Not including fire engines (vehicles) (Cl. 12-13), fire-hoses and nozzles for fire-hoses (Cl. 23-01).

29-01
防火灾装置和设备

注：(a) 包括灭火器。(b) 不包括消防车（交通工具）(12-13 类)、消防水带和消防水带喷嘴（23-01 类）。

104372	Beaters for fire	拍火器
104375	Devices and equipment against fire hazards	防火灾装置和设备
104374	Extinguishers	灭火器
104378	Fire extinguisher tanks	灭火器罐
104377	Fire extinguishing pumps	消防泵
104376	Flame arresters	消焰器，阻火器
104373	Foam sprays [firefighting]	泡沫喷射器 [消防]

29-02
Devices and equipment for accident prevention and for rescue, not elsewhere specified

Note: (a) Including devices and equipment for animals. (b) Not including helmets (Cl. 02-03) and garments for protection against accidents (Cl. 02-02, Cl. 02-04 or Cl. 02-06).

29-02
其他类未列入的防事故和救援用装置及设备

注：(a) 包括动物用的装置和设备。(b) 不包括头盔（02-03 类）和避免意外伤害的保护服装（02-02、02-04、02-06 类）。

104392	Anti-dust nasal filters	防尘用鼻过滤器
104397	Blasting mats	爆炸垫，防爆帘，爆破防护网
104389	Breathing masks	呼吸面具
104584	Bullet proof vests	防弹背心 【10】
104395	Devices for protection against X-rays	X 射线防护装置
104384	Diving bells	潜水钟
104385	Face shields	面罩
104398	Floating barriers for preventing oil pollution	防油类污染浮屏

104394	Gas masks	防毒面具	
104379	Life nets	救生网	
104382	Lifebelts	安全带，救生带	
104381	Lifebuoys	救生圈	
104386	Lifejackets	救生衣	
104390	Parachutes	降落伞	
104388	Protective face masks	防护面罩，口罩	
104396	Rescue bags for transport of persons	逃生救援包	
104380	Rescue chutes	救援滑道，救生袋	
104379	Rescue nets	营救网	
104833	Rescue robots	救援机器人	【11】
104389	Respiratory masks	呼吸面具	
104383	Safety belts for vehicle seats	交通工具座位用安全带	
104393	Safety harnesses	保险带，安全吊带	
104391	Submarine escape devices	潜水艇逃生装置	
104834	Tactile indicator studs for road surfaces	路面用触觉指示路钉	【11】
104387	Welders' masks	焊工面罩	

29-99
Miscellaneous

29-99
其他杂项

105038	Emergency equipment posts	应急设备柱	【13】

Class 30
Articles for the care and handling of animals

Note: Not including animal foodstuffs (Cl. 01), or pharmaceutical and cosmetic products for animals (Cl. 28-01 or Cl. 28-02).

30 类
动物照管与驯养用品

注：不包括动物食品（01 类），或者动物用药品和化妆用品（28-01 或 28-02 类）。

30-01
Animal clothing

30-01
动物服装

104406	Animal clothing	动物服装
104402	Animal pads	动物衬垫
104403	Blankets for animals	动物用毯
104400	Bootees for dogs	狗用毛线鞋
104401	Headwear for horses	马头饰
104399	Horse boots	马护腿
104623	Horse gaiters	马绑腿 【10】
104405	Horsecloths	马衣，马披
104404	Kneepads for horses	马护膝

30-02
Pens, cages, kennels and similar shelters

Note: Not including buildings (Cl. 25).

30-02
围栏、笼、舍及类似居所

注：不包括建筑物（25 类）。

104413	Apiaries	蜂房
104407	Aquariums	水族缸
104416	Aviaries	大型鸟舍，大鸟笼
104414	Beehives	蜂箱
104417	Bird houses	小型鸟屋
104421	Birdcages	鸟笼
104409	Cages for animals	动物笼
104419	Dog kennels	狗舍
104420	Fish tanks	鱼缸
104411	Fowl confining devices	家禽围限装置
104412	Pens for animals	动物围栏
104410	Rabbit hutches	兔箱，兔笼
104418	Receptacles for queen bee rearing	饲养蜂王用房

104415	Terrariums	动物育养箱	
104422	Transport containers for animals	运输动物用容器	
104408	Trap-frames for queen bees	蜂王圈养架	

30-03
Feeders and waterers

30-03
喂食器和饮水器

104579	Bird feeders	喂鸟器	【10】
104431	Bird tables	鸟用食盘	
104425	Cribs for animal fodder	动物饲料槽	
104428	Dog bowls	狗食钵	
104423	Drinking troughs	饮水槽	
104427	Mangers	饲料槽	
104426	Nose bags	草料袋	
105039	Pet feeding bowls with visual recognition	具有视觉识别功能的宠物喂食碗	【13】
104429	Racks for feeding animals	动物喂食架	
104655	Saltlick holders	盐舔架	【10】
104430	Teats for drinking troughs	饮水槽饮水奶嘴	
104424	Troughs for cattle	家畜食槽	

30-04
Saddlery

Note: Including collars for animals.

30-04
鞍具

注：包括动物颈圈。

104574	Bark control collars	止吠项圈	【10】
104448	Bits for horses	马嚼子	
104455	Blinders for horses	马眼罩	
104455	Blinkers for horses	马眼罩	
104451	Breast harness	胸带挽具，缰绳挂具	
104436	Bridles	马勒，缰绳	
104454	Cantles of saddles	鞍后桥，鞍后弓形部分	
104437	Cavessons	驯马鼻勒	
104438	Collars for animals	动物颈圈	
104456	Dog chains	狗链	
104457	Fasteners for stirrup leathers	马镫皮带扣	
104461	Girths	肚带	
104446	Halters	笼头	
104434	Hames for shafts	辕马颈轭	

104459	Harness buckles	挽具扣	
104439	Harness hooks	挽具钩	
104440	Harness pads	挽具垫	
104463	Harness tugs	挽革	
104444	Harnesses	挽具	
104445	Leads for animals	动物用牵具	
104445	Leashes for animals	动物用绳套、皮带	
104447	Longes	练马长绳	
104447	Lunges	套马索	
104449	Muzzles	口套	
104450	Nose bands [harness]	鼻带[挽具]	
104435	Packsaddles	驮鞍	
104458	Rein guards	缰绳扣	
104443	Reins [harness]	缰绳[挽具]	
104462	Riding saddles	鞍	
104653	Saddle blankets	鞍褥	【10】
104653	Saddle cloths	鞍布	【10】
104654	Saddle pommels	马鞍前桥	【10】
104452	Saddlebags	马褡裢	
104433	Saddlebows	前鞍桥，鞍的前穹	
104453	Saddlery	鞍具	
104442	Stirrup leathers	马镫皮带，马镫革	
104441	Stirrups	马镫	
104432	Terrets	鞍环，扣环	
104447	Tethers	拴绳，拴链	
104460	Yokes [harness]	轭[挽具]	

30-05		**30-05**
Whips and prods		**鞭子和刺棒**

104465	Crops for riders	骑手用马鞭
104464	Goads	刺棒
104464	Prods	刺棒
104466	Spurs	马刺
104467	Whips for animals	动物用鞭子

30-06
Beds, nests and furniture for animals

Note: Including scratching posts for cats.

30-06
动物用床、窝和家具 【12】[1]

注：包括猫抓柱。 【12】

104468	Beds for animals	动物睡床、睡垫
104609	Furniture for pets	宠物家具 【10】
104469	Nests	窝
104492	Scratching posts for cats	猫抓柱
104470	Sleeping baskets for domestic animals	家畜用睡篮

30-07
Perches and other cage attachments

30-07
栖木和其他笼子配件

104471	Bird baths	鸟戏水盆
104473	Perches for birds	鸟栖木
104472	Perches for poultry	家禽栖木

30-08
Markers, marks and shackles

30-08
标记用具、标记和脚镣

104476	Branding irons for animals	动物用烙铁
104602	Ear tags for livestock	家畜耳标 【10】
104475	Hobbles for animals	动物缚腿物，动物用足枷
104478	Markers for animals	动物用标记用具
104477	Marks for animals	动物标记
104474	Rings for birds	鸟环
104475	Shackles for animals	动物脚镣

30-09
Hitching posts

30-09
拴柱

104480	Attachment anchors for animals	动物用锚链
104479	Hitching posts	拴柱

1　由"Beds and nests 睡床、睡垫和窝"修改为"Beds, nests and furniture for animals 动物用床、窝和家具"。产品项"Furniture for pets 宠物家具"和"Scratching posts for cats 猫抓柱"由 30-99 类转移至 30-06 类。

30-10
Grooming articles for animals

30-10
动物梳洗用品 【12】[1]

104493	Brushes for animals	动物刷
104486	Combs for dogs	狗梳
104483	Curry combs	马梳
104491	Grooming gloves for animals	动物用梳洗手套

30-11
Litter boxes and devices for removing animal excrement

30-11
动物排泄盒和排泄物清除装置 【13】[2]

104490	Devices for removing animal excrement	动物排泄物清除装置	
105040	Litter boxes	猫砂盒	【13】
104489	Toilet seats adapted for animals	动物用便器座	
104672	Toilets for pets	宠物厕所	【10】

30-12
Toys for animals

30-12
动物用玩具 【12】[3]

104488	Bones for dogs, artificial	人造的狗用骨状制品	【13】[4]
104485	Toys for animals	动物用玩具	

30-99
Miscellaneous

30-99
其他杂项

104482	Brooders	育雏器	
104494	Cat flaps	开在门上供猫进出的猫洞	
104481	Drenching bits	动物灌药用钳口具	
104484	Horseshoes	马蹄铁	
104482	Incubators for eggs	孵蛋器	
104487	Matting for stables	厩席	
104835	Pet carriers	宠物携带装置	【11】
104495	Trays with recesses for the transport of pet animals	宠物运输笼的托盘	

---

1 新增加 30-10 类，产品项由 30-99 类转移至 30-10 类。
2 第 12 版新增加 30-11 类，产品项由 30-99 类转移至 30-11 类。第 13 版小类名称由 "Litter and devices for removing animal excrement 动物排泄用具和排泄物清除装置"修改为"Litter boxes and devices for removing animal excrement 动物排泄盒和排泄物清除装置"。
3 新增加 30-12 类，产品项由 30-99 类转移至 30-12 类。
4 由 30-99 类转移至 30-12 类。

Class 31

Machines and appliances for preparing food or drink, not elsewhere specified

Note: Not including hand-operated utensils, instruments and appliances for serving or preparing food or drink (Cl. 07), or kitchen knives, knives for boning meat (Cl. 08-03).

31类

其他类未列入的食品或饮料制备机械和设备

注：不包括用于分发或制备食品或饮料的手动操作器具、工具和用具（07类）或者菜刀、剔骨刀（08-03类）。

【3】[1]

【12】[2]

31-00
Machines and appliances for preparing food or drink, not elsewhere specified

31-00
其他类未列入的食品或饮料制备机械和设备

【5】[3]

编号	英文	中文	
104557	Baking machines	烘焙机	
104540	Beaters, electric [household]	电动搅拌机［家用］	
105041	Beer pumps [machines]	啤酒泵［机械］	【13】
104531	Beer wort making apparatus	啤酒麦芽汁制作设备	
104504	Bolters, electric	电动筛选机	
104518	Bread molds [machine parts]	面包模子［机械部件］	
104541	Bread slicers, electric	电动面包切片机	
104506	Butchers' machines	屠宰机械	
104503	Butter churns [machines]	黄油搅乳机［机械］	
104529	Centrifugal milk separators, electric	电动离心牛奶脱脂机	
104542	Cheese slicers, electric	电动干酪切片机	
104496	Choppers, electric [household]	电动切碎机［家用］	
104550	Coffee grinders, electric [household]	电动咖啡豆研磨机［家用］	
104559	Coffee machines [except for household purposes]	咖啡机［非家用］	
104538	Coffee roasters, electric	电动咖啡豆焙炒机	
104509	Corers for apples [machines]	苹果去核机［机械］	
104510	Cream-milk separators, electric	电动乳脂分离机	
104551	Crushers-grinders, electric [household]	电动压碎研磨机［家用］	
104545	Crushing machines [household]	压榨机［家用］	
104508	Cutting up machines for fruit	切水果机	

---

[1] 原15-08类的类别标题和所有产品项移至此处，成为新的31类。

[2] 由"Notes: Not including hand-operated utensils, instruments and appliances for serving or preparing food or drink (Cl. 07)注：不包括用于分发或制备食品或饮料的手动操作器具、工具和用具（07类）。"修改为"Not including hand-operated utensils, instruments and appliances for serving or preparing food or drink (Cl.07), or kitchen knives, knives for boning meat (Cl. 08-03).不包括用于分发或制备食品或饮料的手动操作器具、工具和用具（07类）或者菜刀、剔骨刀（08-03类）"。

[3] 在31大类下新增加31-00小类，类别标题与大类相同，原大类下的所有产品项转移至该小类。

104514	Dairy machines	制酪机	
104532	Dough cutting machines	切面机	
104533	Dough mixing machines	和面机	
104546	Drink preparing machines or appliances [electric]	制备饮料的机械或设备［电动］	
105042	Dry-aging cabinets	熟成柜	【13】
104530	Drying machines for butter	黄油干燥机	
104558	Electric graters	电动磨碎机	
104547	Emulsifiers, electric, for cream	电动奶油乳化机	
104606	Fermenting chambers for baking	烘烤用发酵机	【10】
104524	Fish cutting and gutting machines	鱼的剖切和去内脏机	
104517	Flour milling machines	磨面粉机	
104502	Food industry machines	食品工业机械	
104497	Food masticators	食品切碎机，食品搓揉机	
104543	French-fry cutters, electric	电动切薯条机	【13】
104513	Fruit juice extractors [electric]	榨果汁机［电动］	
104549	Fruit squeezers, electric	电动榨果汁机	
104500	Grape crushing machines	葡萄压榨机	
104498	Grinding machines [household]	碾磨机［家用］	
104527	Grinding mills for sugar cane	甘蔗碾榨机	
104619	Honey presses [machines]	压榨式蜜蜡分离器［机械］	【10】
104620	Honey slingers	摇蜜机	【10】
104548	Ice cream freezers, electric	电动冰激凌凝冻机	
104520	Kneading machines	揉面机	
104505	Machines for industrial preparation of drinks	饮料工业制备用机器	
104519	Machines or appliances [electric] for extracting fruit stones	水果去核机械或设备［电动］	
104516	Malt cleaning machines	麦芽清洗机	
104528	Mash tubs	捣麦芽浆桶	
104526	Meat cutting machines	切肉机	
104636	Meat grinders [machines]	绞肉机［机械］	【10】
104496	Mincers, electric [household]	电动切碎机［家用］	
104552	Mixers, electric [household]	电动搅拌机［家用］	
104525	Molds for chocolate and confectionery [machine parts]	制巧克力和糖果的模子［机械部件］	
104507	Oil cake crushers	油渣饼压碎机	
104534	Oil presses, electric	电动榨油机	

104544	Onion choppers, electric	电动洋葱切碎机
104553	Peelers, electric	电动剥皮机
104511	Peeling machines for fruit and vegetables [industrial]	水果和蔬菜的剥皮机 [工业]
104515	Popcorn machines	爆米花机
104543	Potato chippers, electric	电动土豆切片机
104523	Poultry pluckers [machines]	禽类拔毛机，禽类脱毛机 [机械]
104556	Pouring stands for draught beer	啤酒灌注机
104535	Presses for biscuit manufacture	饼干压制机
104521	Presses for fruit or vegetable [electric]	水果或蔬菜的压榨机 [电动]
104539	Separators for flour [machines]	面粉分离机 [机械]
104537	Sieves for flour milling [machines]	磨面粉用筛粉机 [机械]
104536	Sifting machines for flour milling	磨面粉用筛粉机
104499	Slicing machines [household]	切片机 [家用]
104501	Stills for distilling beverages	饮料蒸馏机
104512	Sugar driers	糖干燥机
104554	Vegetable slicers, electric [household]	电动切菜机 [家用]
104522	Wine presses, electric	制酒用电动酒榨机
104555	Yoghurt making appliances, electric	电动酸奶制作设备
104555	Yogurt making appliances, electric	电动酸奶制作设备

Class 32
Graphic symbols and logos, surface patterns, ornamentation

32 类
图形符号、标识、表面图案、纹饰

【9】[1]

32-00
Graphic symbols and logos, surface patterns, ornamentation

32-00
图形符号、标识、表面图案、纹饰

【9】[2]

104836	Get-up [arrangement of boat interiors]	式样 [船内部布置]	【11】
104926	Get-up [arrangement of restaurant interiors]	式样 [餐厅内部布置]	【12】
104924	Get-up [arrangement of shop interiors]	式样 [商店内部布置]	【12】
104561	Get-up [arrangement of the interior of a room]	式样 [房间内部布置]	
104613	Get-up [arrangement of train interiors]	式样 [火车内部布置]	【10】
104925	Get-up [arrangement of window displays]	式样 [橱窗陈列布置]	【12】
104562	Graphic designs [two-dimensional]	图形设计 [二维平面的]	
104563	Graphic symbols	图形符号	
104564	Graphic symbols [comic figures]	图形符号 [漫画图形]	
104565	Logos	标识	
104566	Ornamentation	纹饰	
104567	Surface patterns	表面图案	

---

1 原 99 类被删除，新增加 32 类。
2 新增加 32-00 类。

编译说明

在世界知识产权组织公布的《国际外观设计分类表（第13版）》英文版本的基础上，对其历次修订内容进行整理并编撰在本书中。

1. 按类别顺序排列的产品项列表中，大类和小类的标题采用"英文标题—中文标题—标记"的三列结构，注释采用"英文注释—中文注释—标记"的三列结构进行编排。

2. 小类下的产品项采用"编码—英文产品项—中文产品项—标记"的四列形式进行编排，如下所示。

104680　　Waffles　　　　　　　　　　　华夫饼　　　　　　　　　　　　　　　　　【10】

3. 编码及英文内容均与世界知识产权组织正式公布的英文版本的内容相同，中文内容则是其对应的译文。

4. 本书对历次版本的类别变化和第10～13版产品项的重要变化进行标记。

5. 标记采用"【*】"的方式表达，表示相应条目发生改变，其中"*"是以阿拉伯数字表示发生改变的版本号。"【*】"上未带有脚注的表示其为第*版新增条目，带有脚注的表示该条目在第*版进行过修订，脚注对其修订过程进行说明。

6. 整理第11～13版《国际外观设计分类表》中删除的产品项，以列表的形式编录在本说明之后。

第 11 版《国际外观设计分类表》已删除产品项列表

类别	编码	英文产品名称	中文产品名称
02-01	100064	Underpants, short [for men]	短内裤[男用]
02-01	100064	Briefs [underwear]	贴身的短内裤[内衣]
02-01	100064	Panties	妇女或儿童的短内裤
06-06	100673	Reading desks	斜面读书桌，诵经台
14-03	102491	Teleprinter receivers	电传打字机接收器
14-03	102492	Telegraph repeaters	电报中继器
14-03	102495	Telautographs	电报传真机
14-03	102497	Telegraphs	电报机
14-03	102498	Teleprinters	电传打字机
14-03	102500	Teletypewriters	电传打字电报机
14-03	102527	Casings for mobile phones	移动电话机壳
14-03	104669	Telegraph relays	电报中继装置
16-03	102837	Facsimile machines	影印机
18-02	103002	Copying apparatus [office requisites]	复制设备[办公必需品]
25-01	103959	Drainpipes for walls	墙壁排水管
25-02	104006	Sewer manholes	下水道检修孔
32-00	104560	Get-up	式样

第12版《国际外观设计分类表》
已删除产品项列表

类别	编码	英文产品名称	中文产品名称
02-02	100090	Costumes	戏装，节日装
03-01	100311	Haversacks	背包
03-01	100311	Knapsacks	背包
03-01	100316	Suitcases	手提箱
03-01	100334	Shopping baskets	购物篮
03-99	100398	Carrying devices for babies	婴儿携带装置
06-04	100634	Racks for cassettes for recording tapes	盒式磁带架
06-13	100760	Turkish towels［toilet articles］	土耳其浴巾［盥洗用品］
06-13	100773	Toes muffs for children	儿童用保暖脚套
07-01	100797	Tin bowls	锡碗
07-01	100804	Porcelain [household]	瓷器［家用］
07-01	100826	Bowls for washing fruit	用于洗水果的盆
07-02	100854	Ranges［cooking］	炉灶［烹调］
07-02	100880	Stoves [cooking]	炉灶［烹调］
07-04	100950	Strainers［household］	滤器，漏网，滤盆，滤网［家用］
07-04	100951	Pastry cutters	面团分切器
07-04	100951	Pastry shapes	面团模具
07-04	100958	Table trenchers	桌上木制食物处理盘
07-05	100963	Rotating wash balls	旋转清洗球
07-05	100967	Window dusters	窗户除尘器
07-05	100968	Sad-irons	熨斗
07-05	100971	Dishmops	洗碗具
07-05	100977	Towel driers	毛巾干燥架
07-05	100979	Cloths for wiping or dusting［dusters］	擦抹或除尘用布［除尘器］
07-06	101019	Serviette holders	餐巾座，餐巾托，餐巾架

类别	编码	英文产品名称	中文产品名称
07-99	101095	Kettle racks	壶架
07-99	101096	Cooling bags, balls, plates or sticks	冷却袋，冷却球，冷却板或冷却棒
08-05	101290	Sprays guns for paint	喷漆枪
08-05	101298	Watchmakers' pliers	表匠钳
08-08	101399	Fittings for blinds and curtains	帘帷配件
09-05	101594	Refuse bags	垃圾袋
12-12	102210	Go-carts [children's carriages]	学步车［儿童车］
12-12	102214	Go-carts [for teaching babies to walk]	学步车［教婴儿行步用］
12-12	104651	Rollators	助行车
14-99	102535	Cassettes and cartridges for magnetic tapes	磁带盒
14-99	102544	Fixing devices for loudspeakers [brackets]	扬声器用固定装置［支架］
15-99	102794	Sack or bag filling machines	装袋机
16-01	102825	Photographic cameras [digital/numerical]	照相机［数码的/数字的］
16-02	102828	Diaprojection apparatus	幻灯放映设备
16-05	102851	Cardboards frames [photography]	卡纸架［摄影］
19-01	103039	Pay packets	工资袋
19-06	103170	Pen racks	置笔架
19-08	103230	Tables of directions for use of spices	香料调味品用法说明图表
19-99	103272	Pool coupon checking devices	联合券检查装置
19-99	103275	Currency converters	货币换算器
20-01	103279	Slot machines, automatic	自动贩卖机
20-03	103315	Signs [e.g. mechanical, luminous]	标志物，招牌［例如：机械的、发光的］
21-02	103456	Table tennis [except tables]	乒乓球［乒乓球台除外］
21-02	103463	Golf pegs	高尔夫球座
23-02	103691	Sanitary installations	卫生设备
23-02	103709	Bathroom shelves other than furniture	家具以外的浴室搁架
25-03	104122	Shelters [sentry boxes]	小屋［岗亭］
26-04	104202	Dim lights	暗光灯，磨砂灯泡
26-05	104209	Lamps for cinematography or photography [except flash]	电影或摄影用灯［闪光灯除外］

类别	编码	英文产品名称	中文产品名称
28-03	104294	Bobby pins	发夹
28-03	104309	Curling tongs	卷发钳，烫发钳
28-03	104309	Hair crimpers	卷发器
28-03	104336	Hair wavers	卷发器
30-08	104476	Branding irons [for animals]	印铁 [动物用]

第13版《国际外观设计分类表》已删除产品项列表

类别	编码	英文产品名称	中文产品名称
02-01	100052	Infants' napkins	幼儿尿布
05-04	100453	Ribbons [decorative trimmings]	缎带[缀饰品]
06-06	100668	Doorway and window safety guards for babies	门口或窗户的婴儿安全防护装置
06-08	104644	Garment covers for clothing on hangers	衣架用护衣罩
07-02	100868	Basting spoons, for kitchen use	厨房用涂油勺
07-02	100876	Broilers	烧烤器,烘烤器
07-05	101003	Capsules containing washing products	含洗涤制品的清洗球
07-05	100986	Clothes pins	晒衣服别针
07-05	100966	Drainers [plate racks]	沥水器[餐具架]
07-06	101018	Dish stands	碟座,碟托
09-01	101515	Pots [packaging]	罐,鼓形瓶[包装]
09-02	101527	Canteens	军用水壶
09-03	101542	Preserve cans	防腐罐头罐
09-05	101583	Bags, small [packaging]	小袋[包装]
09-07	101624	Fasteners for packaging	包装用扣件
12-08	102156	Karts	小型汽车
18-99	103032	Document sorting machines [other than for information retrieval]	文件分拣机[信息检索机除外]
26-06	104229	Signalling light for vehicles	交通工具用信号灯
28-03	104326	Perfume vaporizers [except packaging]	香水喷雾器[包装除外]
28-03	104326	Perfume sprayers [except packaging]	香水喷雾器[包装除外]

后　　记

　　从《中华人民共和国专利法》实施之日起，我局确定使用工业品外观设计国际分类法对外观设计专利进行分类。该分类法是根据《建立工业品外观设计国际分类洛迦诺协定》建立起来的，体现在《国际外观设计分类表》（又称《洛迦诺分类表》）中，于1971年起正式生效。《国际外观设计分类表》由世界知识产权组织（WIPO）编发，经过不断修订，已经发布了13个版本。从1985年4月1日至今，我局翻译并使用了《国际外观设计分类表》第4版、第6～12版等8个版本。

　　自第11版开始，世界知识产权组织通过网络平台在线发布最新版本的《国际外观设计分类表》，不再出版纸质版本。第13版《国际外观设计分类表》（以下简称"本版分类表"）共涉及大类、小类、注释及产品项的修订387项。本版分类表在继承以往编排的基础上，整合世界知识产权组织在网络平台上发布的相关内容，延续中文翻译版本的惯例，继续翻译按类别顺序排列的产品项列表。此外，对历次版本的类别变化以及第10～13版中涉及的产品项重要变化进行收集整理，并标注在表中。同时，将第11~13版中涉及删除的产品项编录在本书中，供使用者参考。

　　本版分类表的翻译工作从2020年7月启动，由外观设计分类领域9位资深审查员组成翻译小组，他们是钱红缨、王晓云、方丽娟、瞿怡、周芸、张舒凡、彭程璐、孟雨和刘增。在翻译过程中，翻译小组本着严谨的工作态度，对分类表进行全面梳理，对大类、小类、注释以及产品项逐一进行核实、翻译，使本版分类表在第12版的基础上翻译得更趋准确。在此，对翻译小组成员表示感谢！也对为本版分类表的翻译提出建议的同事表示感谢！

　　虽然翻译小组投入了大量的精力，但是由于翻译人员水平有限，疏漏在所难免，恳请使用者批评指正。

国家知识产权局专利局
2020年12月